GEOFFREY HINDLEY, educated at Kingswood School, Bath and University College Oxford, is a lecturer and writer. He was three times an invited participant at the International Congress on Medieval Studies, Western Michigan University; was visiting associate professor at the University of Florida, Gainesville; and has lectured in Europe and America on European culture, medieval social history and Magna Carta, and the history of music. From 1994 to 2000 he taught English civilization at the University of Le Havre. He is also co-President of the Society for the History of Medieval Technology and Science of Oxford and London. His many books include *The Shaping of Europe*, *England in the Age of Caxton*, *The Book of Magna Carta*, *A Brief History of the Crusades* and *A Brief History of the Anglo-Saxons*.

Other titles in this series

A BRIEF HISTORY OF THE

MAGNA CARTA

The Story of the Origins of Liberty

GEOFFREY HINDLEY

RUNNING PRESS
PHILADELPHIA · LONDON

To Diana and Sophie

Constable & Robinson Ltd
3 The Lanchesters
162 Fulham Palace Road
London W6 9ER
www.constablerobinson.com

First published in the UK by Robinson,
an imprint of Constable & Robinson, 2008

A copy of the British Library Cataloguing in Publication
Data is available from the British Library

UK ISBN 978-1-84529-505-9

1 3 5 7 9 10 8 6 4 2

First published in the United States in 2008 by Running Press Book Publishers
All rights reserved under the Pan-American and International Copyright Conventions

9 8 7 6 5 4 3 2 1
Digit on the right indicates the number of this printing

US Library of Congress number: 2007936638
US ISBN 978-0-7624-3390-2

Running Press Book Publishers
2300 Chestnut Street
Philadelphia, PA 19103-4371

Visit us on the web!
www.runningpress.com

Printed and bound in the EU

CONTENTS

ILLUSTRATIONS

Panel of four royal portraits from Matthew Paris, *Historia Anglorum*, 1250 (© *The British Library Board. All Rights Reserved/Bridgeman Art Library*)

Château Gaillard, Normandy, which King John lost in 1204 (*Author's collection*)

King John's tomb, Worcester Cathedral (*Bridgeman Art Library*)

The Articles of the Barons (*British Library/TopFoto*)

'King John and the Barons at Runnymede', after Ernest Normand's mural for the Royal Exchange, London (*Private Collection/Bridgeman Art Library*)

Magna Carta exemplification of the 1225 text issued by King Henry III (© *The British Library Board. All Rights Reserved. C6257-03*)

'The Court of the King's Bench', Westminster Hall, *c.* 1460 (*Inner Temple/Bridgeman Art Library*)

Sir Edward Coke by Marcus Gheeraerts (*Collection of the Earl of Leicester, Holkham Hall, Norfolk/Bridgeman Art Library*)

The Magna Carta Memorial, Runnymede (*TopFoto*)

ACKNOWLEDGEMENTS

In times so dangerous to constitutional liberties as these, one honours the exhortation of the great William Penn (1614–1718) of London and the Commonwealth of Pennsylvania 'not to give away anything of Liberty . . . that at present men do enjoy, but . . . to understand that it is easy to part with . . . great privileges, which be hard to be gained if once lost.'

In the writing of this book I would first like to acknowledge the encouragement of Ben Glazebrook, chairman of Constable at the time of the publication of *The Book of Magna Carta*, in 1990. My present editor, Leo Hollis at Constable & Robinson, proposed an updated edition, made most valuable comments and suggested the sub-title; Jaqueline Mitchell made a thorough and helpful reading of the text which, together with Eleanor Dryden, she saw through the press.

Even as its eighth centenary approaches, the Charter is

rarely out of the news. While teaching at the University of Le Havre during the 1990s I found interest among colleagues and would like to thank Professor Maryvonne Nedeljkovic for inviting me to address the Centre d'Etudes du Pacific on the theme at its international conference of April 1998. In England I was honoured to be invited to address the Friends of the British Museum on the Charter in March 2005.

PREFACE

Of all the documents surviving from the Middle Ages, Magna Carta, in America known always as 'the' Magna Carta, has a unique fascination. In the opinion of a contributor to the Wikipedia Magna Carta website on 17 May 2007 it is 'An English charter, the most significant and early influence on the extensive historical process that led to the rule of constitutional law today'. In the stolid legal Latin of the document, some sixty-odd clauses regulate strange-sounding privileges and obligations, order the abolition of fish weirs on the Thames, specify rates of composition payments for military service, lay down standard measures for wine and ale, and institute a committee of barons authorized to raise the country against the king should he infringe the terms.

It was a very different world – a world in which all were in theory subject to the power and will of an autocratic monarch, and even the greatest were liable to severe penalties at his whim. However it was also a world in which government and local officials could be fined for incompetence – different indeed. We need only try to imagine the formation of a committee empowered to monitor and restrain the operations of a modern Westminster government and its agents to marvel at what things were once thought possible.

Despite the somewhat different title, this book is in effect a second edition of *The Book of Magna Carta*, which Constable published in June 1990. I have updated the bibliography; added two chronologies, one giving additional material on King John's life and the situation in Europe at the time, the second sketching the presence of the Charter in subsequent events, from England's Civil War to the American Bill of Rights and beyond; added a new chapter on the 'Celtic' realms of Britain; and made a number of other small changes. The aim of that first edition, as it is with this new edition, was 'to journey into the world that gave birth to the Charter . . .'; to trace how 'Magna Carta' acquired its name and 'became part of the common law of England . . . a lawyers' text in cases ranging from civil liberties to commercial law'.

My aim was also to explain how, long before Thomas Paine wrote his tract *Rights of Man*, this medieval document came to be revered as a talisman of liberty in England's trans-Atlantic colonies. The term 'liberty' in this usage embodied the concept not of 'freedom from all restraint', but rather of legal entitlement to certain conducts within the reasonable constraints of life in a community, entitlements considered the birthright of the people of England. In the eighteenth century, unrest in the colonies of the British crown in America was fuelled to a considerable extent by resentment among the colonial landed gentry at what they saw as the deprivation of their liberties as Englishmen by the Parliament in Westminster. Elements of Magna Carta were to be written into some state constitutions and into the American Bill of Rights itself.

Called by the great eighteenth-century parliamentarian William Pitt the Elder 'the Bible of the English Constitution', the
Charter came to be seen as the authority on constitutional
propriety for the best part of two centuries up to the time of
Henry V and was used in practical ways as a document to
which people would appeal in support of their legitimate
rights, and was cited in constitutional debate in England in
the sixteenth and seventeenth centuries. Thereafter it took on a
new life in the English-speaking world. At the heart of the story
is the core principle of civilized political life as now understood
in the western world: that government shall ultimately be held
responsible to the governed.

The book is divided into four sections: *Routes to Runnymede* traces the events international as well as national that led
to the confrontation of king and dissidents; *The Community of
England – and its Neighbours* breaks the narrative, with the
opponents squaring up for the encounter, for a survey of the
country and its population; *Crisis Charter to Legal Charter*
resumes the narrative with quickened pace, as the road from
Runnymede leads through civil war to the new reign and the
adoption of a revised Charter into the law of England; and
Law, Legend and Talisman sketches something of the story of
the past 400 years when the Charter has served as a battle
standard for parliamentarians, a rallying point for revolutionaries against parliamentary tyranny and a lawyers' text in
cases ranging from civil liberties to commercial law.

Note on currency

On the question of marks and pounds I have adopted standard
practice and followed the sources that, use both units without
apparent consistency except for the general equivalence of £1 =
1.5 marks. In the first use of the currencies I have indicated the

two to show how the difference appears in practice. Although the medieval 'pound' is the same word and the same symbol '£' is used as for the pound today, the relative values are so widely different that no useful comparison can be made. The mark as used in medieval English records shares its name with the modern unit of currency known as the D-Mark used in Germany until that country adopted the euro, but there is no other connection.

INTRODUCTION

During the spring and early summer of 2007 the parchment of Magna Carta, deposited in the treasury of Lincoln Cathedral in the summer of 1215, was on display at Virginia Beach, Virginia as part of the quatercentenary celebrations of the settlement of Jamestown. The presentation had entailed a costly dedicated security plan and a number of renovations to the gallery: costs to be expected for the reception of a highly valued object. This same document had last been in the United States in 1987, the 200th anniversary of the writing of the US Constitution.

Why should a piece of English parchment, some 800 years old, be such an honoured guest in the Republic? Partly, no doubt, because for half that time its text has been part of American history. But largely because the Americans seem to venerate the document and the events that gave rise to it in a way that the English have forgotten. It could indeed be said that today English men and women are embarrassed by the very idea of a love of liberty. To an American, however, Magna Carta, described by one newspaper at the time of the 1939 New York World's Fair as 'the ever-living fountain from which flow those liberties which the English world enjoys today', remains the talisman.

On the 1987 visit to the States the 'Lincoln Charter' provided the focus for exhibitions nationwide; more than one of the thousands of visitors it attracted was observed to weep with emotion. A United States Army Air Force serviceman visiting the exhibit at the Pentagon, Washington DC commented to the curator on duty at the display stand: 'I suppose this is what we fight for.'

Magna Carta is a powerful symbol for the sovereign power of the people to impose their will on the government: the embodiment of a fundamental conviction that the expression of the people's will concerning the fundamental rights retained by them should be recorded in a written document. In England, which removed the supremacy of the monarchy only to replace it with the supremacy of the monarch in Parliament, the idea of a constitution supreme over the powers that be at any one time has still to be accepted.

When, in the 1980s, Prime Minister Margaret Thatcher proudly vaunted the English tradition of Runnymede over the French Revolutionary tradition of 1789 and the Rights of Man she was peremptorily derided by London's opinion-formers, though she spoke only the blindingly obvious – a constitutional tradition based on law is more secure than one based on a rhetorical appeal to 'rights'. Cynics commonly assert that the Great Charter of Liberties (as Magna Carta is sometimes referred to) is merely a record of privileges won by an elite for themselves and their like. It may have originated in that intention but the words of the actual document refute the cynics' claim. Clause 1 ends with the solemn assurance '. . . we have granted to all the freemen of our realm for ourselves and our heirs for ever (*in perpetuum*) all the liberties written below, to have and to hold, them and their heirs from us and our heirs'.

Very possibly, had the king lived, the Charter would have been withdrawn and its provisions diluted or sidetracked. But John died and his successors pledged themselves to maintain a reissue that repeated this assurance. By chance of mortality and history, a legal document that may indeed have been intended as part of a cynical exercise in self-interest came to be legally binding.

By virtue of John's sudden and unexpected death the stage was set for a centuries-long constitutional debate as to what might be meant by the term 'freemen' and the words 'for ever'. Although much of the Charter concerned baronial revenues and financial outgoings, the dissident barons at Runnymede would prove to have championed the majority of Englishmen outside their class and below their rank. We shall find that as early as the mid-thirteenth century most of their countrymen were coming to that view.

In one way the barons' concerns are very much in tune with the contemporary British vogue for politics that deal with 'everyday issues'. Their obsession with money and revenue of any kind seems somewhat mundane in the authors of the foundation stone of English liberties, but then such everyday matters are the chief business of Parliament today. With one difference: John's barons kept a tighter grip on the purse strings of government than does the democratic Parliament of the twenty-first century, where profligate expenditure is the norm and accountability a thing of the past.

Intriguingly, in England, where the medieval monarchy guaranteed the grant of liberties, the monarch's authority has long been usurped by that strange constitutional creature 'the Crown in Parliament', the British constitution's ultimate legislative authority, which until the passing of the Maastricht Treaty of 1991 might claim to be sovereign and untrammelled in English affairs. Since that date it has been increasingly, and indeed willingly, subject to European authorities and rulings, so that now more than half the legislation emanating from Westminster is, in fact, European. Westminster would appear, in fact, to be European. It is perhaps something of a paradox that British representatives were prominent among those who drew up the text of the European Convention on Human Rights issued in 1950 by the Council of Europe.

In the summer of 2006 a survey conducted by *BBC History Magazine* showed a majority in favour of 15 June, the date given in the 1215 Magna Carta, as the proposed British National Day. Professor Colley of Princeton University pointed out that since Magna Carta was English it hardly qualified as a British commemorative, while a Scottish radio listener rejected the idea with contempt on the same grounds. No doubt that same Scot was unaware that the first great commentary on the Charter since its promulgation at Runnymede was published in the early twentieth century by a leading Scottish scholar, William Sharpe McKechnie of the University of Glasgow.

A few years later, the first ever dedicated commemorative celebrations of the Runnymede event were planned for the seven hundredth anniversary in June 1915. Professor McKechnie was to have been among the distinguished participants, along with the Russian-born Professor Paul Vinogradoff and Professor Charles McIlwain from Canada. It must have seemed fitting to the organizers that with liberties apparently under threat worldwide the Great Charter should be honoured and celebrated, but hostilities prevented the holding of the international conference.

The story of American involvement with Magna Carta starts with the royal charter granted by King James I to the pioneers at Jamestown, Virginia, in 1607, sponsored by London's Virginia Company of London. It was drafted under the direction of Sir Edward Coke, lawyer, opponent of the crown and champion of Magna Carta. Instructions issued in 1618 by the Virginia Company to Governor Sir George Yeardley came to be known as the 'Great Charter' by Virginian historians and writers (who would proudly boast the General Assembly of Virginia as the oldest such body in the New World). Half a century later the proprietors of the colony of North Carolina authorized the governor to grant land on the same terms and conditions as the 'Great Deed of Grant' of Virginia, which they considered 'a species of Magna Carta'.

The idea grew up over the years that the Great Charter was, in essence, merely a confirmation of rights and liberties to the English people and their descendants from time immemorial and this idea seems to be embodied in the Ninth Amendment of the United States Constitution. Here it is stated that the 'enumeration in the Constitution of certain rights shall not be construed to deny or disparage others retained by the people'. In other words, that the written document, though it specified the limits of government power, was merely recording rights that had existed prior to its promulgation, and in so far as the writing was deficient in stating all those rights, those not stated were still retained by the people.

The point was further enshrined by the United States Supreme Court in the case of Hurtado v. California in 1884:

The concessions of Magna Carta were wrung from the king as guaranties against the oppressions and usurpations of his prerogative. It did not enter into the minds of the barons to provide security against their own body so that . . . in English

> history . . . the omnipotence of Parliament over the common
> law [became] absolute, even against common right and reason.
> In this country [i.e. the United States] written constitutions
> were deemed essential to protect the rights and liberties of the
> people against the encroachments of power delegated to their
> governments, and the provisions of Magna Carta were incor-
> porated into the Bill of Rights.

Thus it was America that gave the world the idea of a written
constitution, a formula taken up by almost every nation in the
world except the United Kingdom.

The history of the 1297 Confirmation of Edward I, subsequent to its purchase by Mr Ross Perot in 1983, is a further
indication of the importance that Americans attach to the
Great Charter. From then on, it was on display, courtesy of the
Perot Foundation, in the National Archives in Washington,
until 2007. On 18 December that year it was auctioned at
Sotheby's New York and was acquired for $21.3 million
(£10.16 million) by Mr David Rubinstein, co-founder of the
Carlyle Group, a private equity firm. His intention was to put
it back on public display. 'Today is a good day for our
country,' he was reported as saying. 'This document stands
the test of time. There is nothing more important than what it
represents . . . It is important that it stay in the US. I have
always believed that the three most important documents were
the Constitution, the Declaration of Independence and the
Magna Carta.' (In the week before the auction, the Bodleian
Library in Oxford exhibited the four versions of the Charter in
its possession, being three of the 1217 reissue and one of the
1225 charter issued by Henry III. Hundreds of people queued
to see the one-day exhibit.)

For nineteenth-century Americans the Charter was the lineal
ancestor of the United States Constitution. In the eighteenth

century 'no taxation without representation' was claimed as a right enshrined in the Charter; today the Charter is also held to embody that other constitutional principle central to the American way – the separation of Church and state.

Even in the twentieth century the influence of Magna Carta upon the American Constitution has been powerful. In 1963 Mr Justice Goldberg, in the case of Kennedy *v*. Mendoza Martinez, commenting on the Fourteenth Amendment, that forbids 'any state to deny to any person life liberty or property without due process of law', observed, 'Dating back to Magna Carta, it has been an abiding principle governing the lives of civilized men that no freeman shall be taken or imprisoned or disseized or outlawed or exiled . . . without the judgment of his peers or by the laws of the land.'

Magna Carta is still seen as the lineal ancestor of Habeas Corpus by many in Britain and the United States. The House of Lords, whose constitutional ancestors actually forced the acknowledgement of liberties from King John, found itself fighting for one of the most essential of them again in March 2005, in opposing government proposals to extend detention without trial. In the United States on 28 April 2004, in oral arguments before the Supreme Court relating to the foreign enemy combatant detainees at Guantánamo Bay, Justice Stephen Breyer had protested the rights of detainees to ' "due process according to law" in the words of the Magna Carta'.

It has been used recently as a talisman of liberties even by British lawyers. In October 2003, appearing before Mr Justice Ouseley in the case of the Chagos Islanders *v*. the Attorney General and Others, Counsel attempted to persuade the court to recognize a new tort of 'unlawful exile', claiming it to be a continuing tort based on rights deriving from Magna Carta. The argument failed, but the old warhorse had been brought once again to the fore. Fortunately, at long last, the rights of the islanders to return to their homeland were confirmed in May 2007.

In February 2005, on his visit to the assembly of the dignitaries of the European Union at Brussels, President George W. Bush observed that his country's Constitution could trace its roots back to Magna Carta. One imagines that this caused a certain amount of irritation among his audience of Eurocrats, who no doubt assumed that, with the United Kingdom's affirmation of the single act of union, their institution superseded any such medieval nostalgia.

In recent decades the Charter has been actively canvassed in the southern hemisphere, notably on a website of the Magna Carta Society, Papakura and Hokitika, New Zealand, where it was cited in a dispute relating to Maori fisheries allocations concerning what might be the nature of an Iwi fishing area. The thirteenth-century document was alluded to when questioning whether the New Zealand Court of Appeal had been entitled to make a particular ruling if the principles of 'due process of law' were adhered to, principles established by Magna Carta. Although this citation relates to the legal grounds for a judgment, it is entirely fitting that it should have been made with relation to a dispute over fisheries in view of the fact that just such technicalities, concerning fish weirs on the Thames, constitute the subject matter of Clause 33 of the Runnymede charter.

In England, the land of its origin, Magna Carta, the world's longest-lived constitutional document, under threat more than once in the past, is now in danger of becoming an ineffectual memory. Using the full plenitude of the powers of the medieval monarchy, King John assured historic liberties to the people of England, *in perpetuum,* 'in perpetuity' – for ever. Surprisingly, thanks to generations of struggle, the principles of no imprisonment without cause shown and no conviction without due process of law were made good, and above all the principle that government is not above the law, it seemed, secured. Today, with the monarchy a cipher in the nation's affairs but its prerogative powers usurped by a government independent of it, England's sovereignty has been surrendered by that government and the sacred principle of Habeas Corpus challenged.

The abandonment of sovereignty and hence the emasculation of the Charter of Liberties came not from the monarch but from the elected representatives of the people. We can be certain that such a surrender of national sovereignty will never be considered by the legislators accustomed to assemble in Washington DC. But then, it seems, the citizens of the republic have long valued the ancient talisman of liberty of the English-speaking world more highly than have the legislators of the United Kingdom.

THE LIFE OF KING JOHN AND
THE FIRST CENTURY OF THE CHARTER

1167   *24 December.* John is born at Oxford.

The same year, the King of Leinster, seeking help against his rivals, visits England, swears fealty to Henry II for his ancestral rights in Ireland and returns to the country with Welsh-Norman barons he has recruited as mercenary allies to prosecute his claims.

1171   Henry II (John's father) leads the army into Ireland and in a few months of successful campaigning asserts his supremacy over the Irish kings and Welsh-Norman barons.

1175   Under the Treaty of Windsor, O'Connor, King of Connacht (Connaught), the reigning Irish High King, comes to an agreement with Henry that recognizes the position of the Norman barons in Ireland.

1176   *May.* The title 'Lord of Ireland' is solemnly bestowed on John at Woodstock. Irish chieftains and Norman-

Irish magnates do homage to him, the rival claim of O'Connor the High King ignored.

1185 *January*. Patriarch Heraclius of Jerusalem arrives in England to offer King Henry the crown of the crusader kingdom. He refuses and forbids John to accept.

April. John lands at Waterford with a strong force and ample funds, and marches overland to Dublin, to mediate in Irish affairs as his father's deputy, but succeeds only in angering the Irish. He squanders the money on riotous living and by the end of the year is recalled. He mocks the Irish chieftains for their dress, flowing hair and beards.

1187 Saladin captures Jerusalem for Islam.

1189 John marries Isabelle de Clare, heiress to the earldom of Gloucester, his first cousin and so within prohibited degrees of consanguinity.

6 July. Henry II dies before fulfilling his vow to go on crusade.

1190 Richard I sails on crusade having first created his teenage nephew Otto of Brunswick (emperor to be) Earl of York.

1192 *October*. Richard leaves the port of Acre intending to return to England.

December. Richard is seized by Leopold, Duke of Austria.

1193 *January*. Prince John travels to Paris to do homage to Philip for the English lands in France.

February. Richard is handed over to the emperor, Henry VI. Philip of France hopes to 'buy' prisoner Richard so as to use his release to bargain for Angevin possessions in France. John returns to stir up rebellion in England while Philip prepares to invade.

April. Richard, now on friendly terms with the emperor,

surrenders England and receives it back as a fief of the empire. His mother, Queen Eleanor of Aquitaine, travels to Speyer with the first instalment of his ransom and celebrates Christmas with him and the emperor.

1194   *13 March.* Richard lands at Sandwich.

The castles of Tickhill and Nottingham, holding for John, are soon retaken.

17 April. Richard has a second coronation at Winchester.

May. Richard is reconciled with John.

1196   Richard builds Château Gaillard overlooking the Seine; it will be his base for the remainder of his life, campaigning to recover Angevin lands in France.

1198   *January.* Lotario di Segni is elected pope. In February he is ordained priest and bishop of Rome. He reigns as Innocent III until his death in July 1216.

1199   Two panels of bishops declare John a single man.

6 April. Richard dies at the siege of Chalus. The succession is disputed between John and his nephew, Arthur of Brittany.

18 April. Anjou, Maine and Touraine recognize Arthur.

25 April. Normandy recognizes John as duke.

27 May. John is crowned king of England in Westminster Abbey.

1200   *January.* The Pope places France under an interdict because of Philip II's bigamous marriage.

22 May. By the Treaty of Le Goulet Philip II of France recognizes John of England as heir to all the English fiefs in France held by his brother Richard and their father Henry II; for his part John acknowledges Philip as his overlord in these territories, but also agrees to pay a huge 'relief' or succession duty. Neither his father nor his brother had even been asked to pay such a levy.

24 August. John marries Isabella of Angoulême.

8 October. John and Isabella are crowned together at Westminster Abbey.

1202   *Easter*. Philip II orders John to appear before the court of French barons in his capacity as Duke of Aquitaine.

28 April. John fails to attend: Philip declares Aquitaine, Poitou and Anjou to be forfeit. Philip knights Arthur of Brittany.

May. Philip launches a campaign against John in France.

July. Arthur does homage to Philip for all John's French lands, except Normandy.

The same month, Philip's bigamous wife having died, the interdict on France is lifted.

Arthur lays siege to his grandmother Queen Eleanor of Aquitaine, at the castle of Mirebeau in Poitou.

August. John raises the siege and takes Arthur prisoner.

1203   The imprisoned Duke Arthur of Brittany, John's nephew and rival, mysteriously disappears. There are rumours of his having been murdered on the orders of King John, or even by the king himself.

1204   *6 March*. John loses Château Gaillard and Normandy to the French.

The Fourth Crusade takes Constantinople.

1208   *March*. Pope Innocent III lays England under an interdict because the king refuses to accept Stephen Langton as Archbishop of Canterbury.

1209   *October*. Otto of Brunswick is crowned emperor (Otto IV) by the Pope.

November. When the interdict fails to force John to the Pope's will, Innocent pronounces the personal excommunication of the king as the ultimate sanction of the Church.

1210 Campaigning in Wales, Scotland and Ireland to assert
–11   English dominance, John achieves notable, but short-lived, successes.

1212 *June*. Llywelyn the Great negotiates a treaty with Philip of France; John, who had been planning to invade France, diverts his army for Wales.

July. Robert Fitzwalter and Eustace de Vescy's plot against John is revealed.

1213 *April*. Philip of France resolves to invade England; his son Louis is to be king.

15 May. At Ewell, near Dover, John makes formal surrender of the kingdoms of England and Ireland to the Holy See; Innocent III returns them under a bond of fealty and homage and a tribute of 1,000 marks a year.

30 May. The English fleet under William, Earl of Salisbury destroys the French invasion fleet at Damme, near Bruges.

20 July. John's excommunication is formally lifted at Winchester, after he reaffirms his coronation oath.

July/August. The northern barons (*barones Northanhumbrenses*) refuse to serve on John's projected expedition to Poitou, France.

October. At St Paul's Cathedral, John's homage and tribute for England is ratified before a papal representative in a charter sealed with a golden bull and recorded on England's charter roll.

1 November. John is reconciled with the northern barons in a meeting at Wallingford.

1214 *1 February*. On the eve of John sailing (at last) for the expedition to Poitou, he appoints Peter des Roches, Bishop of Winchester, as his new justiciar.

15 February. John arrives at La Rochelle, France.

April. John receives token homage from the barons of Poitou.

May. Marriage of John's daughter, Joan, to Hugh of La Marche.

2 July. Prince Louis of France confronts John west of Angers; the Poitevins refuse to fight and John retreats to La Rochelle.

Pope Innocent lifts the interdict on England.

27 July. The Battle of Bouvines proves a crushing victory for the French under Philip II over the allies of John under Emperor Otto IV. Students at Paris hold seven days of 'feasting, leaping and dancing'.

14–15 October. John returns to England.

Christmas. The barons demand that John confirm Henry I's Coronation Charter (1100), which had made vague assurances over baronial rights and pledged to restore the Laws of Edward the Confessor.

1215   *6 January*. John meets the barons in London, but there is deadlock: the barons insist on the restoration of the 'ancient and accustomed liberties'. The king gets a delay until Easter. The parties agree to lay the matter before the Pope 'since he is lord of England'.

8 January. John sends legal representatives to Rome.

4 March. John takes an oath to go on crusade.

19 March. In Rome, Pope Innocent draws up *triplex forma pacis* (the threefold form of peace), a group of three letters drawn up by Pope Innocent which he hoped would resolve the dispute, and writes to the barons forbidding their conspiracies against John.

26 April. The barons assemble at Northampton, then make for Brackley, Northamptonshire.

5 May. The opposition barons make their formal *diffidatio*, renouncing their allegiance.

12 May. John orders the sheriffs to seize the lands and chattels of his enemies and begins distribution of their property among his supporters.

Civil war.

17 May (Sunday). Dissident barons are secretly admitted to London by a city faction.

9 June. John meets Stephen Langton in a preliminary conference at Windsor.

10 June. John faces a baronial deputation in Runnymede when draft heads of the agreement are presumably drawn up.

1215   *15 June*. The date on the Charter, presumed to be the day on which the terms were actually agreed between king and barons. The royal seal was to be attached, probably a few days later, to the Charters to be sent out to the counties. There was no 'signing ceremony'.

19 June. The ceremony of peace. The ceremony is intended to reconcile king and barons, but the dissidents soon take up arms and march on Rochester Castle.

24 June. The first batch of Charters are dispatched to the counties.

22 July. The last batch of Charters are dispatched.

24 August. The Pope annuls the Charter, and condemns the barons' opposition of the crusader-king.

September. Rochester Castle surrenders to the baronial army.

November. John recovers Rochester Castle.

1216   The army of Prince Louis of France arrives in England in support of the dissident barons.

May. Louis himself arrives in England.

16 October. Louis besieges Dover.

19 October. Death of John at Newark.

28 October. Henry III (aged nine) is crowned at Gloucester.

11 November. First reissue of the Charter (at Bristol).

November. The Pope opens the Fourth Lateran Council.

1217   *February*. The new Charter is sent, on Marshal's orders, to Ireland.

Louis is recalled to France by his father, Philip II.

23 April. Louis returns to England but without his father's blessing. He goes first to Winchester, then to Dover, where he raises the siege.

May–June. Chancery rolls record 150 '*reversi*' defecting back from the rebel to the loyalist cause.

June. Louis is in London. Negotiations between Louis and the loyalists break down.

24 August. Defeat of the French invasion fleet in the Channel.

12 September. The Treaty of Kingston ends the civil war and pays off Louis, who leaves England. The terms are so lenient that enemies would accuse Marshal of treason.

November. The first 'Charter of the Forest', dated 6 November: it forms a supplement to the second reissue of Magna Carta, which is undated, but is presumed to have been issued on the same day.

1225   Henry III's Charter is made '*spontanea de sua voluntate*', of his own volition.

1234   *August*. Royal letters are issued asserting that the Charters are granted to both great and small and to all men.

1237   King Henry III confirms both the Magna Carta of 1225 and the Charter of the Forest, so as to get agreement to a tax he needs to raise.

PART I

ROUTES TO RUNNYMEDE

The Charter had its roots in 1154 with the accession of Henry II; he was to check the collapse of royal authority during the 'anarchy' of King Stephen's reign – a golden age for England's Norman baronage. They in any case looked down on him as a *déclassé* foreign interloper, son of a mere count, Geoffrey of Anjou. A turbulent warrior, Geoffrey had married above himself when he won the hand of Matilda, widow of Emperor Henry V and daughter of Henry I of England. He had also, much to the barons' disgust, won the duchy of Normandy.

Baronial snobbery apart, Henry, king of England and lord of Ireland and half France, stands as one of the greatest rulers in European history. By brilliance, an obsession with justice and a huge talent for government, he continued the evolution of England's centralized administration and brought royal justice to an unparalleled pitch of quality and accessibility. The background to 1215 is best understood in the context of

the centralized English state enmeshed in the affairs of continental Europe. In the reign of his son, Richard I, events
evolved in a way that would help shape the future of France as
well as England, and so it is with Richard the Lionheart that
this book opens.

I

THE BROTHERS PLANTAGENET

On Sunday, 3 September 1189, a new king of England was crowned in Westminster Abbey. It was the first time in a hundred years that the crown had passed without controversy or warfare to the indisputable lineal successor. It is also the first coronation for which we have an extended and detailed contemporary account. And in broad outline it served as a model for all coronations over the next 800 years. The participants would not have been surprised. Many looked to the new reign to open a new era in the history of England.

The death of King Henry II two months earlier, lamented by a few, had been a cause of joy for many more. They hoped that the accession of his son Richard would bring the end of unreasonable royal demands and royal encroachment on baronial privilege and jurisdictions, with a return to customs which the Anglo-Norman baronage liked to believe were rooted in an immemorial past. Yet within a year this new king's government, like that of his father, was at loggerheads with the realm, and a generation later his brother John was obliged to agree a document that affronted the very idea of monarchy. A large part of the blame for the turmoil that led to Magna Carta lay with John himself, but discontents and resentments fuelled by Richard were smouldering in the social and political structure of England long before the final conflagration of 1215.

At the time of his coronation, Richard Plantagenet, Count of Anjou and Maine, Duke of Normandy, and Lord of Aquitaine by grace of his mother, Queen Eleanor, was in his thirty-third year. Though he had a surprisingly pale complexion, he was a handsome six-footer, with dazzling blue eyes, long straight limbs, deep chest and reddish-golden hair. Richard was the model of the knightly warrior – even in his faults. He was violent in his rage and jealous of his honour. But he had a generous streak too. A monastic chronicler accused him of 'immoderate use of arms from his earliest youth'. To a stark physical courage, this king joined an intellectual grasp of strategy, logistics and every branch of contemporary military practice, qualities which made him the most admired commander in Europe. Warfare was his trade. When he went to his crowning, it was with the prospect of worthy employment. In October 1187 Jerusalem the Holy City had fallen to the Muslim armies of Saladin, and the following year Richard had made his vows as a crusader. Thanks to the 'Saladin tithe' levied by his father, England had already shipped cargoes of cash to the treasury in Jerusalem. Richard's campaigning was to absorb silver pennies by the barrel load. He had plans. No doubt his counsellors knew what was coming; intelligent courtiers no doubt guessed. But the Sunday-morning celebrations of the coronation veiled the omens.

Attended at his lodgings by churchmen in purple silk vestments and by priests bearing a great cross, candles and thuribles of smoking incense, the king was conducted to the abbey along streets carpeted with cloth of the finest quality and resounding to 'the most glorious singing'. At the great west doors, a procession of nobles bearing the golden regalia of spurs, sceptre and verge fell in behind the royal party. Next followed three earls, among them the short, swarthy and somewhat foppish figure of Prince John, Earl of Gloucester, the king's brother, and a score of other notables.

The royal entourage halted at the high altar. The king now took the oath to protect the Church, to exercise justice and to root out evil customs. Next he was stripped of his clothes down to his undershirt and drawers. Taking the beautiful little silver spoon (last used at the coronation of Her Majesty Queen Elizabeth II in 1953), Archbishop Baldwin of Canterbury now anointed the king with the holy oil, smearing it on his head, exposed shoulders and chest. This was the central ritual of the whole service; it was the act which was seen to imbue Richard with the semi-sacred aura of the kingly office. The ceremony of crowning followed. Approaching the altar, the king himself lifted the ponderous, jewel-encrusted crown and gave it to the archbishop, who in turn placed it on the royal head. Next the archbishop gave the king the sceptre and the dove-tipped verge (the symbolic rod of authority) and led him to his throne. While the archbishop conducted the mass of the day, it seems the crown was held over the king's head by two earls.

A coronation was the most important event in medieval political life. Richard had acted with the authority of king since his father's death; now he was confirmed in the exercise of that supreme power in a ceremony that paralleled the consecration of a bishop. When the great men of the realm swore their allegiance to him, they did so as to a man now felt to have some attributes of the divine. In return that man was pledged to do justice to his subjects in general and to be a good lord to the oath-takers in particular. The only resort against a tyrannical monarch amounted to institutionalized rebellion. By a formal act known as *diffidatio*, a baron renounced his homage of allegiance and went to war against the king. It was a perilous course. Friends and allies in a quarrel against the king were, by definition, hard to come by. A man who put himself outside the king's lordship was liable to find his lands assigned to others. The king's recognized powers were immense and it required an extraordinary combination of oppression, misgovernment and political mismanagement to provoke a general rising.

A successful king carried his great nobles with him in major policy decisions. They were his natural councillors. But the actual administration of the king's government was generally headed by men of humble origins who had demonstrated their executive capacities and who were entirely dependent on royal favour. Two weeks after the coronation, Richard appointed the Norman cleric William Longchamp to be Bishop of Ely and as chancellor of England (shortly after he received the additional post of chief justiciar). Longchamp had already served the king well in the administrative service of the duchy of Aquitaine, but his enemies (he soon made plenty) claimed he was the grandson of a serf. The rise from unfree peasant to bishop in three generations was certainly possible. The medieval Church offered brilliant career opportunities to men of determination and talent from all walks of life. The minor clerical orders, badge of an educated man, were also the entrée to service in a great household or at court. For those who caught the king's eye, anything was possible. Even so, it is generally thought that the slur on William Longchamp's origins was without justification.

His appointment as Bishop of Ely was a classic instance of royal power in action. In theory, bishops were made either by the election of their cathedral chapters or by the provision of the pope. In fact, almost without exception, the electors' role amounted to little more than confirming a royal nominee, while the pope intervened only if he thought the candidate outrageously unsuitable, or to arbitrate. The medieval bishop was a great landowner; the revenue from his estates funded a handsome income to a minister of state at no expense to the Crown; and it might finance contingents of men-at-arms to the king's army. Piety, charitable works or theological profundity were rarely qualities a king looked for in his bishops; nor did he intend that a group comprising some of England's major landholders should be chosen by cabals of cloistered clerics. If his enemies are to be believed, Bishop Longchamp looked like a cross between Shakespeare's Richard III and Tolkien's Gollum; in addition to being low-born he was known as avaricious, unscrupulous, inordinately proud and consumed by ambition. By general report he was also a pederast. Even if we attribute a generous percentage of all this to the character assassins, the man hardly emerges as an obvious ornament to the bench of bishops. But the king rated him as a valued royal minister and the timid chapter at Ely, no doubt wisely, did not dare gainsay the royal nominee. The Pope acquiesced in the appointment.

Like the great men of the Church the barons were, ultimately, subject to the will of the king. A wise ruler aimed at least for the grudging support of these great men, the lay magnates; but if diplomacy and persuasion failed he could fall back on the arbitrary sanction known by the uncompromising formula of 'vis et voluntas', 'force and will'. If a noble fell under the royal displeasure for any reason, he might see his lands summarily confiscated and put in the hands of royal receivers. The slightest hint of sedition, failure to meet feudal dues, the marriage of a ward without royal permission: all were the kind of misdemeanours that could bring crippling penalties. While men might complain at a king's acting by *vis et voluntas*, no one questioned his right so to act. The dissident barons at Runnymede may have hoped to put a stop to it, but modern studies of the administrative records of Angevin kingship have shown that it lingered on after 1215. Naked fear of the king's power could shape the calculation of even the most obstreperous baron.

The career of Geoffrey Plantagenet, the king's half-brother, amply demonstrates how well justified such fear was. An illegitimate son, he had remained loyal to their father while Richard and John had rebelled more than once. Henry II had called Geoffrey his 'only true son', conferred the revenue of the bishopric of Lincoln on him, made him chancellor and promised him the archbishopric of York. In fact Geoffrey, a few years older than Richard, had aspirations far beyond the Church. On one occasion, when drinking with his cronies, he had settled a golden cup cover on his russet hair with the remark, 'Would not a crown look well on this head?' Soon after, Richard ordered the canons of York Minster to elect Geoffrey their archbishop. They complied, Rome having already waived any objections on the grounds of the candidate's illegitimate birth. Outraged protest rumbled through the English Church for years. Geoffrey himself, not yet even in holy orders, seemed to regard York and its revenues merely as a new power base, declaring that any grants made by the king within the ecclesiastical province would stand only with his will and consent. Richard brought him to heel; Geoffrey was stripped of his lands and ordered to undergo ordination as a priest. Three weeks after the coronation, 'unwilling and complaining', he finally complied. His lands were restored two months later, when on the promise of a payment of £3,000 he was 'to have the king's love'. With such power in things both temporal and spiritual pertaining to the king, it is small wonder that a medieval coronation was a ceremony of high solemnity and deeply felt symbolism.

When the rites in Westminster Abbey were completed, King Richard, now sanctified in the awesome powers of his office, changed out of the heavy ceremonial robes into a rich and elegant tunic and cloak and went to his coronation banquet in Westminster Hall. More than 900 sat down at table. By tradition it was an all-male occasion, women, even the wives of the nobles, being barred admission. But the guest list also excluded some of the richest and most important men in the kingdom. The nearest that even the greatest among the merchant princes of London came to participating in the festivities were the kitchens and pantries, where the senior dignitaries of rival gilds and merchant bodies squabbled over precedence to serve at table. Still richer men than they were forbidden entry even to the precincts of the palace of Westminster. These were the members of the city's Jewish community.

From about the year 1100, when their ancestors came over from Rouen, the Jewry of London had played an ever increasing role in the finances of England. Free of the Christian prohibition of usury, they were of central importance in the still primitive banking system. They enjoyed the dubious privilege of coming under the special 'protection' of the king. In fact, Jewish moneylenders operated under tight royal licence; like the gentile merchant community, they were 'permitted' to grant 'voluntary' gifts of money, or tallages, to the Crown when required to do so, like Christians; but unlike Christians their heir in the eyes of the law was the king himself. Jewish money was vital to the shaky royal finances. Nevertheless, on that coronation day in September 1189, Richard had given strict orders to the staff on the entrance to the hall that these 'enemies of Christ' were to be barred entry.

The great banquet was just beginning to swing when news came of some kind of commotion at the gates. Unaware, one supposes, of the royal arrangements governing admissions, a deputation of leading Jews, eager to honour their royal patron on his big day, had attempted to gain entrance with gifts and salutations. The guards had apparently forced them back, and the London mob carousing outside the palace enclosure were piling into the scrimmage. A bloody riot ensued. Longchamp, deputed as royal troubleshooter, was sent to investigate. But mob rule prevailed. By morning the Jewish quarter and neighbouring districts were smoking ruins and many leading figures of the community were dead. The king was incandescent. His reasons, in ascending order of importance: the special peace surrounding the court had been grossly violated; people specifically under royal protection had been killed; and, most serious of all, the royal exchequer would be badly out of pocket. With the creditor's bonds belonging to the dead financiers gone up in flames, the identity of their debtors and the amounts owing to their estates, and hence to their royal heir, could not be determined.

Bizarrely (and squalidly) enough, the perpetrators, who had thus damaged the royal finances, boasted that the mayhem they had wreaked on these 'enemies of Christ' was their contribution to the coming royal crusade. Jewries in other cities and towns, such as Stamford, Norwich and Bury St Edmunds suffered, as mobs decided to make their contribution to the king's crusading venture. At York, inspired by the ravings of a fanatical hermit, the mob included even members of the local gentry, among them intending crusaders who had no doubt equipped themselves with loans from Jewish moneylenders.

Ten years before, Sir Roger de Estreby of Lincolnshire had petitioned Henry II to implement a seven-point programme which, he claimed, had been revealed to him by the Archangel Gabriel and St Peter. Interestingly, some of the points anticipate Magna Carta but for Sir Roger one feels item seven was the crucial one: the king should expel the Jews from England, having first seized their chirographs (IOU counterfoils) and returned them freely to the borrowers. Sir Roger's hauberk was in pawn to Aaron of Lincoln.

At York such deeds of transactions were held in the cathedral minster's archive. The town's Jews fled for sanctuary to the king's castle, Clifford's Tower, chased there by the mob. Some of the fugitives martyred themselves in ritual suicide rather than face forcible conversion. Others consented to convert, only to be slaughtered as soon as they left their refuge. The mob next raided the minster and burnt the records.

Money for the crusade was in fact Richard's overriding priority, and the methods he used to raise it set new standards in royal rapacity. They were a major cause of the grievances in the build-up to Magna Carta. The decade-long reign of Richard I saw more money extracted from England's taxpayers than had been taken in any previous ten-year period. On the Tuesday following the coronation Richard put up for sale every possible asset. Estates from the royal domain and privileges of every kind went on the market. Profitable positions such as county sheriff or offices of state were farmed out to the highest bidder. Every operation by the office-holder, every petition by an applicant, was an opportunity for making money. William Longchamp had paid £3,000 for the chancellorship. Men already in place had to pay handsomely to keep their positions – or new men would buy them. Richard boasted 'I would have sold London could I have found a buyer.'

This king, who spent fewer than six months of his reign in England, never considered the country as more than a source of funds. In ten years he piled immense additional demands on the normal day-to-day outgoings of government. First the financing of the crusade; then the money for his ransom; finally funds for campaigning in France to defend his family's ancestral lands there against the designs of the French king. Richard left an empty treasury and a government encumbered by debt. His brother entered on a soured inheritance.

However, in early 1190, as Richard embarked his crusading army at Dover, John had little cause for complaint. He had been created Count of Mortain in Normandy, given a free hand in Ireland, and granted numerous castles and rich fiefs in England. Ignoring Church protests that the two were too closely related, Richard had allowed John's marriage to their distant cousin Isabelle de Clare, heiress of the great Gloucester estates. The revenues of Somerset, Dorset, Devon and Cornwall, Derbyshire and Nottinghamshire were all assigned to him. Here were the makings of a principality and a princely revenue and John prepared to rule as a sovereign prince. One thing Richard had not done, however, was to nominate an heir. Should anything happen to the king, the question of the succession would be critical. Crusading was dangerous and Jerusalem was a long way from England.

Richard's generosity to his brother, in terms of lands and revenues, seems feckless: the family history may hold a clue. Their father's reluctance to delegate lands and responsibilities to his sons had served as their pretext for more than one rebellion. Queen Eleanor had eagerly abetted her sons. The feuding family of the Angevins was the wonder of Europe. It boasted the devil among its ancestors and even intelligent observers were prepared to credit the legend. For his part, Philip of France backed son against father at every available

opportunity. John, the youngest, had been his father's favourite, yet he had joined the last rebellion and in so doing had
broken his father's heart. But King Henry had not granted the
boy estates on which to maintain his self-respect and, as John
'Lackland' ('*Jean sans Terre*'), he felt himself a laughing stock.
The fact that, despite his magnanimity, Richard did not name
his brother his heir before setting out on the hazards of
crusading far from Europe, might suggest that he feared such
a formal designation could tempt John into trying to make it a
reality. Avidly ambitious, John, like all the 'Devil's brood', had
learnt disloyalty at his mother's knee; before their father died,
his elder brother had allied himself to the arch-enemy France.
Evidently, betrayal could be the road to power. Later Prince
John would reveal a fascination with and a talent for governing. Just now, in his early twenties, he wanted money by the
sackful – and power.

The vast English territories he now disposed of were a
starting point. He soon set up an administrative structure,
complete with justiciar, chancellor and seal-bearer, which
mimicked the royal government. His chief adviser, Bishop
Hugh Nunant of Coventry, had a reputation to match Longchamp himself. When he catalogued the sins of a lifetime on his
deathbed no confessor, it was said, could be found willing to
absolve him. With Hugh at his right hand, John stood ready to
champion any baron with any grievance against the royal
minister. Chancellor Longchamp obligingly provided justification for such grievances.

People naturally expected a man with such power to practise
nepotism on a grand scale. Men sighed resignedly when the
upstart from Normandy handed out profitable appointments
to his relations. But when Longchamp married them to great
English heiresses whom he controlled as wards of the
Crown, resignation turned to fury. Longchamp boasted of

his contempt for the great men of England and humiliated even the men that Richard had appointed to work with him as his colleagues. One such, the powerful Hugh le Puiset, Bishop of Durham, Earl of Northumberland and royal justiciar for the north, was dispossessed and forced into retirement. William Marshal, one of Richard's most revered advisers and a man respected by the whole baronage for his knightly prowess, was relieved of the important castle of Gloucester. Bishop Godfrey of Winchester was forced to give up lands, castles and honours for which he had paid the king £3,000 only the year before. The chancellor added these to his own already considerable holdings and revenues. These included the immense temporal revenues of the archdiocese of York; Geoffrey Plantagenet was still awaiting consecration so that the see was technically vacant and its non-ecclesiastical revenues went to the Crown. Since the king, apprehensive about the use to which Geoffrey might put them, was opposing the consecration, it might be indefinitely delayed. Meantime the revenues were at the disposal of the chancellor. Many considered him a still greater threat to the king's authority and to the kingdom.

Their view was not unreasonable. In the spring of 1191, Longchamp came to a private understanding with King William 'the Lion' of Scotland. In March news reached England that Archbishop Baldwin of Canterbury had died on crusade. Now the temporalities of the southern province of the Church joined those of York under the control of the power-hungry chancellor. The fact that he had also been appointed the Pope's legate in England tempted the ambitious minister to aim for outright control of the Church throughout England. However, complaints about his deputy's high-handed behaviour were streaming into Richard's travelling court on the other side of Europe. The king decided on a major policy change. He now asked the Pope to expedite the consecration of Geoffrey as

Archbishop of York. At the same time he dispatched Walter of Coutances, Archbishop of Rouen, to England with letters authorizing him to partner Longchamp in the administration of the realm. But now the chancellor-justiciar, with thousands of mercenaries and numerous castles at his command, decided he was powerful enough to challenge even documents under the royal seal. Accordingly he ignored Archbishop Walter, demanding proof of the 'authenticity' of his letters of appointment. Walter looked for an ally against the dangerous minister. Prince John, who was certainly not about to let anyone else usurp the authority of his absent brother, was the obvious candidate.

Indeed, no one in England was more worried by Longchamp's ever advancing power. In simple, practical terms, his seizure of Gloucester Castle had been an overt threat to the prince's holdings in the west country and his swelling resources and influence were still more threatening in the long term. Now John eagerly canvassed opinion among the leading magnates. Most promised him their support in the event of a confrontation. Thus, improbable as it might seem in the light of later events, Prince John emerged for a time as champion of his brother's authority and champion also of the baronage of England against the excesses of a royal government officer out of control.

The confrontation duly came. Longchamp accused the sheriff of Lincoln of corruption and demanded he surrender the castle there, which happened to be of considerable strategic importance. The sheriff sought protection at John's court and left his wife, Nicholaa de la Haye, in charge of the castle's defences. They were in good hands. A castellan's wife was expected to know her husband's business and Lady Nicholaa was respected for courage and competence. She held off the besieging army and Prince John took advantage of the breathing space to seize the neighbouring castles of Nottingham and Tickhill. Longchamp decided to seek terms.

Under the mediation of Archbishop Walter, the rivals, each backed by large forces of armed men including contingents of Welsh bowmen, met at Winchester. Three senior bishops nominated arbitrators drawn from the rival camps. These were sworn to deliberate to 'the honour of each party and the peace of the realm' and to settle any future disputes. The prince and the chancellor undertook to abide by the arbitrators' decision.

Castles were a major concern for the treaty arbitrators at Winchester. Lincoln, the cause of all the trouble, was returned to the sheriff – though he was ordered to answer the charges of corruption. Prince John surrendered Nottingham and Tickhill to the custody of Archbishop Walter, though they would be reassigned back to John should the chancellor cause further trouble. Longchamp remained in office but was now forced to accept the archbishop as his colleague in government. The treaty dramatically curbed his powers in another matter, with high significance for the future. Henceforward no one, whether bishop, earl or simple freeholder, was to be dispossessed merely 'at the pleasure of the justiciars or ministers of the Lord King'. Any such case was to be settled in the courts, 'according to the legitimate customs of the realm', or by the king himself. No one at this point dared question the monarch's personal exercise of his '*vis et voluntas*'. It was another matter altogether when royal ministers invoked it as a routine procedure of government. Opponents of the royal government appealed to the ancient custom of the realm and a senior churchman acted as adviser and mediator. The treaty at Winchester foreshadowed Runnymede in a still more important respect. It set up a committee to monitor the government's observance of its terms and to enforce redress if it broke them.

In September Geoffrey Plantagenet, now duly consecrated Archbishop of York, landed secretly at Dover. Longchamp had issued an order banning his entry into the country and the wife of the constable of Dover Castle was none other than Longchamp's sister. It was probably she who forced the events that followed. The archbishop had sought sanctuary with the monks of Dover priory. It was here, on Wednesday 18 September, that he was given orders to leave the kingdom. He refused. Without further ado, armed men dragged him from the church by his feet, his head jolting over the mud and cobbles of the ill-made streets. Imprisoned in the castle, he solemnly excommunicated his abductors. It was barely twenty years since Archbishop Thomas of Canterbury had been martyred on the steps of his own altar. It was useless for Longchamp to protest that he had not ordered the sacrilege: all who heard of the outrage were united against him and his supporters. In effect, the head of the royal government was under siege from popular opinion.

Prince John leapt to his half-brother's defence, and sent to Dover to demand he be released. The castellan refused without direct orders from the chancellor. Together with Archbishop Walter of Coutances, John rallied the guarantors of the Winchester treaty. Bishops, barons and the chancellor himself were summoned to assemble at Loddon Bridge, between Reading and Windsor, to 'deliberate on certain matters concerning the Lord King and the realm'. At this point Longchamp ordered Geoffrey's release. The wronged prelate relished a triumphal progress to London where he preached opposition to the chancellor before heading west for Loddon Bridge. When he finally rode into the pavilioned encampment there, John welcomed him with effusive displays of brotherly love. The next morning, majestically in cope and mitre, Geoffrey, tears in his eyes, fell to his knees to implore the assembled dignitaries to right his wrongs. Then Archbishop Walter read a letter from the king that empowered him to supervise the election to the see of Canterbury and to depose Longchamp as chancellor should he refuse to consult with his fellow justiciar. It was all very affecting and, for Longchamp, ominous.

At the last moment on his way to the Loddon Bridge conference, perhaps fearing for his personal safety, he had turned away and headed for Windsor Castle. Now, in desperate straits, he sent a member of his circle, William de Briouze (Braose) to Prince John, with offers of a handsome bribe for his support. It was the right idea – John rarely refused offers of money – but the timing was wrong. Revelling in his unaccustomed role as champion of an oppressed nobility, John was also anticipating the removal of his rival from the scene of active politics. The bribe was virtuously rejected and Longchamp summoned to answer the charges that had been formulated against him. Instead, 'sparing neither horse nor spurs', he raced for London, the key to England.

The chancellor had his supporters among the city factions but the mood of the times was against them. To support him now would mean shutting the gates against England's two most popular men in Church and state – both brothers of the king himself. The chancellor and his party dashed for the Tower, while the citizens went out with torches and lanterns to welcome Prince John. The next day, summoned by the bells of St Paul's, the citizenry assembled to hear again the wrongs done to Archbishop Geoffrey and the misconduct of Longchamp, who was now mewed up in his 'refuge' by bands of citizen militia. To general acclaim he was pronounced deposed from his office as justiciar, and Walter of Coutances was appointed chief justiciar in his stead. As for John, he was hailed as *rector totius regni*, 'governor of the whole realm'. A grateful prince made formal recognition of London as an independent 'commune'.

Longchamp's humiliation was not over. Attempting to escape from England disguised as a woman, he was fumbled and rumbled by a fisherman, on Dover sands. On 29 October 1191 John authorized a ship to take him to France. In fact he retained the office of chancellor and, in 1193 regained Richard's favour when he arranged the terms of the captured king's ransom with the emperor in Germany.

Having seen off his rival in England, John was now ready to try his luck in France. The time was opportune. In December, King Philip returned from the crusades. By leaving Richard of England to champion the cause of religion in the Holy Land he hoped to be able to exploit his rival's absence from Europe to take over his French lands. But a planned invasion of Normandy had to be abandoned when the French magnates refused to make war on a crusader. Philip guessed that the crusader's brother would have no such scruples. For years he had pitted the Angevin brothers against their father; now he confidently expected to play the same game between the brothers themselves. Overlord of the family's French territories, Philip now offered them to John – leaving the prince to make good his claim as best he could. Fascinated by the prospect, John assembled a force at Southampton. Even French chroniclers, such as Rigord de Saint-Denis, hostile though they were to Richard, were shocked by John's treacherous dealings with his brother's enemy, their own king. But John probably felt he was following family precedent. Eight years before, when Richard had refused their father's order that he hand over Aquitaine to John, King Henry had ordered him and his brother Geoffrey to war against Richard.

By mid-February 1192, all was ready. But the expedition never took place. The seventy-year-old Queen Eleanor, herself Duchess of Aquitaine in her own right, had got wind of this plan to oust Richard, her favourite son, from half his inheritance. Braving the wintry waters of the Channel, she crossed over to England. Convening four successive meetings of the Great Council, she forced John to abandon his treacherous scheme under threat of confiscation of all his English lands.

Having mobilized the lay magnates against her unscrupulous youngest son, the ageing but imperious queen turned her attention to conditions in the English Church. Here the air was thick with ecclesiastical thunderbolts. Once out of England, Longchamp, in his capacity as bishop, had appealed to the Pope. By return, he received bulls of excommunication against John's advisers the Archbishop of Rouen and the Bishops of Winchester and Coventry, and against John himself. Meanwhile, in the course of an ecclesiastical dispute in the northern province, the Bishop of Durham had been excommunicated by Archbishop Geoffrey of York. Not even Hugh of Avalon, Bishop of Lincoln, reckoned the most saintly of the English bishops (John was a pall-bearer at his interment), paid much attention to these ecclesiastical tantrums. Others ignored them altogether. Walter of Coutances confiscated the revenues of Longchamp's Ely diocese and he, in retaliation, laid the diocese under an interdict. With all this politicking among the clerics, the souls of ordinary Christians were in mortal peril. None of the Ely clergy could celebrate mass and bodies lay unburied in the fields. Visiting some of her manors in the diocese, Queen Eleanor saw the condition of affairs at first hand. She was able to enforce a reconciliation among the southern bishops; Durham and York continued hostilities. By the end of the year, however, news reached England of more serious developments – at least in the political sense.

In October, King Richard sailed from Palestine. He had recaptured much territory for the Christian kingdom of Jerusalem, and though the Holy City itself remained in Muslim hands, had won a hero's reputation. But news from England compelled a return to Europe to defend his beleaguered territories and, if possible, settle the disputes in his troubled kingdom. He had decided to travel overland rather than take the long sea route through the Mediterranean, round the Iberian peninsula and up the Atlantic coast of France to the Channel. To avoid the hostile territory of France he took ship up the Adriatic and then made his way through the Alpine passes into the lands subject to the emperor Henry VI. Even here it was necessary to travel in disguise, for the route lay through the territory of Leopold, Duke of Austria, a fellow crusader whom Richard had deeply insulted after the capture of the city of Acre. Leopold had planted his standard on the walls; Richard, considering this presumptuous in one who was not of royal blood, had hurled it into the moat. Such was the affair of honour that would bring the crown of England into pawn and the diplomacy of Europe into frenzy.

Travelling disguised as a monk, it seems that Richard was betrayed by his great height and by the excessive deference shown to him by his companions. At all events, he was seized by agents of Duke Leopold as a suitable case for ransom. The duke sold him on to Emperor Henry VI, who found he had an auction on his hands. (News of these bizarre events would presumably have been received with glee if they reached the Muslim world: the royal hero of the Christian cause against Islam being held to ransom by the Holy Roman Empire, head of western Christendom!) Richard's ministers found themselves competing for the return of their sovereign with the king of France. Philip first reckoned that with Richard in a French prison he could force him to renounce the Angevin French inheritance as the price of release. But when it seemed the emperor was going to deal with England after all, he offered to pay him to delay

Richard's release for a year, during which time he calculated he could overrun 'English' France and instal John as a puppet vassal.

In January 1193 John hurried to Paris to do homage to Philip for the English lands in France. He bustled back to England to foment civil war, confident of Philip's help. The attempts to rehabilitate John's black reputation have pointed to his undoubted ability for administration, his concern for the administration of justice and his capacity for hard work. To contemporaries he seemed devious, untrustworthy and, in the last resort, cowardly. In a world where character counted for more than competence, these things mattered. When we consider that while John was negotiating with his brother's enemies, the English government was straining its resources to ransom its king, we can perhaps understand one reason at least for John's unsavoury reputation.

The ransom had been agreed at 150,000 marks (£100,000) – a sum almost beyond the range of contemporary accounting. It was impossible to audit the returns of the tax collectors. Extortion and embezzlement were rife. A country drained by demands to finance the crusade was now ransacked for cash for a king who, some may have thought, should have had more sense than to get captured in the first place. Yet the first massive instalment was found, and in March 1194 King Richard of England was back in his realm and presiding over a royal council at Nottingham. The honour escort of German knights who accompanied him were stunned by the city's opulence; they reckoned their emperor would have pitched the price higher had he been better informed.

John had fled to Normandy. His grandiose treason had collapsed from lack of support. In March the king presided over a Great Council which stripped the prince of his lands. John Lackland once more, he was summoned to trial in forty days on a charge of treason. It never happened. Travelling through Normandy in May, Richard had a meeting with his brother. He gave him the kiss of peace with the words, 'Think no more of it, brother: you are but a child who has had evil counsellors.' The 'child's' lands, however, were not at once restored. Taught loyalty at least for the time being, John displayed considerable ability as a captain of mercenaries in Richard's campaigns against Philip of France, prosecuted to secure the Angevin ancestral lands there against the French king's depredations. At home, the exchequer toiled away at its familiar task, the extracting of large sums of money from an ever more fractious baronage, which it shipped overseas to fund those campaigns.

Near forty years old, Richard the Lionheart – he seems to have acquired the nickname on crusade, either because of his bravery or because of his brutality – was again soon in his element, fighting in a righteous cause: the vindication of his own knightly honour and the defence of his family lands. Affirmed king of England once again, on the advice of his barons, to wipe out any doubts following his act of homage to the emperor, in a ceremony reminiscent of the 'crown wearings' of the Anglo-Saxon kings, at Winchester in April 1194, he immediately afterwards set off for Portsmouth and thence for France, never to see England again. Mobilizing alliances among the lords of territories on France's eastern borders against Philip, he displayed political skills to match his soldiership. In the year 1196 he commenced the building of Château Gaillard on the Seine; technically an outstanding complex of fortifications, it was complete in three seasons. Then, in September 1198, commanding a small force of battle-hardened mercenaries he routed the main French army near Gisors. King Philip led the flight across the little River Epte and, as the bridge broke under the weight of his knights, himself 'drank of the river'. While he was being hauled up by his heels on to the bank Richard was claiming three Frenchmen as prisoners. Four months later he signed a five-year truce with the French king. A new trouble was looming among his fractious vassals in his mother's duchy of Aquitaine.

Adhémar, Viscount of Limoges, was among the ringleaders. On 26 March, directing the siege of the viscount's castle of Chalus, Richard was terribly wounded in the eye socket by a bolt from the bow of a sharp shooter on the castle battlements. The wound festered and on 6 April, after days of unrelieved agony, the king died, the victim of gangrene. He bequeathed his jewels and the bulk of his personal treasure to his German nephew, Otto of Brunswick (whom he had created Earl of York and who, people said, looked very like him); the remainder of his treasure he left to be divided among his servants and the poor; the 'realm of England and all his other lands' he left to his brother John.

The will of a dying king weighed heavily in the choice of his successor; especially when, as in this case, the law was not clear. Richard's territories, stretching from the northern frontiers with Scotland to the foothills of the Pyrenees and a border with Spanish Navarre in the south, were held by a cluster of titles and governed by a patchwork of local customs and traditions. The crown of England was the prize title, followed by the golden rose ducal coronet of Normandy and the great ducal sword of Aquitaine, held by right of his mother. It was as Count of Poitou that Richard had claimed the allegiance of Adhémar of Limoges; in the family's hereditary land of Anjou he ruled also by virtue of his title of count. The law governing the succession varied from territory to territory.

In England opinions as to the law of succession differed. The fashionable legal view tended to the idea that descent of the crown lay in the senior male line, what today we would call strict primogeniture. On this basis the haughty, twelve-year-old Arthur, posthumous son of John's older brother Geoffrey Duke of Brittany (killed at a tournament in Paris in 1186), had the better claim. Indeed, Archbishop Hubert Walter of Canterbury urged that it be accepted. The other chief advisers of the dead king, William Marshal among them, declared for John. In Normandy, by ancient custom, the younger son is nearer to the land of his father than is a nephew; moreover, they pointed out, their dead master had made his will plain. The archbishop, we are told, warned Marshal that he would live to rue his decision. But the choice was inevitable. In any case Arthur, a ward of the king of France, had never been to England and despised the English.

As soon as news of his brother's death reached him, John rode straight to Chinon on the Loire, the traditional treasury of the House of Anjou. Arthur's mother, Constance of Brittany, entrusted her son to the care of King Philip, raised an army of Bretons and at Angers on Easter Day convened an assembly of the barons of Anjou, Maine and Touraine, who pledged their allegiance to Arthur as their count. On 25 April at Rouen, John was solemnly invested as Duke of Normandy, while in England a council of the nobility held at Northampton under William Marshal and the Archbishop of Canterbury declared for John as their king.

He was crowned in Westminster Abbey on 27 May 1199. Significantly, Isabelle of Gloucester was not at his side. The Church had always contested the legality of their union and John now wanted freedom of manoeuvre in the royal marriage market. He was in fact contemplating a Portuguese marriage, to counterbalance the friendship between Philip of France and the Pyrenean kingdom of Navarre, which threatened the territory of Aquitaine, held for the Angevin cause by the septuagenarian duchess, John's mother Eleanor. Two panels of bishops were appointed, one in England and one in Aquitaine: both found the king to be a single man. (A history of John written during the reign of Henry VIII, whose marriage to Catherine of Aragon was unilaterally declared null by the Archbishop of Canterbury of the day, saw the Angevin king as a champion of the kingdom against papal tyranny.)

The immediate problem in the summer of 1199 was the rebellious condition of Anjou, Maine and Touraine. Lying between Normandy and Aquitaine, the territories' support for Arthur of Brittany posed a considerable menace to John's dominion in his French lands. Volatile and moody, John was a sound strategist and capable in an emergency of vigorous military action. Late in 1199 he saw that the key to his French problems lay in those rebel territories. Ignoring a French raid into Normandy, he drove southward into Maine and in September seized Arthur and forced him to sign peace terms at Le Mans. Philip had been outmanoeuvred and now he came to the negotiating table. However, in the interim Arthur had escaped and joined the French king. At the Treaty of Le Goulet (Brittany) on 22 May 1200 John was recognized as heir to Richard's French territories, in return for homage to King Philip as his overlord there and the payment of a relief (a standard feudal inheritance levy) of 20,000 marks. John was now undisputed lord of the Angevin inheritance. Portuguese ambassadors were at his court and prospects for the southern alliance looked promising. Above all he had peace. He had also broken alliances with his nephew Otto of Brunswick and the Counts of Flanders and Boulogne which his brother Richard had rated so highly. Did John perhaps think that Philip had abandoned his attempt to drive the Angevins out of France?

But Philip was a man dedicated to a mission. For more than two centuries his family, the House of Capet, had amounted to very little. The founding father, Hugh Capet, elected king in

987 by an assembly of nobles, for the most part men more
powerful than he and determined to remain sovereign in their
own territories, was effectively limited to his own lands in the
Ile de France. By contrast the Norman dukes, proud of their
Viking ancestry, effectively controlled northern France, while
the dukes of Aquitaine ruled an immense territory which had
once been a kingdom in its own right. Lesser men like the
counts of Anjou rapaciously extended their own bailiwicks
with barely a nod in the direction of Paris.

Yet all these ambitious barons honoured the fine old political fiction that, with the overthrow of the line of Charle-
magne in the lands of the western Franks, the Capetian at Paris
had succeeded to his position as their feudal overlord. Almost
all went through the ritual of homage and some even paid
reliefs to enter their inheritances. Meanwhile, the descendants
of Hugh Capet methodically produced sons and had them
crowned kings, during their fathers' lifetimes, in the sacred city
of Reims with the holy oil presented in legendary times to St
Rémy by the Blessed Virgin. They stolidly extended their
modest influence wherever possible and so, by degrees, accumulated attributes of actual power to the aura of kingship,
which no one had ever denied them.

Then, in the mid-twelfth century Henry Count of Anjou,
and, through his father, Duke of Normandy, husband of
Eleanor of Aquitaine, father of Richard and John, united
north and south, Normans and Aquitanians, and added them
to the crown of England. Half of France was now subject to
western Europe's strongest ruler. This was the nightmare
clouding the inheritance of Philip when he came to the throne
of France, just fifteen years old, in 1180. His insignificant
appearance and youthful inexperience suggest that the dynasty
was doomed for ever to mediocrity. But the slow seepage of
custom and precedent accumulated by his forefathers had

filled a reservoir of royal prestige and power, and Philip soon revealed qualities of political cunning and tenacity of purpose fully equal to the sometimes neurotic brilliance of the Angevins. The destruction of their power in France was his lifetime's work. It was John's misfortune to face the first French king with the resources, ability and determination of a world-class statesman.

The Treaty of Le Goulet was a classic Capetian stratagem. Couched in traditional feudal terms which no reasonable man could dispute, in fact it strengthened a legalistic obligation which could be developed as a lever of power. Even King Henry II had done homage for his French lands. Homage was, after all, the cement of feudal society. Should he refuse it to his French overlord, his own barons might jib at swearing allegiance to him. But neither Henry nor Richard had dreamed of paying any reliefs. The money would have to be extracted and no French king of their acquaintance had dared raised the matter. However, with Arthur at his court Philip had a valuable bargaining counter. At Le Goulet, for all its conventional technicalities, King John had made an unprecedented and binding admission of the French king's once theoretical overlordship, sealed for the first time in cash.

English critics of the treaty dubbed their king John Softsword. The borders of Normandy gleamed garishly with the fresh-hewn stone of his brother's new castles, Château Gaillard, Richard's 'saucy' castle on the Seine, the queen of them all. To replace the often reluctant and amateurish feudal levies, he had regularly deployed columns of professional mercenaries. Breaking the convention of a spring–summer campaigning season, he had waged war all the year round, looming up out of winter mists to steal unfair victories from startled and indignant opponents. Normandy and the Angevin exchequer, it is true, had been temporarily bankrupted in the process. As

Richard had cheerfully bragged, 'there's not a penny left in Chinon', and now John discovered how nearly the jest spoke truth. Richard's five-year truce with Philip of France had died with him and John needed time to raise the 20,000 marks stipulated as the relief to be paid under the terms of Le Goulet. It might be a hostage to the future; its payment would certainly embitter his subjects already so heavily mulcted by his brother, but to default was out of the question. That might well provoke hostilities from Philip of France. To quote one twentieth-century commentator, 'if John had tried a firm sword, it would have shattered in his hand'.

Peace with France in the north seemingly assured, in July John embarked on a progress through Aquitaine, towards the Pyrenees. He commissioned a return embassy to the Portuguese court. As he moved south, receiving homage from counts and nobles, inspecting castle garrisons and relishing the strange luxuries of southern cuisine, the city of Angoulême was preparing for a brilliant marriage between Isabella of Angoulême and Hugh le Brun of Lusignan, Lord of La Marche. Their families, two of the greatest in Poitou, itself the northern dependency of the vast duchy of Aquitaine, had been at loggerheads for years. The marriage marked a dynastic reconciliation that should bring peace to the local region but which might hold dire implications for their joint feudal overlord. The lands of bride and groom, about to be united by the marriage, would form a block of territory between royal France in the east and the Atlantic coast in the west that would effectively split the duchy in half. The Lusignans were no friends of the Plantagenets and John had cause to worry.

He was well south of Bordeaux when, in mid-August, he retraced his route to arrive at the city of Angoulême in time to join the throng of fashionable guests at the wedding. The bride was a dazzling, very young beauty. The king's first sight of her was as she was led into the church by her father. By his authority as overlord of both families, John stopped the proceedings and took the bridegroom's place at the altar steps. So goes the story, and the actual events may have matched it. Certainly John and Isabella were married only days after his arrival in the city, plans for a Portuguese union apparently forgotten. Instead, in the political balance, John could set the break-up of a potential threat from an Angoulême–Lusignan accord with the bonus of a breathtaking bride. Passion and policy seemed married that day. Contemporaries were to say that he had been bewitched – even historians think he may have been in love. But he had won, too, a remorseless enemy. Count Hugh left Angoulême swearing vengeance.

It was John's second marriage; his first, to Isabelle of Gloucester, had been annulled in 1199 (they shared a common ancestor in Henry I). The king held on to her lands but, equally, he maintained a numerous household for her in a residence for some years at Winchester Castle and was generous as to revenues and gifts. There were objections to the new Isabella as bride also. In the first place she and Hugh had gone through a form of betrothal that would have constituted full marriage had the union been consummated. Her date of birth is unknown, though her parents are first recorded as man and wife in 1191; so she could have been under age, even the then accepted age of twelve, and Hugh had held back on grounds of decency. Historian Nicholas Vincent has noted what a bonus it would be for critics of the king if the charge of 'child-molesting' could be added to all his other character failings! Isabella's first recorded child, Henry (later King Henry III), did not arrive until 1207.

As he returned to England, John felt in control; always a dangerous mood for him. He had won himself a beautiful if dangerous 'child' bride ('she should have been named Jezebel

rather than Isabel' was the view of chronicler Matthew Paris –
but then he accused her of incest and sorcery), forced Philip of
France to terms and he imagined he had cowed the troublesome
lords of Poitou. In the first years of his reign he had toured most
of his continental lands and was presiding over an Angevin
empire that was at peace. In fact, the situation was unstable.
Queen Eleanor's agents were reporting new rumblings of discontent among the Poitevins. She sent couriers across the
Channel, urging her son to come and rally his supporters. John,
in characteristic style, preferred to humiliate his enemies still
further. He ordered his officials to harry the Lusignans and 'do
them all the harm they could'. Punitive measures of this kind
were the standard way for an overlord to discipline unruly
vassals. In England, as yet, there was no one to contest such
overbearing action. In France the case was different. The
Lusignans appealed against John as Duke of Aquitaine to the
king of France, their supreme lord and John's also.

Philip undoubtedly had the authority to summon John, as
lord of the duchy, to answer complaints against him by his
under vassals in the royal court of France. But he hesitated. He
had domestic problems of his own and did not wish to
confront his powerful royal vassal if that could be avoided.
Instead he required John to give his personal assurance that he
would give the Lusignans a fair hearing of their case in the
Aquitainian court. Confident that he had correctly assessed the
political mood in Paris, that the situation was back to normal-
ity as it had been under his brother and father, and that he
could flout the theoretical supremacy of the Capetian monarchy as an outmoded legal quibble, John went back on his
assurance. Seething with frustration, Philip recognized that he
now faced the great showdown with the Angevins at a time not
of his own choosing. If he left the Lusignans to their fate,
Capetian claims to the sovereignty in France would be

crippled; if he challenged John, war could be guaranteed and victory was far from certain.

Grasping the nettle, Philip issued a summons against John to stand trial as a vassal of France for failing to render justice to his sub-vassals of Lusignan. Although it was issued against him in his capacity as a nobleman of France, the summons fascinated contemporaries. Whatever the technicalities, here was one king solemnly claiming jurisdiction over another. At Le Goulet, John had formally acknowledged Philip to be his overlord in France, but that was a very different matter from standing in the well of his court as an accused lawbreaker. The hearing was set to open on Tuesday 28 April 1202. The barons of France assembled in formal session, for the Duke of Aquitaine could be tried only before a court of his peers (a right, be it noted, that Magna Carta would grant to every freeman of England). The appointed time came and went.

John had promised to attend the hearing and even to hand over two castles as security. He fulfilled neither undertaking. Now, at the behest of King Philip, the barons formally pronounced him contumacious for failing to obey the citation of his liege lord. He was declared to have forfeited his fiefs of Aquitaine, Poitou and Anjou. The king proclaimed that the mutual ties of feudal obligation between him and John were severed. Next he knighted Arthur of Brittany and invested him with the Angevin lands that the court had adjudged forfeit. In July 1202 Arthur did homage for them. Meanwhile, French troops invaded Normandy.

Strictly speaking, it was not John 'Duke of Normandy' but John 'Lord of Aquitaine' who was contumacious. Having decided on confrontation with his overmighty vassal, Philip was declaring all-out war. The initiative made sound strategic sense. The Lusignans were now fighting alongside Arthur in the south against a small force led by Eleanor of Aquitaine. For his part, John was confident that the great border castles would protect the duchy and he marched south to the support of his mother. Approaching eighty, the shadow of her legendary beauty still able to inspire men to follow her imperious will, she had raised herself from her sick bed in defence of the Angevin heartlands.

On 29 July, when he was just south of Le Mans, the king was met by a courier with desperate news. The Lady Eleanor was in imminent danger of capture – she and her little army were standing at bay in the castle of Mirebeau en Poitou, some 80 miles (129 kilometres) to the south. Early in the morning of 30 July, John, at the head of a body of crack horsemen, set off at the steady hand gallop of an Angevin prince in a hurry, and at cockcrow on 1 August he saw the village of Mirebeau in the valley below him. John raised the siege and was master of the place. His mother was free and all the rebel leaders were in his power, Arthur at their head; he had been taken prisoner by William de Briouze, who handed his prize to the king. Contemporaries considered it near miraculous: as in 1200, King Philip had to withdraw from Normandy. Angevin power had never seemed greater. Presiding over a triumph to match anything achieved by Richard, John proceeded to throw it away.

Vindictive in victory and mistrustful of loyalty, he shocked opinion with his ill-treatment of the prisoners and drove new men into rebellion by insulting those who had helped him with his triumph. As for Arthur, he was never seen in public again. In 1203, gruesome reports as to his fate began to circulate. Ralph of Coggeshall in England heard that John had given orders that the young man be blinded and castrated (the penalty, incidentally, exacted by the forest laws of Richard I for poaching the king's deer). The abbot of Coggeshall Abbey in Essex found such action against one of noble blood to be both 'detestable' and 'execrable', but mutilations were fairly standard practice for the disposal of, for example, rival claimants to the imperial Byzantine throne. At Constantinople in the 1190s the emperor Alexius III Angelus had deposed and ordered the blinding of his brother Isaac II. Similar bestial measures were known in Ireland where, in 1141, Dermot MacMurrough established his position as king of Leinster by killing or blinding seventeen rivals. John's French contemporary Simon de Montfort the Elder presided over systematic atrocities against the Albigensian 'heretics' in the south of France with the consent of the Roman Catholic Church – a body, one must always remember, that considered burning alive a conventional and proper punishment for any flagrant offender against the faith. In his discussion of John's undoubted reputation for cruelty, a recent historian observed that 'compared with Hitler and Stalin . . . John seems quite tame'. The comparison is surely bizarre – in the company of those two monsters even Genghis Khan might uneasily feel himself outclassed. By the standards of his own time, while hostile churchmen might carp, John's practices were often matched by his contemporaries. Returning from crusade in 1192, his courts having found a number of Jews guilty of ritual murder, Philip of France had the wretched victims burnt at the stake.

Whether in fact he was brutalized, Arthur could hardly expect his freedom. The legendary name he bore made him a hero to the Celtic Bretons. King Philip had named him lord of John's French inheritance; and when we consider that he had made war on his own grandmother, it is clear that this arrogant fifteen-year-old was no plaster saint. He had played an unscrupulous game for high stakes and lost. Gossip soon reported that John had killed him. Evidence was never forthcoming; though it seems that William de Briouze later claimed to have been present at Rouen Castle on the night that the king himself, in a drunken rage, murdered his nephew. As to King Philip, he never accused John of the crime. He merely proposed to talk terms about the release or ransom of the teenage Duke of Brittany, whenever he might be produced. Few mourned, and none was surprised at the disappearance. Yet the killing of a kinsman was dirty work for a king and John's reputation fell another notch.

But the removal of Arthur, by whatever means, seemed to yield practical results. By the end of 1202 John was master of all the rebel strongholds in Poitou. Many of the minor leaders of the rebellion were sent to England, where they were incarcerated in Corfe Castle; they died in an attempt to overpower the garrison. The principal Lusignans were closely confined. But a new threat loomed from John's former allies at the taking of Mirebeau, who were disgusted by the contemptuous way they had been treated. To counterbalance this, he reinstated the Lusignans in exchange for hostages and oaths of allegiance. With John, such cynical horse-trading passed for statecraft. William Marshal and other advisers looked on horrified as he resurrected the rebellion buried only months before. Abandoning their hostages to their fate, the Lusignans were soon hunting once again with the Bretons who, though leaderless, were united in fury at the persistent rumours of Arthur's murder.

John never learnt to win the loyalty of his barons, whether English or French, and he lacked the force of personality and habit of success with which Richard had held men loyal even when they were reluctant. The triumph of Mirebeau was followed by months of desultory, ill-directed activity. But in the spring of 1203 King Philip made a regal progress down the Loire, through the heart of Angevin territory, giving support to rebels against John and receiving the tributes due to a liege

lord. He returned to the attack in Normandy and won a
startling success when Vaudreuil, a key fortress only a few
miles down river from Rouen, surrendered with scarcely a
fight. Its craven commander was Eustace de Vescy, who would
later be a leader of the dissidents at Runnymede.

So far, John's strategy in France had been based on the
assumption that his position in Normandy was secure. Its
castles were up to date and the defenders were, for the most
part, hardened mercenaries. Rouen, one of the greatest cities in
all France, seemed steadfast in its loyalty, thanks to civic and
trading privileges guaranteed to it by ducal charters. Since the
conquest of England, just as those who had crossed over in the
conqueror's army had retained family lands in Normandy, so
many of the duchy's great barons had acquired lands in
England. And yet traditional family ties were being seriously
weakened and loyalties to the king-duke strained. The proud
days when Norman dukes of the old line boasted a royal
crown as well as the ducal coronet were long past. Now both
titles were held by the Angevin house, mere counts by origin –
men who were considered by the old school of Norman
nobility as outside upstarts who now tyrannized the duchy
as they did the kingdom. Richard had compelled loyalty by
force of character and military prowess. His use of mercenaries
was resented but tolerated as a military necessity. John not
only appreciated their – undeniable – military qualities, but he
seemed to favour their routier captains above his noble Norman advisers. He even seems to have preferred their company,
appointed them to positions of trust and responsibility and
allowed them to pillage the countryside to pay their men. 'King
John lost the love of his people here in Normandy,' wrote a
contemporary, 'because that wolf Lupescar [the most hated of
the mercenary captains] treated them as though he were in
enemy territory.' In place of the honoured lord protecting

grateful vassals against an invader, John himself often seemed like a hostile commander fighting to maintain a beachhead in enemy territory.

In autumn of 1203, King Philip of France prepared for a renewed offensive – it would prove the last. With a vast train of siege engines, he led his army to the walls of the fortress town of Les Andelys, squatting below Château Gaillard; supposed by most people at the time to be impregnable, its function was to bar the way to Normandy to French kings seeking conquest. With all the formalities demanded by the customs of war, Philip laid siege to the place.

The great castle was well supplied, well garrisoned and commanded by a professional English castellan utterly loyal to John, his commander-in-chief. It was as well because thanks to lack of resources in eastern Normandy, John's attempt to break the siege failed. By this time the duke-king was travelling in his French territories with a heavily armed escort. He found little support and having failed to raise the siege, announced his intention of going to England to raise an army, certain that Gaillard could hold out until his return in the spring. On 3 December he slipped out of Rouen before daybreak; on the 5th he took ship from Barfleur.

John spent Christmas with his young queen at Canterbury. Men said that his infatuation with her sapped his energies, but in January he was presiding over a council of barons at Oxford. Many held lands in Normandy; a few who did not privately wondered whether their duty to aid the king in his wars entailed service overseas. Almost all held their lands by 'knight service'; i.e. the obligation to supply a specified number of armed knights on campaign for a set period of time, or provide the monetary equivalent – the composition payment known as scutage (literally 'shield money'; compare 'escutcheon', a heraldic term for a shield). John 'accepted' payment from the assembled magnates of $2\frac{1}{2}$ marks per knight. It was the highest ever recorded up to that time. Levies on towns and merchant shipping and the sale of honours and privileges brought in further funds, and supplies were sent across the Channel in preparation for the spring campaign.

The king seemed in confident mood. On 6 March he gave orders for the trapping of game in the New Forest, which was to be shipped over to Normandy with his hunting gear, dogs and falcons, to ensure his sport during the lulls in the fighting. Gaillard had held out for six months and was provisioned for a few weeks more. If all the castles of Normandy were to prove so stalwart, John's chances of holding the duchy were reasonable. Rouen was heavily fortified and the west of Normandy was as yet untouched by war. It was there that John planned to mobilize his counter-attack, while Philip battered the walls of the castle and the city. A drive straight to a second attempt to relieve Château Gaillard might have been a wiser as well as a bolder strategy. In fact both options were closed by the shattering news that the fortress had fallen – on the very day in fact when John was arranging for his sporting facilities.

The siege and capture of Château Gaillard is one of the epics of medieval history: at the end of six months and two weeks, the garrison numbered just 156 effectives; even then, the stubborn and emaciated defenders refused to make a formal surrender and had to be systematically disarmed. Worse was to follow. With a flash of strategic insight King Philip bypassed the heavily fortified defences of Rouen, and marched through southern Normandy to join forces with his Breton allies in the west. By June he had taken most of the strong points of the duchy and, by promising to confirm the town's privileges, had won the submission of Rouen itself. Apart from a brief rising in favour of John at Dieppe, Philip's takeover of the duchy was unopposed and leading Normans willingly collaborated with the royal government.

King John and the Normans

The speed of collapse in John's position in Normandy seemed a miracle to contemporaries. Militarily, Philip seems to have proved the better tactician and strategist; modern economic studies tend to the conclusion that financially the antagonists were fairly equally balanced; while in terms of military hardware the castles of Normandy were well up to withstanding siege. But the principal reasons for the collapse were surely two factors of morale: in the first place, John lost Normandy because of the implacable determination of the French king that he should; secondly, the barons of Normandy, its natural defenders, had loyalties divided between two overlords, and no compelling motivation to prefer the overlord across the water to the one down the road to Paris, who could harass them at will.

Take those castles: a military tool for John; ancestral homes and emblems of family prestige to his Norman barons. Nowhere in his vast dominions did King John inspire respect or loyalty; here in Normandy the general background hum of distrust was reinforced by the loyalty owed to family. Reluctance to provoke the anger of the French king merged into willingness to collaborate with him and so to betray the English king. According to the *History of the Dukes of Normandy* (eleventh-century), English soldiers garrisoning castles in Normandy reckoned Norman garrisons surrendered too easily. Some in England even attributed the fall of the duchy to the sedition of its Norman constable, while even a Norman chronicle named two prominent Normans as traitors. As head of the Norman people or '*gens*', descendants of Rollo the Norseman and renowned throughout Europe for their triumphs in the south of Italy and the kingdom of England, the duke should have inspired special loyalty. As Count of

Mortain since 1189, John was a leading Norman magnate. He also held tracts of the ducal forest of Lillebonne, known to the Romans as *Julia bona* and site of the great amphitheatre whose ruins may still be seen. Much of its stone was robbed to build fortifications, among them no doubt the famous castle where it is said William the Conqueror took his decision to invade England. For all that though, John's ancestry was not Norman, not even ducal, and he had a mixed reception even in the southern region of the duchy bordering the county of Anjou. Here Count Robert of Sees, a prominent malcontent, brazenly defected to the cause of the French king. Philip rewarded him well after the fall of the duchy to France in 1204. At this time some nobles decided to wind up their affairs in France and move to England.

Philip had been chipping away at border territories even before John became king-duke; John's territory was already diminished before he brought war to the central province around Rouen, which had been at peace for fifty years, and his mercenary routiers based at Falaise, birthplace of Duke-King William, preyed on the countryside and pleasured themselves on the wives and women kinsfolk of Norman knights. And yet, notoriously, John often preferred their company and counsel to the duchy's nobility. So he forfeited the trust and respect of his natural supporters and if King Philip's advance was sometimes faltering and dilatory, the hearts and minds of the Norman lords in their fortified ancestral homes were already lost.

The loss of Normandy would haunt John for the rest of his reign. Perhaps it was, in the long perspective of history, inevitable. But whereas King John withdrew across the Channel to prepare sophisticated strategic schemes, his brother Richard would have stayed in the field, rallying his Norman liegemen and directing action for further efforts and the harassment of the French. Over the next ten years, John was to devote much of his effort to an attempt to recover his position in France, but to little effect. The English found themselves taxed as never before to replenish an exchequer drained by Richard and strained by John's wars. The end of the Norman connection meant that the baronage was less willing than ever to assist the king in his overseas campaigning. John's favour-itism towards his mercenary captains, tolerable when exer-cised to the discomfort of Norman lords in time of war, became insufferable when those same mercenaries were given positions of profit and honour in England. Above all, the loss of Normandy, and the French occupation of much former English territory in France, meant that the king was in England most of his time, directing the government in person and intervening at will in his barons' conduct of their affairs. Almost all the excesses of royal power complained of in Magna Carta had been committed by the governments and ministers of King Richard. But since he was an absentee king, opposition could press home its case without resorting to rebellion. John was more or less permanently in the country, so became the target of discontent.

The roots of the great Charter of Liberties were traced back, even by contemporaries, to the authoritarian but efficient rule of John's father. Before him, in the days of anarchy under King Stephen, a magnate sometimes enjoyed such freedom of action within his own domain that he could indeed have looked upon himself as a 'king within his own land', to use the words of Edward Jenks, an early-twentieth-century critic of the Great Charter. In his view its object was to return to these good old days of privilege. But those days had gone for good thanks to Henry II. The systems of government he introduced were taken to the point of excess by the harassed officials who governed England because of the incessant demands for cash from his brother.

In an age when office-holders were expected to recoup their expenses and to make a comfortable income from the revenues they collected, corruption, as we understand the term, was built into the system; but that did not lessen resentment of extortion among the ranks of those who had to pay. In the field of law, Henry II's reforms produced an ever more standardized national regime which encroached upon the feudal jurisdictions of the great magnates; even so they had retained a pretty free hand within their own domains. But under John royal justice was exerted with increasing consistency at the expense of private jurisdictions. When this was added to the rising level of financial exactions and the increasing efficiency of the central administration, all under the personal direction of a king whom few had cause to respect and many had cause to fear, repetitions of the baronial solidarity which had brought about the humiliation of William Longchamp were, perhaps, predictable. That they produced a constitutional upheaval whose tremors are still detectable today was the result of events and developments tracked in the chapters that follow.

2

THE SMACK OF FIRM GOVERNMENT

With the Norman ports in French hands, John had to rethink his entire strategy. Moreover, King Philip was renewing his attacks into Aquitaine. Its northern county Poitou was quickly overrun up to the walls of the port of La Rochelle before the French advance faltered. While the place held for John, the landing of a major English expedition against central France was still a practical proposition; but mounting such an expedition would take time, and in the meanwhile Philip was militarily free to march on Angoulême. Such a move, however, would be politically sensitive. John held the territory by right of his wife, Isabella, who was a peeress of France, so that any intervention by the French king would provoke hostility among his baronage, many of whom held lands by marriage.

South of Angoulême, the minor lords of Aquitaine were rallying to John. There was no special love for the king of England, merely alarm at the prospect of exchanging his distant rule for the intrusive administration of Paris. English treasure, proceeds of the funds collected for the aborted Norman campaign, now poured into Bordeaux to pay for a Gascon army to hold the line and spear a counter-attack.

The loss of Normandy had altered the logistics as well as the strategy of overseas campaigning. For well over a century, what we might call 'The Anglo-Norman Channel' had been virtually the private preserve of the king-dukes. Merchant shipping was raised as need arose for military expeditions. Henry II maintained a fast royal galley in constant readiness for urgent communications and the 'Cinque [i.e. 'five'] ports', chief among them Dover, were required to provide a military service of fifty-seven ships for fifteen days a year in return for various priviléges. New ports were occasionally added to the original 'five', but having lost automatic control of the seaways, John planned for a more effective naval force of his own – in short, a fledgling 'royal' navy. He set about raising one with all the energy and attention to detail of which he was capable.

In 1205 he granted the ports a charter which confirmed their privileges, but also restated their military obligations, discharged since Anglo-Saxon times. The ships and crews they provided, merchantmen rather than custom-built naval vessels, were valuable as troop transports; but these ships could also, since naval warfare at the time differed little from encounters of armed men in land battles, serve as well as fighting platforms. But the era of naval battles of manoeuvre was dawning and John, who always aimed, so far as possible, at professionalism in warfare, was preparing to reshape England's naval forces. In 1205 he ordered London yards to lay down keels for several new war galleys and building continued apace throughout the reign. Between 1209 and 1212, for example, twenty new galleys and thirty transports and other ships were launched at the king's expense. England was becoming a maritime power.

A stream of orders and directives, still filed away in London's Public Record Office, reveal the urgency and efficiency with which the new force was built up. Harassed minor officials found themselves ordered 'from the same hour that these letters reach you', to labour night and day in the king's service to see to the completion of the job specified. At the head of the hierarchy, chief keepers of the ports maintained supervision of the merchant arm of the services, acted as overseers for the technical specifications of the royal naval establishment and, in short, fulfilled many of the functions of an admiralty administration. Richard had established a maritime depot near the royal castle of Porchester on the Solent. John developed it with magazines to house stores and a new breakwater to harbour his fighting ships. For 750 years Portsmouth would hold pride of place among England's royal naval dockyards.

The chief commander of the battle fleet was William Longsword, Earl of Salisbury and half-brother to the king – the only one of his barons, it has been said, with whom he was on back-slapping terms. In May 1213 at Damme, near Bruges, the new royal navy, commanded by Longsword, in a pre-emptive strike, destroyed most of the ships of an immense invasion fleet assembled there by Philip of France. It was still not a true naval battle; the king's ships still acted as transports and the battle was won by soldiers attacking their opposite numbers on the beach. But it was a crushing victory none the less. Rather than see the undamaged remnant fall into English hands, Philip destroyed them too. His invasion plans had, in any case, to be scrapped for the time being. Just two weeks before, in a ceremony near Dover, John had formally surrendered his kingdom of England and lordship of Ireland as fiefs to the representative of the Holy See, receiving them back under a bond of fealty and homage and for a token tribute of 1,000 marks a year. It was a capitulation to Europe's spiritual overlord that made any attack on his new liege subject problematic in the extreme. It had taken John barely seven years to create his formidable naval force. Such efficiency, while it played a vital role in this case in the country's defence, also reflected a growth in government bureaucracy which men at the time resented.

England had long been a most thoroughly governed state. The court of the exchequer administered royal revenues with an efficiency which, it has been said, was 'the wonder and envy of Europe'. Continuous records date back to the pipe rolls of the 1150s – so called because the parchment documents, one stitched to the tail of the one before and all rolled for storage, looked like pieces of piping. Chancery officials had perfected formulas for royal writs based on sophisticated Anglo-Saxon examples, models of brevity and precision. Officials throughout the country, from humble port reeves responsible for harbour dues, to sheriffs administering whole counties, implanted central directives with an effectiveness unmatched by continental regimes. The legal system applied routine procedures, or 'writs of course' to matters once ruled by traditional local custom.

By the time of John, the great officers of state – chancellor, justiciar, treasurer – were professionals fascinated by the possibilities of the machine they controlled. Lucid and detailed handbooks of procedure from his father's time, while displaying characteristic English respect for tradition, set an equally English pattern for pragmatic innovation. The servants of the king had already begun to acquire the *esprit de corps* of a civil service. The best efforts of an unruly baronage would prove unable to strangle the sturdy infant. It was during John's reign that the royal chancery began to follow the exchequer practice of keeping regular records.

The governmental machine creaked occasionally. While the various functions were well differentiated, the personnel who carried them out were not. All ministers were officials of the royal court and dealt with business of all kinds as it came to hand or as the king directed. Government was the monarch's personal business, with the consequence that functions were not precisely distributed, so confusion could arise. The fact remains that any English king interested in the administration of his realm had a powerful apparatus at his disposal. John had the intelligence and energy to exploit its full potential. In the view of his recent biographer R. V. Turner, the king's ability and dedication to the job of kingship could stand comparison with the achievement of his father Henry II. To his subjects' great dismay, John loved the work. As Abbot Ralph of the Cistercian House of Coggeshall in Essex was to note, 'this king governed indefatigably'.

In the months immediately following the collapse of the English position in Normandy and in the midst of planning an expedition to Gascony, John initiated a full-scale reform of the currency. At the same time, he issued a tariff of standard fees payable at the chancery for the issue of documents under the Great Seal. Authenticated charters and a variety of other official documents were increasingly valued as titles to lands and privileges, but for years past the charges made by the clerks had risen extravagantly. John made large reductions in the tariff but he ruled that only charters he had confirmed would be accepted by the courts.

Swelling relentlessly, the royal archive pipe rolls, carried on packhorse or wagon, were just part of the baggage train of miscellaneous paraphernalia – kitchen stoves and utensils, the king's bed (and dressing-gown; John was the first English king known to have had one), the chalices and furniture of his chapel, his bath tub and personal wardrobe – which followed

John from royal manor to castle, on his incessant tours of England. This was personal government in action. For all the divinity that hedged a king, a surprising number of his English subjects could have glimpsed John at least once in their life. As noted, after 1204 he was in England most of the time. His father had followed a yearly itinerary which included half France, while his brother had spent most of his reign in Palestine, in an imperial gaol or on campaign in Normandy. Law cases that had been settled in the justiciar's court at Westminster under his predecessors were now heard by the king himself in his court, the royal quarters or wherever the king happened to be at the time. Administrative acts and rulings were all registered in chancery and other documents – little was left to memory and nothing left to chance.

Thanks to the efficient management of the royal exchequer, the king was able to keep an ever firmer grip on royal finances and on the county sheriffs who administered them on what amounted to a franchise system. Men bid for the post of sheriff since it was paid not on a regular salary basis but by the difference between the dues they could collect and the annual levy owing to the exchequer. This levy, or 'farm', fixed under John's predecessors, remained unchanged year after year while, because of inflationary tendencies, the monetary value of the services due to the king was increasing. The late twelfth century saw an increase in the money supply. New silver lodes opened in the Alps in the 1160s meant an increase in coinage output across Europe, so that by the 1180s English mints were producing six times as many pennies as in previous decades. In an attempt to restore the situation Richard's governments had charged certain sheriffs a *crementum* over and above the fixed farm.

At a time when the concept of inflation was not understood (England was still far from being a fully fledged money-based economy), royal claims to need increasing revenues merely to keep pace with legitimate expenditure tended to be regarded as evidence of irresponsibility, extravagance or simple greed. Moreover, given his ambitions to recover his lost French lands, John's revenue needs were increasing in real as well as relative terms. He extended the demand for the *crementum* to all the shires and even imposed additional incremental payments. The response of the sheriffs was predictable – to meet these new obligations they increased their exactions whenever they could. As a remedy for this abuse we find in Clause 25 of Magna Carta: 'All counties, hundreds and trithings [i.e. the 'ridings' of Yorkshire and Lincolnshire] excepting those of our demesne manors [i.e. those directly owned by the king himself] shall remain at the old rents, without any additional payment ['*incremento*'].'

But no one was clear as to the real value of shire revenues, since the farms had been established in the reign of Henry II. The country was clearly prospering, but despite the measures by the administration to increase yields the king's share of the revenues was less than it should be. The royal administration introduced various reforms to increase yield to the exchequer.

Following the loss of Normandy, clerks who had held jobs such as castle paymasters in the duchy returned to appointments in the English administration, some of them as joint sheriffs of the larger more populous counties. One such was Brian de Lisle, in 1205 appointed castellan of Knaresborough, who later became chief forester of Nottinghamshire and sheriff of Yorkshire. De Lisle appears to have been nothing more than a loyal if tough government servant. But as baronial opposition mounted, John began to give shires, castles and forest wardenships to another group of French refugees – the mercenary captains whose military support had proved more reliable than the feudal loyalty the king reckoned he could demand from his barons.

Their job was to clamp down on any hint of rebellion. Like the sheriffs they displaced, they took their pay by ruthless exploitation of shire revenues. It was an example of the way in which John managed to transform accepted operations of government into apparent tyranny. Traditional though it was, the system of farmed revenues tended to oppression even in the hands of reasonable officials; by handing it over to men whose profession had hardened them, whose ambitions encouraged them and who as foreigners were doubly open to hostility, John ensured that his government, which had previously been resented no more than any other medieval government, earned particular loathing. While the populace feared them as they did all the royal officers, the baronage hated them as foreign newcomers who had edged them out of their natural preserve as king's advisers.

Few of these interlopers were more hated than the clan of Gerard d'Athee, named in Clause 50 of the Great Charter itself, in which John promised to remove them all from any office in England. Appointed sheriff of Gloucester and Herefordshire, in 1209 Gerard was succeeded by his nephew Engelard de Cigogné, who later became constable of Windsor Castle and warden of the nearby forest of Odiham. A more distant relation of Gerard's, Philip Marc, may have provided later ballad-mongers with a model for the sheriff of Nottingham in the Robin Hood legends. His appointment as sheriff ran concurrently with the career of Robert Hod, 'fugitive', recorded in the Yorkshire county rolls and proposed by one modern historian as the origin of Robin. Marc was appointed sheriff of Nottinghamshire and Derbyshire and castellan of Nottingham in 1209 and had custody of Sherwood Forest itself. Strategically well placed for the north of England and north Wales, Nottinghamshire was also rich in royal demesne lands and forests. As a provincial treasury, Nottingham Castle received the proceeds of the levies made in Ireland, Yorkshire and Northumberland for the campaign year of 1210 and would be a vital royalist strongpoint during the civil war.

Up to the middle of John's reign cash revenues, accounted for at the exchequer in Westminster, were stored in the ancient treasury of the Saxon kings at Winchester. The needs of the travelling court had to be supplied by cumbersome and costly convoys of wagon-loads of silver pennies trundling along England's inadequate and often dangerous roads. In 1207 John began a modest policy of decentralization with provincial treasuries at towns such as Bristol in the west and Nottingham in the midlands.

At the same time, the tightening of government procedures and the placement of John's household officers in positions of administrative responsibility made for an ever firmer royal grip on finance. The king's accounts came to be heard by officials ('auditors') of the chamber, that is, at the court where the king happened to be, rather than in the exchequer. More and more money accounted for in this way tended not to be convoyed on to Winchester, or even one of the new treasuries, but to be diverted to the king's immediate use. In place of silver pennies, the treasurer received chamber receipts, or 'writs of liberate' – he knew where the money had gone but was of course much the worse off when having to meet accounts presented by merchants or landowners whose goods or services had been requisitioned in the royal service.

The chamber, once the private accounting department of the royal household but now in process of becoming a department of state, sometimes took receipt of major nationwide taxes, and it was common for Church revenues to be paid into it. Above all, it was to the officials of the chamber that feudal levies, like those paid for the wardship of heirs and heiresses, were handed over. Access to cash was the constant objective of government. The flexibility and quick returns of chamber accounting offered very real practical advantages; the drawback was that it personalized public administration at its most sensitive point – raising of money.

Taxation is generally resented, even when its objective may be popular, and, as the historian Frank Barlow has observed, John's purposes were seldom popular. From that fateful year of 1204 his overriding objective was the recovery of his family's hereditary lands in France. The English baronage had little interest in the project. Although proud of their Norman descent, very few families still retained actual property interests in the old duchy. The king's oppressive efficiency at raising money was the more resented because of its objective; the fact that the money itself was actually handed over to his personal officers of the chamber merely rubbed salt into the wound of baronial indignation.

So far, it may seem that the chief reason for John's evil reputation was, to use modern jargon, a matter of perception. There was, unfortunately, rather more to it than that. Vindictive by nature, he could also be brutal. The classic case concerned the fate of William de Briouze and his family.

Ruthless and unscrupulous, de Briouze held large estates on the Marches of Wales where he summarily dealt with any Welsh troubles on his borders. A loyal henchman of King Richard, he had been quickly favoured by John, who in 1201 granted him the vast lordship of Limerick in Ireland for 5,000 marks to be paid in easy instalments. As a royal favourite, William could reasonably hope not to be pressed for payment. The next year, at the capture of Mirebeau, William won further credit when he handed over the young Arthur of Brittany, whom he had taken prisoner, to the king. But he was too close to the royal councils for his own good. The death or disappearance of Arthur under mysterious circumstances started ugly rumours that the king had had him killed, even murdered him with his own hands. It is possible that de Briouze knew the truth of the matter and may in an unguarded moment have told his wife.

William's growing power seems to have given John pause for thought; in 1208 he determined to bring him to heel. A favourite method of disciplining his baronage was to demand their children as hostages. When the royal officers arrived to take the de Briouze children in charge, Matilda, de Briouze's wife, 'with the sauciness of a woman' we are told by Roger Wendover, the chronicler, refused to hand them over, saying, 'I will not deliver up my sons to your lord, King John, for he basely murdered his nephew, Arthur.'

Over the next two years, the de Briouze lands in Wales were harried by John's new sheriff of Gloucester, Gerard d'Athee; the lands in Ireland were ravaged by an army led by John himself; and William's wife and eldest son were in all probability starved to death. At any event they were incarcerated at Windsor and never emerged alive. By this time, William himself had fled to France where he died in exile in 1211. The given pretext for this appalling sequence of events was that William had defaulted on the payments of his 5,000-mark debt for his property of Limerick and that when the king's officers had entered upon his lands to distrain for the debt he had forcibly resisted.

There is no direct evidence for the death of Matilda de Briouze and her son, but the starvation story is found in every chronicle of the period and is probably true. To many barons the fate of de Briouze himself must have seemed yet more worrying. Envious they may have been, yet he had been one of the most powerful of all the English baronage and high in royal favour. The terms of the Limerick loan had been repeated in many other cases (one baron had been allowed to make repayments for a similar proffer on such generous terms that had they ever been completed the debt would have been discharged in 1917). If such a man could be destroyed by the will of the king, then who was safe?

The truth was that John trusted only men who were completely dependent on him. Patronized by his father and more or less openly despised by his brother, he never really grew up. He never learnt the self-assurance of dealing on equal terms with mature men whose personal interests might be at odds with his, but who would expect to remain loyal to their king if he played his part within the terms of the mutual feudal bond. The mere fact that the reign was fifteen years old before the opposition united in open rebellion is proof not only of the power of the Crown and the extent to which patronage could buy men's compliance but also of a genuine desire among the great families of England to live at peace with the king if at all possible.

According to J. R. Green, in his immensely popular *Short History of the English People* (London, 1874), 'Hell itself was defiled by the fouler presence of King John'; though it must be said that he was paraphrasing the judgement of chronicler Matthew Paris, a hostile near-contemporary of the king. His treatment of the de Briouze family was vicious even by the standards of the day, and it was not the only well-authenticated example of the king's brutality. In addition, he was a notorious womanizer, numbering among his mistresses the widowed Hawise, Countess of Aumale, as well as women of low birth named in the records as Suzanne and Clemetia. John is known to have had five bastards; a daughter Joan (who married Llywelyn of Wales) and four sons, hardly remarkable for a medieval monarch and modest indeed when compared with the twenty-one sired by his great-grandfather Henry I. John may have debauched the wives of the nobility – the charge has never been fully substantiated – but perhaps more important to understanding his unsavoury reputation was the way he mulcted their men folk.

Money matters

Magna Carta is much concerned with money. The idea of liberty and freedom with which it resonates in later history carried far less weight with the framers of the document than the detailed, legalistic and now frankly arcane subtleties of 'scutage', 'wardship' and 'relief'. If we exclude the clauses dealing with the liberties of the Church, the general principles governing the relations between the king and the barons and those relating to the barons' Welsh and Scottish allies, half of what remains has all the inspirational quality of an accountant's appeal against an assessment by Revenue and Customs.

The barons had good cause for their practical concern. John exploited any traditional feudal payments or 'incidents' and continued to exercise prerogatives which his barons could not force their tenants to respect. His treatment of widows was a classic instance of his mercenary application of these financial rights of lordship. Where his father had made comparatively modest demands on widows, who had to buy his consent for their remarriage or their freedom from that obligation, John was extortionate. The rights of widows were a prominent concern of Magna Carta.

A major point at issue between the king and his barons concerned scutage, payable by barons in place of the military service owed by the terms of their land tenure, terms often settled as far back as the Norman Conquest, 150 years earlier.

A specified number of fully equipped, mounted men-at-arms, ready to serve at the king's request for a period of forty days, was agreed for each estate or 'honour' following calculations as to how many the revenues of the land could in fact fund on these terms. The land in question was said to constitute an 'honour' of that many 'knights' fees'. The barons who held the land directly from the king and supplied the due military force of fully equipped tenants were said to be tenants-in-chief: they might also, in modern terms sub-let, in feudal terms sub-infeudate, part of their honour to lesser men on condition that these would discharge the military obligations that went with the land – recruiting and equipping, in their turn, the necessary number of men.

From an early period it had been possible for a baron, rather than sending some or all of his tenants to the wars, to make a cash payment equivalent to the cost to the king of raising and equipping the necessary force. He recovered this money from the rents of his estates or by levying his sub-tenants. Over the years various factors led to the reassessments of the service owed (*servitium debitum*), generally in the barons' favour. A tenant-in-chief made his own arrangements with the royal officers; some sent men-at-arms for part of the service owing and paid cash for the remainder. Gradually the fractional quota of knights sent came to be accepted as the actual full *servitium debitum*. Estates changed hands by marriage or their tenure changed with successive sub-infeudation, so the service owed changed again. With improvements in agriculture, the clearance of forest lands, whether authorized or not, and improved exploitation of land such as by the pasturing of sheep on waste grazing land, the values of properties increased. Knight service gradually became a bookkeeping anachronism relating neither to the original assessment nor to the real value of the land.

John's problems were compounded by a decline in the value of money; no doubt to be partly accounted for by the increase in the supply of money (see page 48). Theoretically, payment of the scutage due enabled the king to raise mercenary men-at-arms to fill the quotas of the exempted landowner. This may once have been possible, but while the value of money declined, the scutage rate remained fixed. It has been calculated that the daily wage for a man-at-arms was three times what it had been in his father's day. King Richard made a small increase in scutage; John raised it still further; even so he never managed to establish an economic rate. When in 1213–14 he tried to levy a scutage at three times the traditional rate he was met with blank refusals. He therefore resorted to various devices to increase the yield: he levied it far more frequently than his predecessors, and on at least one occasion for a campaign that never took place. Since a landowner made a profit by paying rather than serving, John followed his brother's practice of imposing a fine or surcharge over and above the scutage rate.

No doubt his demands were rapacious and the campaigns they were to pay for unpopular, but the redress the barons sought to impose at Runnymede was beyond reason. Clause 12, one of the most famous of the Charter, laid down that no scutage might be levied at all 'unless by the common consent of our kingdom'. This was plain contrary to feudal law and custom. The barons held their land in exchange for military service. Scutage was merely its monetary equivalent, as we have noted. In fact, since either service or payment was due on the tenure of land it was in effect a type of land tax. Carried to its logical conclusion, Clause 12 meant that if the consent of the kingdom was not forthcoming, the baron held his land outright. The clause was omitted from reissues of the Charter.

Scutage was just one of numerous levies allowed to the king. On the death of a tenant-in-chief, his successor had to pay a 'relief'. A reasonable rate was considered to be £100 – John generally charged exorbitantly more. Then there were the aids – gifts of money which he could demand on three recognized occasions: the cost of his ransom if he were captured in war; the expenses of knighting his eldest son; and the expenses for the marriage of his eldest daughter.

In addition, an unscrupulous king might make large profits from his rights of wardship and marriage. A juvenile heir, incapable of his feudal military service, had to yield management of his estates to a royal agent; such agencies were regularly sold to the highest bidder, who squeezed all he could from the estate during the heir's minority. An heiress or widow could marry only with the king's consent, on the theory that her lands might otherwise go to one of his enemies. Naturally, such consent had to be bought. John and his predecessors had mulcted to the full those assets that the law and their control of public policy put into their power. Much of Magna Carta was concerned with bringing these aspects of royal government under restraint. In fact, the system, even when stretched to its utmost, seemed unable to bridge the gap between expenditure and income.

3

CHURCHMEN, CHARTERS AND POLITICS

In his chronicle *Flores historiarum*, Roger of Wendover (d.1236), claimed that the idea of setting out their grievances against the king in the form of a charter was suggested to the barons by Stephen Langton, Archbishop of Canterbury. The occasion was an assembly of lay and ecclesiastical magnates convened in London in August 1213 to discuss the state of the realm and the measures to be taken to restore things following the years of papal interdict imposed on England because of King John's refusal to accept the Pope's appointment of Stephen Langdon as Archbishop of Canterbury (see pages 68–70 below) (the king's personal excommunication was considered the final sanction for the same offence). In a ceremony held the month before in Winchester, Archbishop Langton had formally lifted the personal excommunication of King John. As part of the proceedings the king had sworn that he would love and defend the Church. It is certain too that he made solemn promises to abolish bad laws and restore good ones, 'such as those of King Edward' (i.e. Edward the Confessor); to guarantee every man his rights; and to give every man justice according to the proper justice of his own courts.

Now, in London, Langton held a great service in St Paul's Cathedral and preached a sermon on the text 'My heart hath trusted in God'. The archbishop had returned to England only a few months before after years in enforced exile, having been refused access to his see of Canterbury on the king's orders. To most Englishmen he was an unknown quantity, but he evidently had his critics for when he announced his text a voice from the congregation – a King's man presumably – shouted out, 'It is a lie. You never trusted in God.'

Langton was too shrewd a man of affairs to rely merely upon simple faith. There were those who would have said he was too shrewd a man of affairs altogether. At times in the events that led to Runnymede, he appears as the loyal friend, almost accomplice of the barons, at others he stands back as a dispassionate mediator. By persuading John to promise to judge all men in accordance with the just judgments of his own courts, he was demanding a promise to abide by the rule of law and to abandon the ancient royal rights of *vis et voluntas*, a notable concession for any medieval monarch.

After the service, according to Wendover, Langton took some of the great men aside for a private conference. He told them of his meeting with the king and went on, 'A charter of King Henry I has now come to light with which if you wished you could recover your lost liberties and your former condition.' Next, 'he had a document placed before them and had it read out', and when the reading was finished and the document understood by the barons 'they rejoiced with exceeding great joy'. There and then they took a formal oath in the archbishop's presence that when the time was ripe they would take up arms in defence of those liberties. For his part, the archbishop promised his loyal support to them 'as far as in him lay'.

Roger Wendover is the only source we have for believing that the episode ever took place, and this is the last we hear of Henry I's charter in the context of Magna Carta. There have been objections against Wendover's account on the grounds that Langton's sermon contained no hint that he was contemplating any cooperation with opposition barons against the king. But it would surely have been astonishing if the sermon had contained any such suggestion. Pope Innocent, through the person of Langton himself, had just formally welcomed the king back into the bosom of the Holy Church; the kingdom of England was now, by John's own act, a feudal fief of the Holy See; and the service in the cathedral was in part a celebration of the outcome, after years of hostility and hazard, of debates to reunite the king, his subjects, and the Church. It was hardly the time for the head of the Church in England to moot, publicly, a possible conspiracy against the Lord's anointed. A twentieth-century commentator, J. C. Holt, proposed to discount the entire story on the grounds that it was merely hearsay. But in private Langton could well have gone as far as is reported, in which case such an 'off the record briefing' could have reached the public domain in a chronicle only as a result of 'hearsay', that is as a 'leak'.

There are two elements in Wendover's account to support its plausibility. First, there is the report that the barons 'rejoiced' after the document had been 'read *and understood*' (my emphasis). Roger surely does not mean that these great men were simpletons. As a class they were quite used to dealing with legal technicalities in the administration of their estates; some were already developing estate management offices modelled on the royal chancery and exchequer. However, few had a mastery of Latin and they would expect clerks to render any technicalities into Norman French. There was nothing in Henry I's charter beyond their mental grasp – once it had been translated so that it could be 'understood'.

With the setting presumably the chapter house of old St Paul's, one can perhaps visualize the scene. The archbishop waits for the select band of great men to gather round him. First he favours them with an account of his interview with John at Winchester, no doubt affording them a moment's grim amusement that their slippery monarch had given his unsupported oath to mend his ways and that the churchman had accepted the assurance. But then he spreads out the parchment bearing the coronation charter of a century back and they are intrigued. Charters in legal Latin are familiar enough to them, as we have noted, in their dealings with their tenants. No doubt the implications behind Langton's suggestion that they might be able to hold the king to similar legal commitments are beginning to spark a response. Everything depended on what this old charter actually said. When it had been read out in full and the Latin explained in Anglo-Norman French, they were electrified – with 'exceeding great joy'.

The second pointer that we may have a report of an actual meeting comes in the description of Langton's reaction to the oath sworn by the barons, that he promised his support 'as far as in him lay'. This is in marked contrast to the action of the churchmen who had assembled with John and the barons at the time of the London commune back in 1191 to oppose the tyranny of William Longchamp. Then, all present, clergy included, had sworn an oath of loyalty to the commune together (*conjuratio*). No doubt those present at the August 1213 meeting knew something of that earlier ceremony. The fact that their archbishop did not join their '*conjuratio*' but merely promised support to the best of his ability might have suggested that he was a schemer guarding his back. The charge of untrustworthiness levelled by the heckler during the sermon could square with such a suspicion.

The king's hostility to the kingdom's leading churchman went back to the time of Langton's appointment to the archbishopric by Pope Innocent and his consecration in June 1207. Modern governments may be tempted to inveigh against meddling clerics: their medieval predecessors often had good reason to. Bishops then were more than moralists; many were officers of state. When John came to the throne, the government of the kingdom had for years been in the hands of his brother's trusted counsellor and companion on crusade, Hubert Walter. Appointed Archbishop of Canterbury in May 1193 at Richard's request, he was also Richard's justiciar and the Pope's legate in England. John made him chancellor of the kingdom; he was a model of that typically medieval public servant, churchman/government minister, and is reckoned among the top three or four heads of government before the age of Gladstone.

Of course, by agreeing to serve as chancellor and archbishop at the same time Walter discounted Thomas Becket, whose refusal to do so had led to his martyrdom. In fact, Hubert Walter proved a worthy churchman who saw to the good administration and reform of the Church in his province. By and large the bishops who served John's government followed his example. Even de Gray of Norwich, the most trusted and efficient of royal servants, ended a long-running grievance of the monks of Norwich Cathedral and also appointed an excellent deputy to run his diocese. Often dismissed as a time-serving king's man, had he in fact become archbishop of Canterbury in succession to Hubert Walter, as John wished, he might well have proved of similar stature. In fact, when the archbishop died in 1205, John is supposed to have said 'At last

I can be king,' but he continued to rely on capable ministers, chief among them another bishop, his justiciar, Peter des Roches, Bishop of Winchester (England's richest see; the earliest audited accounts outside the royal household, from 1208, survive here).

The age was past when churchmen were the only literate people in western Europe. While the king probably could not write and certainly did not 'sign' the Charter, we know he could read, like his father Henry II who was a friend of scholars. A newly popular proverb held that an unlettered king was but a crowned ass. Lay literacy was certainly on the up, but the Church still provided the natural career structure for men of talent outside the landowning baronage and would do so for centuries.

The system had drawbacks for the Church and corresponding advantages for the lay administration. Chronically short of funds as he usually was, the royal or baronial employer in need of clerical staff or estate managers, officers of state or humble clerks, could take them on at no expense by the simple expedient of appointing them rector of a prosperous parish, canon of a cathedral or even bishop. The new office-holder received the full revenues while a deputy or vicar (Latin, *vicarius*, 'substitute') did the work at a wage often approaching the ideal of 'apostolic poverty'. Observing the politics of medieval 'ecclesiastical' Europe one is sometimes caused to think that the souls of the faithful were never less well served than at the height of the 'Ages of Faith'.

The typical educated secular priest of the twelfth century, as opposed to his monastic colleague, was the royal clerk. Hence, some bishops might be officers of state, all were considerable landowners, duty bound to send military contingents in time of war; in 1215 such forces amounted to about 13 per cent of the total owed by all English landowners. Some clerics still served on the battlefield in person – Peter des Roches was lampooned as *Wintoniensis armiger*, 'warrior of Winchester' – and the mace or cudgel was thought to be a typically ecclesiastical weapon as the clergy were not supposed to shed human blood. Given that churchmen, though but a small minority of the population, owned or controlled an estimated 25 per cent of the land, it is really not surprising that kings made use of these resources as best they could in the service of the crown.

Kings, electors and ecclesiastics

Kings insisted on scrutinizing, approving and usually as good as controlling the elections to the bishoprics and archbishoprics of their realm. When a see fell vacant by the death of the incumbent, convention allowed the administration of the lay revenues to pass to the sovereign for the duration of the interregnum. Inevitably a monarch took advantage of such situations to divert a portion, generally a sizeable portion, to the royal exchequer. (During the vacancy at Lincoln from November 1200 to July 1202, the Crown acquired a net profit of £2,649). Popes were willing to connive at any reasonable royal intervention. King John, of course, went too far. The result would be a conflict which, if Church teaching were to be believed, would imperil the souls of all his subjects and put the king himself in jeopardy of eternal damnation. A dispute over the election to Canterbury on the death of Hubert Walter began the trouble.

Considering that there is no mention of bishops in the New Testament it was, even to some people in the twelfth century, surprising that they existed in the Church at all. (These people, called Waldenses after a merchant from Lyons, Peter Waldo, who founded them, believed in various impractical things, such as apostolic poverty for churchmen, and disapproved of other things such as the excessive wealth of the princes of the Church. Peter and his followers were properly condemned and persecuted as heretics. (Their successors formed a Protestant sect that is still active.)

Church law laid down the correct procedure for the appointment of a bishop. Ideally it was to be by election in a free vote of the staff, or chapter of a cathedral. Papal approval of the conduct of the election was followed by the formal installation of the successful candidate. However, it was also accepted by convention that the election could take place only with the agreement of the monarch who would, in due course, make it clear to the electors which candidate he favoured for the job.

The system tended to run smoothly enough. So long as the king chose men of decent life, as well as administrative competence, the pope could be expected to concur in their election. Since many of the clerks in a cathedral chapter were likely themselves to be royal place men, i.e. clerics employed in the government service, they could be expected to vote for the king's man. Henry II was known to order a cathedral chapter to hold a 'free' election naming the royal clerk who was to be chosen. People regularly spoke of the king 'giving' a bishopric to a favoured candidate. Recording the succession of John de Gray, the king's secretary, to the bishopric of Norwich in the year 1200, the chronicler Roger of Howden said that he achieved the promotion 'by the gift of King John'.

De Gray was neither a saint nor a theologian but he was no doubt a perfectly respectable Christian as well as a first-rate government servant. To King John he looked like ideal archbishop material. Accordingly, when Hubert Walter died in July 1205, the king knew whom he wanted for his successor at Canterbury and naturally hoped to have his way. However, the case called for a certain amount of finesse.

Many of England's cathedrals were staffed by monks, not by regular clergy, and Canterbury, served by the monks of Christ Church priory, was one of them. Since monks lived apart from the world and were therefore not potential candidates for government service, monastic cathedral chapters tended to be somewhat more independent at election time than canons and priests. At Canterbury, moreover, the monks had been in a long drawn out dispute with their archbishops and now wanted the next incumbent to be one of their own number. However, they found their supposedly exclusive right to conduct the election was being disputed by the bishops of the archdiocese. Both sides appealed to Rome to give a ruling; the king postponed any further action in the matter until November. That was quite proper, but he also had not the slightest intention of allowing the premier appointment in the English Church to be held by a monk out of his control. Meanwhile, the revenues of the province would legitimately flow to the royal coffers.

So far, the affairs of Canterbury were following the orderly and correct pattern. A clerical dispute as to the mode of election was being referred to the Pope, no candidate had as yet been put forward and the king was doing nothing to pressurize the electors. However, John felt it would be perfectly reasonable to let his wishes in the matter be made known at the papal court. Royal agents were ordered to take advantage of the delay caused by the appeal as to electoral procedure to canvass the qualities of Bishop de Gray, the royal candidate, along the corridors of power in Rome.

When news of these manoeuvres reached England, a faction of the cathedral monks who had no wish to be governed by the worldly John de Gray held a secret election from which their sub-prior, Reginald, emerged as archbishop designate. He still required papal approval of course and was dispatched by his brothers with instructions to reveal his nomination, but only if this were absolutely essential to thwart the king's candidate. It seems the monks had put forward Reginald as a pawn to check the king and spur the Pope into nominating his own candidate from among their number.

But the pawn had aspirations. On arrival at Rome, Prior Reginald proclaimed himself as archbishop elect and petitioned the Pope to confer the pallium on him, the formal act of recognition. When news of this reached England, King John flew down to Canterbury in a whirlwind of rage; the monks promised on their honour that no formal election had in fact taken place and, surprisingly, seem to have convinced the incandescent monarch. Under his direction, however, they now went on to the election of de Gray; the southern bishops gave their blessing and a second delegation of monks proceeded to Rome to ask Pope Innocent III to confirm their new choice. Prior Reginald contested the legitimacy of de Gray's election.

Crisis, Canterbury and Rome

Pope Innocent ordered a re-run there and then by the body of Canterbury monks now at Rome. When the result came out evenly balanced for de Gray and Reginald he proposed a new candidate of his own choosing – Stephen Langton, an English cardinal priest in Rome and a graduate master of the University of Paris, where he had taught for many years. The Pope's candidate received the unanimous voice of the wearied monks. Innocent, bent on general reform in the Church, was delighted to have won his way with so little effort. Langton was known across Europe for his lectures on the duties of a bishop, and in Church circles is remembered, among other things, as the man who divided the books of the Bible into the chapter divisions we still accept.

John was neither impressed nor amused by Innocent's triumph. He did not, he said, know Langton; he did not want him and he would not accept him. Nor would Langton's long residence in Paris have done much to endear him to the sworn enemy of the king of France. The election to England's premier see had been conducted abroad and without his licence to elect having been granted. This and numerous other arguments were rehearsed in a fuming petulant letter of the kind that a king 'by the grace of God' should never have addressed to 'Christ's vicar on earth'. The Pope rejected them all, told the king that he must accept the outcome of a perfectly valid election, and went on to warn him that as a loyal son of the Church he must accept the consecration of Langton as Archbishop of Canterbury.

The principles governing the election of bishops had been laid down at the third Lateran Council, barely thirty years earlier, and Innocent, who was a renowned canon lawyer, was not about to overturn a perfectly satisfactory canonical procedure to suit the whim of a mere king. For his part, John expelled the monks from Canterbury and refused an entry permit into England to the new archbishop.

It was all extremely distressing. But things were about to get very much worse. While Innocent accepted that the issue was a matter of prestige for the king, and was willing to give him time to accept the 'divine ordinance', he was not prepared to wait for ever. At Viterbo, in June 1207, a year and more after the resounding events just described, he formally consecrated Cardinal Stephen Langton as Archbishop of Canterbury. In August the bishops of London, Worcester and Ely received instructions to order the king to accept the fact, on pain of having his kingdom laid under a general interdict. In

November Innocent himself wrote to the barons of England, advising them of their responsibilities in the event of an interdict being promulgated.

Pope Innocent is generally rated one of the most brilliant men ever to sit in the chair of St Peter; nevertheless, it is apparent that he would not have lasted long as a baron of King John if this letter represents his assumptions on the efficacy of opposing that monarch on a matter of morality and right behaviour. The theory was that in the event of an interdict on a kingdom, the great men of the realm, while mindful of their loyalty to the king, had also to bear in mind their higher loyalty to God and beg the king to return to the arms of the Church. Pope Innocent enjoined the English baronage to urge John to abandon his hostility to 'our venerable brother Stephen', Archbishop of Canterbury. He explained that they need have no fear of temporarily offending the king because he would in due course return to his senses and come to look upon them as 'very dear friends for the sincerity of [their] counsel'. To no one's surprise, except, possibly, Innocent's, the king remained adamant. Accordingly, on 24 March 1208, the interdict came into force. On papal orders England's clergy interrupted their normal ministrations and England's Christians found themselves denied the benefits of religion. This state of affairs would continue until 2 July 1214 when, John having paid part of the compensation for funds taken from the Church in England during the interdict, it was lifted.

Interdict

Similar actions had been taken before, notably against the Spanish kingdom of Leon in 1198–1204 and France in 1200. Even so, churchmen were far from clear just what was entailed; though the ban on the ringing of church bells for the duration would no doubt have been noticed and regretted. Their instructions were to refuse to carry out all ecclesiastical services except the baptism of infants and administering confession to the dying. After four years priests were authorized to administer mass to the dying (the *viaticum*). Marriage was affected, though at this time the blessing of the Church was not yet considered essential. For ordinary folk a 'church wedding' commonly meant a ceremony held in the church porch before the wedding party went in to celebrate mass before the altar. While the interdict continued, the mass was no longer possible, but the marriage was still valid – the essential act was the pledging of the troth between man and woman, preferably before witnesses.

An interdict was an ecclesiastical bludgeon liable to stun both the innocent and the guilty. The silence of the church bells was the most obvious effect of the ban but it does not seem that church building programmes were stopped and alms giving continued, as did Sunday markets. The most serious spiritual impact on the population at large was, in theory at least, that the mass, with its commemoration of the Last Supper, could no longer be celebrated (though even here the case was not so severe as it might be felt by practising Roman Catholics today). Some priests recommended people take communion three times a year; at the Lateran Council of 1215 Pope Innocent laid down the minimum of an annual participation for adult Christians. Evidently many did not communicate even that often. For most it was felt to be sufficient to be in the church at the moment the host was elevated. Since this event would usually be hidden from view by the chancel screen the congregation depended on the ringing of the bell that signified the elevation. King Henry II was notorious for arriving just in time for this part of the ceremony and leaving immediately after the bell had sounded. The idea behind the interdict was that John's subjects, dismayed at being cut off from the benefits of religions, would urge him to refrain from 'walking in the counsel of the ungodly' and return to his senses, confident that not only would he consider them good friends for their pains but that he would also rectify his conduct and so enable the kingdom to return to the body of the Church. But of course, so long as the king persisted in his stubbornness many good men and women would suffer.

Such was the theory. However, unfortunately for the Pope, it seems that more or less everybody of any consequence in England saw the matter from the king's perspective. From contemporary reports it would appear that, at the beginning, most of the clergy as well as all of the laity supported King John. Few people outside Church circles had heard of the long-time expatriate Stephen Langton; many were incensed that a king of England, even King John, should, as it appeared, have his choice of the greatest churchman in the land overruled; the barons also wondered uneasily how safe their own rights to nominate friends and relations to church appointments ('livings') under their control now were. To the peasant farmer, of greater consequence than the local priest's power in the consecration of the elements of the mass was his mastery of the necessary blessings for animals and crops, for the cursing of caterpillars and other pests. There must have been many rural parishes where these essential rites were continued.

At all levels there was resentment that clerics were withholding their services yet still receiving payments. By way of counter-attack, John began seizing Church property. If the Pope's men obeyed the Pope, so did the king's men obey the king.

Realities in the 'Ages of Faith'

Directed by the king's sheriffs, lay administrators moved in on the great properties of the Church and took over the running of the estate offices so that the revenues flowed to the crown. Even at parish level it was not difficult to find the men needed to make an accurate assessment of the lands and fees owing and to assign a meagre living allowance to the local priest, supposing the living was not held by a royal appointee. Tithes, the levy on the laity for the maintenance of the clergy, continued to be paid and the government appointed men to guard tithe barns.

The next stage was to make the clergy administer their own confiscations. A week or two after the formal acts of seizure, the government announced that any senior churchman might recover control of his estates on payment of a fee – like a sheriff's farm. The prior of Peterborough, for example, was allowed to regain the administration of the great abbey's lands, with a known return of some £1,000 per annum, for an annual payment to the crown of £600. And of course there were the Church properties that had fallen vacant – by 1211 these amounted to no fewer than seventeen abbacies and seven bishoprics.

Nor was this the end of the king's exploitation of the golden windfalls blown down in the storms of papal anger. He entertained himself, and the country too one imagines, by ordering a round-up of all clerical concubines, variously known as hearth companions, housekeepers or lady friends, to be held in custody until ransomed. Whether it was the honour of a clearly uxorious, if officially celibate clergy, most of the ladies were bought back by their reverend lovers. In fact, the pressure for clerical celibacy in the western Church which came largely from reformers in the Church itself was, in terms of Church history, comparatively recent. While sexual abstinence was always expected of monks and nuns, clerical marriage had existed in the western Church in one form or another for most of the first millennium, though theory might require the partners to abstain from sex. Then in the 1000s agitation for reforms in many aspects of Church life brought the question of married clergy to the fore. By the 1130s it was official Church teaching that marriage, whether celibate or not, was incompatible with priestly office.

All in all, the six-year interdict relieved John of some of his financial worries (when it was all over he agreed compensation should be paid, but fixed the sum as low as possible and paid up on only a third); nor does it seem to have deeply oppressed the citizenry. We find little in the records or chronicles – and mostly those that do exist are written by members of the clergy – to indicate its impact. As to the establishment, neither secular nor clerical notables made any serious attempt to force the king to enable his kingdom to return to the embrace of Christendom, despite their Christian duty to do so. All but two of the bishops removed themselves from the scene, either by death or via the less final exit of the Channel ports. Four bishops died during this period, leaving their sees vacant for the duration and at the mercy of the royal administrators. Langton was already overseas and forbidden to return. Bishop de Gray of Norwich had been appointed the justiciar in Ireland. Seven bishops went into voluntary exile: to remain might suggest complicity in the king's defiance. Winchester was the only see with a resident bishop – Peter des Roches, who remained true to his royal patron. With the Church in this parlous state the spiritual well-being of the English was surely in jeopardy. It was for John's lay noble advisers to pressure him to change his policy. And yet not one of the barons seems to have complained.

Nor does it seem that the ordinary clergy were unduly

concerned at the moral blight that had descended on the country. Chroniclers emptied many an ink horn to blacken the name of the king and to deplore the depredations on the Church and Church property but have next to nothing to say about the actual religious impact of it all. Year in, year out, men and women lived without the blessings of Holy Communion. They married without the full benefits of the rites of the Church, and were buried in unconsecrated ground. No doubt this was felt as the most serious deprivation. There are reports of bodies left unburied in churchyards; some parishes opened new burial grounds where the dead would have to lie unsanctified until the interdict were lifted and the ground could be consecrated. People may have been fearful and depressed, and yet nowhere in the records do we find mention of any form of unrest on the part of the populace at large.

Then, in November 1209, Archbishop Langton, acting with the full authorization of Pope Innocent, excommunicated John by name with all the elaborate terrors of the pronouncement. By Church teaching this meant exclusion from the consolation and fellowship of the Church in this world and the threat of eternal damnation in the world to come; it also released the barons from their oaths of allegiance and, indeed, required them to make war upon their sovereign until he should submit. They did nothing of the kind.

In fact, in the eyes of many people the Church had devalued the coin of its own sanctions by deploying them more as political weapons than as spiritual discipline. Not even the plight of England's bishops stirred the lay magnates into action. After all, they were great landowners too; yet for some five years they were harried into exile and their lands were exploited for the king's benefit. The more thoughtful among the baronage may have wondered about the implications for their own position. Yet, when presented by the Pope with legitimate reason to disavow their allegiance and, indeed, prompted to rebellion for the sake of their own immortal souls, the magnates reckoned their own interest lay rather with the service of Mammon than of God.

The Pope turns to the big battalions

Used in isolation, the interdict had failed miserably as a weapon of international politics. When rumour whispered that the Pope was actually planning to pronounce the formal deposition of the king and to call in Philip of France to enforce it, rebellion began to look like a practicable option. As the year 1212 advanced, John sensed the shift of balance against him on the international scene.

At the beginning of the year he had been preparing to launch a major offensive against France. Then, in June, news came that Prince Llywelyn of north Wales, nominally his liege man but now proclaiming his allegiance to Philip, was in rebellion. The planned invasion of France was abandoned and preparations made to divert the vast resources of men and armaments against Wales. By mid-July, John had changed his plans once more. The danger from Wales was now dwarfed by reports of French preparations for a major offensive against England and news of formidable unrest, at last, among opposition English barons, particularly threatening in the north.

The army for Wales was diverted. John marched north forcing leading magnates to surrender hostages for their good behaviour. Robert Fitzwalter and Eustace de Vescy, powerful men in the Yorkshire baronage, hurried abroad into exile. Both were probably implicated in the plans to murder the king during the proposed Welsh expedition, though they were later allowed to return and readmitted to the king's 'goodwill'. Part of the price of peace with the Church in 1213 (see below) were pardons for the leaders of the plotted rebellion. In his few months of exile, however, Fitzwalter sought out the English bishops overseas and protested his loathing for the service of an excommunicate. A year after his return he would be posing as Captain of the Army of God against the king.

For the moment, however, John had contained the threats to his position. But he needed closure. Above all he needed to stop the French king. Marching under the banners of a papal champion, Philip's cause would provide the cloak of piety for English rebels, beginning to contemplate action against the king for reasons of their own, but afraid to act alone. Eight years back, albeit reluctantly, Innocent III had given his blessing to the sack and capture of Constantinople, Christendom's bulwark against Islam in the East, by the armies of the Fourth Crusade. His was a bellicose pontificate and if spiritual sanction could not bend the English king to his will then military force must be the necessary last resort. Late in 1212 Archbishop Langton was commissioned for England with letters declaring John formally deposed and Philip of France the Pope's commander in the invasion of the kingdom. The letters were never published.

With the advice and support of the ever-loyal William Marshal, the king of England had pulled a master stroke that humbled his pride and so benefited his immortal soul, while at the same time delivering a check to the French king. John's agents at Rome proposed the complete submission of England to the Pope's will. Innocent now sent a second embassy for England. It was headed by his legate Pandulf, who overtook Langton on the road and in the Pope's name instructed him to hold back the letters of deposition for John and of authorization for Philip. Now followed astonishing negotiations and a still more astonishing public humiliation for the king, at Dover. There, on 15 May 1213, a penitent John proposed to render the kingdom of England and Lordship of Ireland to Rome, as feudal fiefs of the Apostolic See. In fact, Christopher Harper Hill points out, the terms were exactly the same as those that Pope Gregory VII, who blessed the Norman invasion of England in 1066 as a crusade, had proposed to William the Conqueror – without success.

John made the proposal in the form of a charter (which actually designated Ireland a 'kingdom'). He swore allegiance in the presence of a large concourse of barons and pledged himself to pay an annual tribute. Innocent was enchanted. 'You now hold your kingdom by a more exalted and a surer title than ever before,' he wrote, 'for the kingdom is become a royal priesthood.' The destruction of the French fleet at Damme that same month put an end to any possibility of a French invasion that year. And when, in May 1216, Philip's son Louis led an army to England, Guala the papal legate excommunicated him as an aggressor against a papal vassal, and without the support of his father who was unwilling to cross the Pope at that time.

The humiliation at Dover did not of itself avert the French invasion in 1213 but it did dislocate future French policy against England. It had still greater advantages on the home front. In the summer of 1213 Langton arrived in England authorized to reimpose the interdict if John failed to respect his undertaking, but eighteen months later he was condemning all leagues and conspiracies against the king. In due course Innocent would declare Magna Carta null and void on the grounds that any such dispute was now to be settled by the Pope himself as the feudal overlord of the kingdom and as an affront to his favourite son in God. Subsequent pontiffs would stand staunchly in the king's corner, supporting Henry III and Edward I, when called upon, against baronial demands for the charters to be observed. On the down side, England continued to pay the tribute, the last payment being made as late as 1333, though with many years of arrears still owing. More seriously, submission to Rome meant the papal promotion of Italian clerics to many of England's most lucrative English clerical appointments. The relationship was finally repudiated in 1366.

4

THE ROAD TO DISASTER

If John had bought the friendship of the Pope by rendering his kingdom as a papal fief, his standing at home was still uncertain, while the situation overseas was positively dangerous. By John's about-face in his policy towards Rome England joined a group of states which acknowledged Rome as feudal overlord. The kings of Sweden, Denmark, Aragon and Poland were all, for one reason or another, papal vassals and retained the status for various lengths of time. In England's case the vassalage lasted for the best part of 150 years and while in the short term it may have thwarted the French king's hopes of posing as a crusader against England it had not deflected that monarch from his purpose.

King Philip had been at war with the Angevin family for some thirty years. During that time he had withstood John's father, outwitted his brother and roundly defeated John himself. The lands of Normandy, surrendered 300 years before to the Viking chief Rollo and for the past 150 years an immense and threatening beachhead of the English crown, were once more a full province of France. Philip was with reason confident that the recovery of full sovereignty in Aquitaine was only a matter of time; meanwhile he saw an opportunity to root out the devil's brood in its nest. Twice before he had been on the verge of an invasion across the Channel. Now, with opposition to John still seething below the surface of Church-induced amity, the moment seemed entirely propitious.

At the very least, a French expedition would deter John's designs for a campaign in Poitou. But much more was at stake than mere strategic diversion. The objective was nothing less than the overthrow and extirpation of the house of Anjou and the annexation of England as an appanage, i.e. a personal family estate, of the French crown, to be fief of the eldest son of the monarch. In April 1213, the very month in which John must already have been at work with his advisers on the dramatic demarche which would surrender his realm as a feudal fiefdom to the Pope, King Philip held a great council at Soissons, to determine the legal relations between the two countries when his son Louis should be crowned king of England.

All the parties to the negotiations had apparently forgotten the rights of the emperor in the case, for had not King Richard, twenty years ago, surrendered the realm into the hands of Emperor Henry VI to receive it back as a fief from him? Some said the cession had ended with the death of Henry, others were not so sure. But Philip, surnamed 'Augustus' by admiring courtiers and likened by them to the Roman emperors of old, had grandiose ideas of his own.

Meanwhile, with the English king harassed by his baronage and Otto of Brunswick fighting to maintain his claims as Emperor Otto IV, Philip could reasonably, it seemed, plan his schemes for the aggrandizement of his family and the enlargement of France. While the constitutional and legal experts in Soissons debated the details of Anglo-French relations following the conquest, shipwrights, quartermasters and chandlers were working on the final preparations for a vast fleet of ships assembling under the hands of skilled mariners and pilots in ports along the coast of northern France and French Flanders.

The conquest of England would complete plans for a greater France already being realized across the Channel. Normandy had been absorbed in 1204–5, but the little county of Boulogne, northwards along the coast, was still able to assert its autonomy from the French crown. In the year 1211 Philip had trumped up a pretext for a quarrel with Count Renaud and expelled him from his lands, which thereafter remained part of France.

Small though it was, the county of Boulogne was a vital piece of the political geography of north-western Europe. Bordering on Flanders and looking across the Channel for friends against the French king, its counts were natural candidates for an English alliance. Renaud, aiming to recover his family inheritance, had busied himself by recruiting support for England in Flanders itself and further afield. France had always claimed the suzerainty of Flanders, and now Philip felt himself fully strong enough to exercise it.

At the time that Philip had been expelling John's garrisons from Normandy, Baldwin, the Count of Flanders and newly elected Latin Emperor Baldwin I of Constantinople, was leading the Catholic armies of the Fourth Crusade against the Byzantine rulers whom they had expelled and the Bulgar enemies of the state. But Baldwin was taken in battle by the Bulgars, and died, probably poisoned, in a Bulgarian prison. His daughter Joanna and her husband inherited Flanders, with its rich but turbulent towns. The new count was glad of assistance from the powerful French king against the citizens, but resentful of his claims to suzerainty.

When, in 1213, Philip authorized his son Louis to seize the town of St Omer and ordered Flanders to join the invasion of England, the count's patience ran out. He refused any further collaboration until his town was returned. Contemptuously, Philip sent an army against him, laid siege to Ghent and brought his invasion fleet into the fine harbour of Damme, port to the great Flemish merchant city of Bruges. The count looked around for friends and sent messengers to England.

The country was in a strong state of preparedness. John was not short of capable and willing soldiers in a war against a French invader; but above all, thanks to the planning and investment of the earlier years of the reign, he had a navy of well-found ships and seasoned seamen. Morale was high, thanks to a cross-Channel raid on Dieppe, and the crews were fully prepared for action when the messengers arrived from Flanders.

A council of war chaired by the king decided to answer the count's appeal for aid in handsome fashion. Seven hundred men-at-arms and a large body of mercenaries were embarked in some 500 ships and the whole flotilla set sail on 28 May, just three days after the call had come. With the Earl of Salisbury in command, the English reached the mouth of the River Zwyn in two days, despite contrary winds, heading for Damme and apparently unaware that it was crowded with a French armada. One contemporary put their number at 1,700 ships.

The French commanders and military were on shore, leaving the ships in the charge of skeleton crews to manoeuvre them when tide or wind threatened. The bulk of the invasion fleet lay at anchor ready to sail on the next tide, supplies stowed and the equipment and baggage of the French knights lashed in place until they should be off-loaded at an English beach, ready to accompany their victorious owner to some castle or manor house in the home counties. Other boats were hauled up above the tide mark, undergoing some last-minute repairs or cleaning.

The English commander ordered an immediate attack. A quarter of the French fleet was sent drifting out to sea or on to the sandbanks, looted or set ablaze, before sundown. The raiders got clean away, with scores of prizes and more booty, gloated one chronicler, than had been seen in England since 'the days of King Arthur'; they had brought with them the Count of Flanders. King Philip himself ordered the destruction of the beached transports and the scuttling of all the other vessels not already destroyed, for fear of a commando raid by the enemy; and his nobility were poorer by a ransom-worth of armour and luxury equipment. John's royal navy had more than paid for itself in its first engagement, and the most serious invasion England had confronted since the Conquest was over before it could begin.

The French undertaking

This Flanders enterprise had been just the kind of war-making the baronage enjoyed: a quick jaunt into enemy territory, little danger, no casualties and immense booty. But now the king tried to mobilize forces for yet another attempt to recover his French inheritance. Reactions varied from sullen reluctance to outright refusal.

Exultant in his victory at long range over the French, John was anxious to take the fight into enemy territory. The barons demurred. He was an excommunicate; they had served already by standing guard; and, the final objection, many and especially those from the north argued that the conditions of military service by which they held their lands did not carry the obligation to serve in Poitou, which was where, for reasons of strategy, John was proposing to launch his grand attack on France.

John stormed northwards, bent on a punitive expedition and infuriated by the resistance in the north to his demands for support. The idea that the terms of military service might be open to interpretation by the courts seemed simply outrageous. It was the basis for the whole system of landholding; the rebels, in his view, had insolently presumed to question a matter beyond question for the king to decide. But he did, eventually, relent. No action should be taken until judgment had been given; he announced his intention of postponing the expedition to the spring of the following year, 1214. He marched north nevertheless. Months of uneasy tension followed as he displayed his strength, and churchmen did what they could to arrange a compromise.

These efforts may have included the document which is known to historians as the 'Unknown Charter of Liberties'. For centuries it lay in the French royal archives virtually unnoticed until its publication in France in the 1860s; even then it was unknown to English scholars, until the historian J. H. Round published an article on it in 1893. The parchment carries no date and it seems one can only guess as to when the text originated: it may be a copy made by a French clerk of an English original and it is accompanied in the Archives du Royaume (Archives of the Realm) by two copies of the 1216 Magna Carta. It is tempting to think of it as a record of the reconciliation talks between John and the northerners in November 1213: certainly the clause excusing military tenants of the king from any service overseas outside Normandy or Brittany is suggestive. Perhaps the document was the first outcome of Archbishop Langton's suggestion to the barons that they present their grievances in charter form. The fact that it is divided into chapters (or clauses) is an intriguing reminder that Langton was the first man to propose chapter divisions for the books of the Bible.

The first clause reiterates the fundamental promise that the king had given to the archbishop at Winchester in July 1213, not to 'take men without justice'. The remaining ten chapters deal with matters raised in the Charter of 1215. There is no suggestion that John gave his consent, at this time, to any of the clauses in this 'Unknown charter' – we cannot even be sure that he saw it. One theory linked it to the Charter of the Forest charter of 1217, but it seems most likely to date from the period leading up to Runnymede (January to June 1215), perhaps being a schedule of the demands sent to John by the barons from Brackley in April; perhaps notes on the developing discussions between the Articles of the Barons and the Runnymede Charter. But there is no way of knowing. The fact that this and the 1216 and 1217 versions are in the French archive at all prompts speculation that the copyist may have been a clerk in the travelling chancery of Prince Louis of France.

Be that as it may, as the new year of 1214 opened the king and his military advisers were readying themselves for one of the most momentous campaigns in the history of English arms, with a recalcitrant baronage loitering resentfully in the wings of the action. John sailed for France in February. No judgment had been rendered on the question of service overseas – it is improbable indeed that the issue had been submitted to any court of law. A significant number of great tenants-in-chief had neither turned up in person nor sent their knight service, nor offered to make scutage payments.

William Marshal was among those absenting himself but he, honourable as always, could not attend in person because he also held land from King Philip of France and so would have been taking the field in person against his other liege lord. He did, however, send a contingent of knights and, remaining in England, served as the king's loyal representative there. Otherwise, the home government was in the hands of the capable Peter des Roches, now justiciar. Archbishop Langton also remained, as did William Briwerre, sheriff in many shires and notorious for his ruthless exploitation of the office. John left behind a band of able, tough and essentially loyal ministers; but not one of them represented the aristocracy of old, Anglo-Norman blood.

Likewise the royal army, professional and capable as it was, also presented contemporaries with an unedifying spectacle, being largely made up of 'low class soldiers of fortune'. King John, always more concerned with results than with show, was generally more at ease in the company of these hard-living, fast-riding professionals than that of his touchy, self-absorbed barons concerned principally with family fortunes and dynastic politics. But these were the men who ultimately counted in the kingdom he left behind, and in his absence they would have ample time to mull over their grievances and to pray for a royal disaster.

The campaign began well. As John sailed west, heading to round Cape Finisterre en route for the port of La Rochelle, still secure in English hands, his half-brother William Longsword, Earl of Salisbury, victor at Damme, sailed east, heading once more for Flanders with a large force of English and Flemish soldiers. His supply train carried a large hoard of treasure. Where John aimed to buy the loyalty of the disaffected nobles of Poitou, nominally his liegemen but in fact absorbed in their eternal private feuds, William had the job of recruiting and financing allies to the Low Country/ Rhineland confederacy which had begun the previous year with the defection of the Count of Boulogne from the French cause.

John had in mind a grand strategy. While he harried the French king from Poitou to the south-west of Paris, his nephew Otto of Brunswick, claimant to the crown of the Empire, was to sweep upon France from the north-east with the combined allied forces. It was strategic thinking on a scale to match the Duke of Marlborough's march the length of Europe to link with Prince Eugene of the Holy Roman Empire on the battle-field of Blenheim in August 1704. At this first attempt the Anglo-Imperial alliance faltered disastrously.

John and Otto had a common problem, namely to bring their forces to the starting tapes. Throughout the spring and early summer of 1214 the king was marching and counter-marching, involved in a seemingly endless series of sacks, sieges, raids and skirmishes to bring the Poitevin nobility to heel. At their head was the Lusignan family, still angered at John's seizure of Isabella of Angoulême as his bride years before. All the time, John was conscious of Philip and the French army poised in strength to the north and of his need to force the issue. In May he launched a lightning campaign which, by dint of hard fighting and quick responses to a changing situation, was entirely successful. As a result he was able to force Hugh de Lusignan to seek terms and to contract for the marriage of his son to John's baby daughter. At last the king was free to mobilize all his forces against the French. Early in June, with the Poitevin lords behind his banners, we find him marching into Angers on the Loire ready for the final push towards the Ile de France. Two weeks later he was in sight of the situation aimed for at the beginning of the campaign all those weeks before. The main French force in the area, now under the command of King Philip's eldest son, Prince Louis, was brought to bay. Triumphant, John was ready, as he thought, for the decisive battle.

But his sword broke in his hand. Unwilling no doubt to engage in open war against the heir to the French throne, the Poitevins deserted. John was forced to abandon a campaign on the verge of probable victory. Reduced to the remnants of the expeditionary force with which he had commenced operations months before, and knowing as he had then that it was quite inadequate to face the French forces now massed against him, John was forced to defeat at La Roche aux Moines outside Angers on 2 July. He withdrew, back to La Rochelle. From there he wrote to England reporting all well, and asking for reinforcements. None came.

This, of all moments, was the one chosen by Otto of Brunswick, styled Emperor Otto IV, to launch a grand assault that was to have been coordinated as far as possible with the English king's operations. But the trap had been sprung. Philip of France, after an apprehensive five months, at last saw his way clear to battle. His back secure from any English threat, and with his feudal levies and town militias marching alongside each other, he took the offensive. The continental coalition whose conflict was to decide the fate of England's king clashed at the epic Battle of Bouvines on the marshy plains near Tournai in Flanders, on 27 July. Battle on that day could not be avoided, even though it was a Sunday and the religious conventions forbade fighting on the Lord's day. Set-piece battles of this type were the exception at a time when warfare largely comprised campaigns of sack and pillage or protracted sieges. It was the first major battle the kings of France had fought in a century. Against the odds, it must have seemed, it was a crushing French victory.

One of the decisive battles of European history, it ended the imperial pretensions of Otto and guaranteed the future of the new monarchy which Philip had established in France. It also dealt a crippling blow to King John's policy against his Capetian rival. Rather than recognize the reality, he lingered on in France, apparently hoping for reinforcements from England. By October even he must have seen that such hopes were absurd. That month the royal galley put into Dartmouth harbour with the king and his retinue aboard.

In fifteen years the king had seriously antagonized leading members of the lay baronage in one way or another; he had ridden roughshod over the rights and privileges of the Church; he had plunged his subjects into years of spiritual deprivation; and despite adroit manoeuvring that had recovered him the good will of Rome, his senior archbishop still distrusted him and, it seems, was even prepared to nudge the barons into dissidence.

But John was still indisputably king. As such, he retained the awesome rights and powers of his office and the sanctified charisma allowed to God's anointed. In practical terms he still enjoyed the loyalty of a number of his barons, among them William Marshal, the most venerated lay figure in the king-dom, and control of a government machine without parallel in Europe. Even 1214 had one comfort. In July, the month of Bouvines, the Pope had lifted the interdict.

The fatal flaw in John's armoury, and for a medieval king it was the most serious, was his failure to win lasting glory on the battlefield and the charismatic prestige that went with it. He had won numerous tactical triumphs but nothing on the grand scale. A king who won great victories could expect loyalty, almost no matter how extortionate his government might be. Richard had demonstrated this. By contrast, John's barons had begun to deny him even the traditional feudal obligations of war service.

During the king's absence, his justiciar Peter des Roches had operated the full rigours of the well-hated Angevin system of government. Unrest was stirring in much of England with opposition particularly strong in the north. Talk about the charter that had been granted by Henry I would be combined in the months ahead with talk about the still more ancient customs of the old English saint-King Edward the Confessor, customs lost which had once been enjoyed. Such rallying cries seemed to give rebellion the respectable gloss of principle and by looking back beyond the Conquest members of the Anglo-Norman baronage seemed to identify themselves with the Community of England.

At the beginning of 1215, with the northerners spreading the atmosphere of rebellion, many undecided barons who might have thrown their weight behind the king had he faced outright military challenge, held back. Royalists and dissidents were almost equal in the support they could muster, but in fact almost half the English magnates remained aloof throughout the struggle that was to ensue, even when it broke into civil war. As the thirteenth century advanced war would break out on more than one occasion. These conflicts have sometimes been known as 'the Struggle for the Charters'. The principal participants being the great magnates of the realm, their interests were naturally at the centre of the contest, but as it advanced it would come to benefit the community of the realm of England as a whole.

PART II

THE COMMUNITY OF ENGLAND – AND ITS NEIGHBOURS

By the 1220s the Charter was being described as a charter for the 'Community of England'. In 1191 Londoners had sought to establish a 'commune' on the model of continental cities. In 1215 the barons at Runnymede proposed to enlist 'the commune of the whole land' ('*communa tocius terre*') to coerce the king. Such ideas hardly amounted to definable constitutional constructs, but the maturing concept of a community of the realm was accompanied by a growing sense of nationhood.

For the great nineteenth-century historian Bishop Stubbs, the Charter was the first public act of the 'English nation'. The pre-Conquest English had been recognized as having a separate identity in the world of Christendom. Now, 150 years on from Hastings, the sense of communal identity was reasserting itself so that the barons, in appealing to the laws of Edward the Confessor, were claiming their place in that tradition. When the Charter speaks of the 'commune of the whole land' it means the population of freemen within the boundaries of England. The Charter is an award not to a section of society, whether Church or nobility or townspeople, but to the whole society. In this real sense the barons of 1215 were the champions of the liberties of the realm. By the 1260s, Professor Holt argued in *Magna Carta and Medieval Government*, the community of the realm, from peasants to gentry, was prepared to accept that that had been their role.

This community embraced a patchwork of towns and settlements, manors and villages, scattered over a heavily wooded landscape interspersed with sparsely populated areas of countryside, heath and marshlands, all of which were locked into their local identities by the clinging conventions of tradition and custom. It was also a country of two language groups, Norman-French, the language of the ruling elite, and Old English or Anglo-Saxon, the submerged language of the majority. In 1191 Londoners upbraided the royal (Norman-born) chancellor William Longchamp for addressing them in French. In fact Longchamp was out of order even by the practice of the establishment. Depending on his audience, unless he was addressing a congregation of Latin-literate clergy, Abbot Samson of Bury St Edmunds delivered his sermons either in French or the English dialect of Suffolk.

In addition, the diverse orders of society each had their own sense of communal solidarity: the nobility with its evolving knightly code, acquiring the ideas of chivalry; merchants with their guilds. Even the despised Jews had their synagogues and officials. Because Magna Carta deals not only with the land-owning elite and the Church, but also with merchants, Jews, women, forest-dwellers and even the humble villain (peasant farmer), to explore its meaning is to investigate that community of England. It was bordered, north and west, by neighbours equally confident in their identities.

5

THE ORDER OF NOBILITY

One hundred and fifty years after Hastings, the baronage of England was an ethnically mixed bunch. Norman, Fleming, Breton were just some of the roots of their family trees and many would have married English or Anglo-Danish wives. At this time, the term 'English', besides meaning people of English ethnicity, could also denote those whose place of birth – *natio* (a twelfth-century usage in university listings from the Latin *'natio, nationis'*, 'being born, a tribe, or race of people') – was England; a third of the students at the university of Paris whose origins were known were English. Thus some Norman barons whose estates lay in England, while they might be insulted at the suggestion they had English blood in their veins, would consider themselves Englishmen by contrast with cousins who held the family lands in Normandy.

Since it was the barons who forced the Charter from the king, the bulk of its provisions, naturally enough, concerned them whether directly or indirectly. The document apparently drawn up among the barons as an agenda preliminary to their negotiations with the king and known as the 'Articles of the Barons' – like the Unknown Charter of Liberties divided into chapters, or clauses – gives a clear indication of their priorities and goes straight to the chief grievance of the baronage: the king's arbitrary increase of the dues owing to him under various feudal obligations.

The chief ground for complaint was the rate at which he levied the payment known as 'relief', which had to be paid to the king before an heir could enjoy the revenues of his inheritance. No one contested that, as the ultimate owner of all the land in England since the division of the country by William the Conqueror, the king could reasonably demand such a payment. The question was, what was a reasonable amount?

The king could often intervene in the succession to an estate quite legitimately. In the thirteenth century, for example, a comparatively small minority of English baronies passed continuously from father to son. In many others the father died childless, so the property passed to collateral heirs; the more distant the claim or the more complex the issues involved, the more important the overlord's consent, and the claimant who paid the higher relief had been liable to succeed. With a characteristic appeal to past practice, Clause 2 of the Runnymede Charter lays down that payment shall be according to the 'old relief' at the rate of £5. The ruling was not always applied, but this was the rate at which the king's exchequer agreed the claim of a certain William Pantoll in the 1230s.

The 1215 Charter next took up (Clause 3) the question of relief in the special case where the king had enjoyed the wardship of the lands in question for an heir who was under age. On the principle that all land was held in exchange for military service and that an heir who was under age could not discharge that service, the

Crown was entitled to take the estate of a tenant-in-chief (one holding directly from the king) into custody or wardship and administer its revenues until the heir came of age. The theory was that reasonable moneys should be set aside to provide for the living expenses of the heir and the guardian or custodian of the estate was to take only reasonable charges and aids from the property. In fact John was liable to top off his over-exploitation of the estate by demanding payment of relief as well. This practice was forbidden by the Charter.

The exercise of wardship presented the Crown, and other lords administering the lands of under-age tenants, with rich opportunities for what one might call asset-stripping. It was not uncommon for the custodian to appropriate all the revenues, setting aside a pittance for the heir's personal requirements and spending nothing on the maintenance of the property. On coming of age, an heir could expect to find dilapidated houses and farm buildings, once profitable mills in need of repair, livestock on neighbours' land because boundary fences had not been maintained, and ploughs and other implements sold off. Even worse, the estate's labour force might have been seriously depleted ('the men wasted' in the expressive terminology of the Charter) by reducing the value of the villeins in various ways to the profit of the guardian. Any lord had the power to 'tallage', i.e. levy payments on, a tenant at will, the victim having no right to refuse. The prosperous peasant of villein status was virtually defenceless against such exactions. In one case, the guardian of the wardship reduced two villeins to beggary by his extortions. Another way to raise money from the prosperous villein was to release him from traditional hereditary labour services owed to the heir's family, in exchange for a money payment.

From the rights of heirs, the Charter made a natural transition to those of widows (Clauses 7 and 8). Next, having dealt with family revenues, it turns to the question of debtors, whether to the Crown or to Jewish moneylenders (Clause 10), so important a part of the Crown's revenues. Given the various legitimate feudal incidents (the obligations attached to the holding of land, office, estates or manors) a baron might be liable for – scutage owed for military service due, the arbitrary fines or tallages which could be levied on towns or serfs, and fines or 'aids' – a sizeable proportion of the baronage must have been more or less permanently indebted to the Crown.

Feudal incidents are the matters dealt with next. 'No *scutage* or aid,' reads Clause 12, 'shall be imposed . . . without the common counsel of the kingdom, except for the ransoming of our person, the knighting of our eldest son, or the first marriage of our eldest daughter.' These were standard feudal levies. When John's brother had had to be ransomed some twenty years before, while there were numerous complaints about the corruption and injustice of the collection, no one questioned the government's right to make it. Yet even these customary dues were to be levied henceforward within reason, while for 'extra-ordinary aids' as they were called – effectively imposed 'voluntary' grants – the Charter demanded that the king take counsel.

Later generations would invoke this clause as proof that the Charter had established the principle of no taxation without the consent of Parliament. It did not: Parliament as such did not exist at the time. The barons did attempt to establish as a principle that scutage could be levied only by consent, but that was merely fantastical. Since land was held in return for the guarantee to provide armed men for the king's wars, the king had to be free to impose money payment in lieu on anyone unwilling to fulfil the obligation. This was one of the clauses dropped in the revised version of the Charter that would be issued on the boy king Henry's behalf in 1216.

Next, after digressing briefly on the rights of London and the towns and boroughs of the kingdom (Clause 6), the 1215

Charter went on to specify who should be summoned to the council and how the summonses should be made out – in the view of later generations this spelt out the doctrine of parliamentary representation. In fact it seems clear that the aim was to ensure that only the familiar personnel of the royal council – the great churchmen and the greater barons and, of lesser landholders, only those who held land direct from the king, tenants-in-chief – should be involved.

After dealing with a technicality concerning the 'performance of service for a knight's fee', the Charter moves to a major bone of contention, the question of where lawsuits of 'common pleas', as opposed to private pleas that might involve the king himself, should be held: Clause 17 specified that they should no longer 'follow our court but shall be held in some fixed place'. At this time royal justice, like every other department of government, tended to follow the court. Nothing could be done outside the royal household and that household never lingered long in one place. John's father, Henry II, had transformed the administration of justice in England by offering an alternative to local justice based on custom and regional traditions. Anyone anywhere who could afford the paperwork could have his case tried in the royal as opposed to the local court, where the interests of the local lord might affect the issue. The drawback was that this royal justice could be had only where the royal judge happened to be. If, for example, King Henry, holding his court at Windsor, decided he wished to move to his hunting lodge at Woodstock and the home of his mistress the fair Rosamund, then to that destination would travel the royal court and with it the royal justices and with them the royal justice they handed down. Clause 17 of Magna Carta aimed to stabilize the system somewhat.

With Clause 20 the Charter reached an issue of interest to all classes of society; this was the question of 'amercements'.

These were payments levied by the courts for certain misdemeanours, mistakes in local court procedure, failures by local
communities to comply exactly with the requirements of the
king's justices or the inefficiency of local officials. (In passing
one notes that life in John's England cannot have been all bad
if administrative officials could be fined for inefficiency!)

A local law officer who failed to ensure that the finder of a
dead child appeared for questioning would find himself
amerced; failure to examine the body of a man who fell to
his death in a quarry could lead to the penalization of a whole
neighbourhood. It was surely a tribute to the thoroughness of
royal justice that such local details could be taken notice of,
and no one questioned that the guilty parties had put themselves at fault, or in the king's mercy (*in misericordiam regis*).
The objection was to the fact that amercements could be
imposed for really petty offences but might be set for quite
excessive amounts, or that they might be levied for purely
notional offences. That, in short, fines supposedly meant to
tighten up the administration of justice or keep local government running smoothly were being used simply as another
source of government revenue.

Assessment was purely at the discretion of the king's justices
and in the normal run of things the average man could be
expected to be amerced at least once a year for one or another
petty offence.

The wording of the clause deals precisely with the grievance;
a man is not to be 'amerced for a slight offence, except in
keeping with the degree of the offence'. But there were two
important provisos. No matter what the offence, no one was to
be fined so heavily as to be left destitute. The freeholder should
not be obliged to sell his land to clear the debt to the court; the
merchant should not be obliged to sell his stock-in-trade; and
even the villein should be spared his 'wainage'. Whether this

means his agricultural implements or is in fact a corruption of the French word '*garnage*' and therefore means 'tillage' is of little importance. The intention is clear. Villeins should not be amerced so heavily as to lose their means of livelihood.

This apparently touching concern for the well-being of the peasantry does not necessarily mean that the barons had a social conscience. The villeins were a vital element in estate economy, being bound to do labour services and to pay tallage at the demand of their lord. The clause seems intended to ensure that royal exactions should not so impoverish estate workers that they could no longer meet their obligations to their lord's bailiff. In other words, the clause is primarily intended to ensure that the king respects the vested interests of his barons. And that this was the intention emerges beyond doubt in the 1217 version of the Charter, which introduces a saving clause to protect the royal interests in peasant labour. The relevant text now reads not 'a villein shall be amerced [reasonably]' but 'a villein *other than our own* [my emphasis] shall be amerced [reasonably]'; where 'our own' means the king's own. The king was to continue to enjoy the right to exploit the peasantry on his own estates with unreasonable amercements, even if his justices when imposing amercements now had to respect the livelihood of peasants on the estates of others. Arbitrary assessments handed down by the king's courts were to be curbed in another way: no amercements whatsoever could be levied, 'except by the oath of the honest men of the neighbourhood'. A following clause stipulated that 'earls and barons' should likewise be amerced only according to the degree of the offence and only then by their peers.

We can assume that most of the great men on both sides of the Charter dispute, opposition or loyalist alike, lived most of their lives in debt and probably died in debt. England was still in the process of becoming a fully fledged money economy so that cash flow was a chronic problem. The estate of a Crown tenant was likely to be encumbered at his death with arrears of unpaid scutage, outstanding instalments owing on aids, or impossible commitments contracted to 'have the king's good will'. The heir and family of the deceased could expect to be harassed by visitations from the local sheriff and royal bailiffs intent on seizing whatever lay in their path on the pretext of selling it in the interests of their royal master.

In most cases far more was taken and sold than was needed to clear any outstanding debts. The surplus either stuck to the hands of the agent or was dispatched to the royal coffers. Clause 26 concerning debts owing to the king on the estate of a deceased landowner aimed to stop all this, by providing that the king's officer was empowered in the first instance merely to catalogue the goods and chattels and to sell nothing until the exact extent of the indebtedness to the Crown had been established.

The next clause deals with intestacy. In general it had been the practice for the goods of anyone who died without leaving a will to be confiscated by the Crown. Under the terms of the Charter's Clause 27 the chattels were to be distributed by his kinsfolk and friends, presumably among themselves but under the supervision of the Church. It was the custom among churchmen in the Middle Ages to encourage people to leave endowments for religious purposes. Since they were in fact in a position to withhold extreme unction from the dying, or at least were perceived to have that power, it was not usually difficult for them to persuade a man to do his duty. If he died intestate, the Church as well as his relations would be deprived. One class of persons necessarily died intestate, namely felons, but they were a special case.

Under Clause 32, the Crown promised to hold the lands of those who had been convicted of felony for no more than a year and a day, after which time the lands were to be handed over to the lord of the fief (*redantur terre dominis feodorum*).

By ancient custom the land of a criminal formally indicted and sentenced for a felony went to his feudal lord, while the chattels were the perquisite of the lord who had tried him. In the course of time the Crown had encroached on both these customary rights. There was no problem when the felon was a tenant-in-chief, that is, the king was his immediate lord. When, however, he was the liegeman of some other there was immediate conflict. It became recognized that if the felony in question was treason the mesne (i.e. intermediary) lord lost all rights in the land. Where it was for some lesser offence he had, in theory at least, the right to property and chattels. But John frequently refused to yield up lands once occupied.

Even if returned after the customary 'year and a day', the lands would be in a ruinous state, for during that period the king's officers were entitled to seize whatever might be of profit to their royal master and to lay waste everything else. It is apparent from contemporary legal texts that the words were taken quite literally. Houses and outbuildings were thrown down, gardens destroyed, meadow land ploughed over, woods uprooted and livestock sold off. Presumably the idea was that no one should profit from the legacy of felony. The right to 'year and a day' exploitation was a valuable perquisite of the crown and Henry III is known to have sold it in certain cases.

The Charter covers a miscellany of other abuses, like royal demands for money in lieu of service on a castle garrison when the knight was willing to put in his time. No doubt John preferred professional soldiers to rustic Sir Gawains, but it was the gentry's right to serve, and the week or two spent with the territorials, so to speak, could be a welcome break from the routine of life. Always on the grab, John even plundered the revenues of religious foundations endowed and hence 'owned' by mesne barons. The charters making such foundations were careful to reserve various valuable property rights including that of wardship of the estate between the death of one abbot and the election of another. Clause 46 aimed to stop the king's practice of intervening to exercise such baronial wardships. Finally, in this summary of the baronial defence of their revenues, we come to two now obscure but then vital matters: the question of petty serjeanties and of the writ *praecipe*.

The concept of 'petty serjeanty' is still met with in the 'peppercorn rent'. Any baronial estate was liable to comprise a patchwork of properties large and small acquired over the generations by various means, from various lords and for various services or annual token rents. It might be the annual render of a hunting knife or a sheaf of arrows or even the service of counting the lord's chess pieces and stowing them back in their box. Claiming that a holding from the king must take precedence over any other, John had enforced where he could the 'right' to the wardship of an entire estate even if the Crown's holding in that particular estate was only a fraction of its obligations; for example, just one or two parcels of land might be held by the king on some lesser tenure, while its principal obligation, the rendering of knight service, was owed to an intermediary or mesne lord, who in his turn had to render knight service to the royal army when required by the king. By enforcing his claim to the entire revenues of the estate during the period of the wardship, on the basis of the Crown's fractional interest, John deprived the lord of any of its revenues (the bulk in fact) that were rightfully his. If, during the period of the wardship, John had reason to call on the knight service of the kingdom, he nevertheless expected the mesne lord to supply his obligation on the estate, even though the revenues owed to him for it were at the time being diverted to the royal coffers. Clause 37 denied the king's claims in the matter.

Even more important to the baronial interest was Clause 34 whereby 'the writ which is called *praecipe* shall not henceforth be issued to anyone [in a case] whereby a freeman may loose his court'. In England, as elsewhere in Europe, private jurisdictions such as the lord's manor court existed alongside the system of royal jurisdiction. However under the late Anglo-Saxon kings and the Normans it was the one polity where freemen could expect relatively impartial judgments from public tribunals. Henry II was able to build on this to introduce changes so that it was possible for anyone with the money to access royal justice by the purchase of a writ, the writ *praecipe*, which could redirect a case due to be heard in the lord's court to a proceeding in the king's court. For the petitioner this meant a judgment independent of local influence or prejudice; for the lord of the court it meant a loss of revenue and authority. The choice of the word 'freeman', meaning here a local worthy of sufficient standing to hold his own court, shows how wide-ranging the term could be in its application. John had been active in extending royal justice to humble landholders.

A simplistic view of medieval history used to distinguish two phases in the evolution of the nobility from the earlier 'robber barons' to the chivalric knightly era. If we accept that there is a grain of truth in the idea, then the year 1200 can be considered the watershed between the one and the other. The earliest recorded tournaments date from the mid-eleventh century – they were in fact battles without a cause except the love of fighting and the ambition for plunder. The earliest, be it said rudimentary, code of rules is attributed to a French knight Godfrey de Preuilly who died in the year 1062, fittingly enough in the course of one his own tournaments. Well into the next century, tournaments continued to range over fields of play several square miles in extent, with hundreds of participants organized into ad hoc war parties.

The sport was popular in southern France with its code of courtly love, as well as the north. The notion of the troubadours as exquisite if ineffectual lutenists is belied by verses from Bertran de Born which, roughly translated, conclude:

> I love the gay time of Easter . . . the leaves and flowers . . . The joyous songs of the birds . . . The knights and horses in the meadows in battle array. We are going to have a marvellous time. Trumpets and drums and horses . . . when men of good breeding think only of killing . . . nothing thrills me like the . . . sight of the last dead with the pennoned stumps of lances in their sides.

If there was no war in progress, a battle could soon be set up. Honour played little part in these conflicts. Many an experienced combatant stood aloof from the fray until well on into the day and then, choosing his moment to maximum advantage, would ride down some exhausted but well-caparisoned young tournier, strip him of horse and armour and hold him hostage. Booty and ransom was the aim for most and fortunes could be made.

The most famous knight of his age, William Marshal, ended his days as England's revered elder statesmen and champion of the boy king Henry III after John's death. The younger son of an obscure Wiltshire gentleman, he was aged about twenty-two when he won the gratitude of Eleanor of Aquitaine fighting in her cause. Her husband Henry appointed him tutor in chivalry to their eldest son Henry, 'the young king'. In due course the once landless adventurer was chosen to induct the heir to the throne into the order of knighthood.

Marshal was the last great man to build his career in the tourney field. Noble families were increasingly loath to risk wealth and social status in such brawls. By the time he retired, the events were being more rigorously regulated. Europe's first organized sport was in the making. The robber barons, if not actually transmogrifying into Galahads, were learning to love King Arthur.

6

LONDON, CITIES,
TOWNS AND COMMUNES

In 1215 London could already look back on more than a millennium of history. The settlement on the Thames antedated the Romans. At the time of the Norman Conquest, Winchester, the treasury of the House of Wessex, was England's chief city; from the time of St Edward the Confessor Westminster was the coronation place of the English kings. London never became a royal city in the sense that Paris was, but it was always the country's metropolis. In the late 1980s, archaeological excavations revealed that the place was considerably larger at the time than had been previously supposed, with a population that may indeed have made it the largest city in northern Europe. As we have seen, the German knights who escorted King Richard I back from his captivity were astonished by the wealth of the place.

A decade before, the writer William FitzStephen rhapso-
dized on the forest of ships congesting its port, the rich furs of
its citizens, the splendour of its buildings, the number of its
churches; but the image that lives in the mind from his
description is of the young men wrestling and playing at
pitch-the-stone and similar games in Finsbury Fields, and
the citizens going off on a spring morning to hunt in the
woods of Middlesex. This was the time too when any apprentice or young Londoner able to hire a horse or rich enough to
own one would try his skill at mock jousting, in the fields
outside the city gates. In an emergency the city could raise a
respectable fighting force. London was a valuable ally in any
civil conflict and its wealthy citizens, commonly known as the
'barons' of London, were capable of exerting important
influence.

To this day, outside the City proper, London has the feeling
of a cluster of villages rather than of a single metropolitan
area. Early medieval London can best be described as a
collection of communities, townships, parishes and lordships,
each of which had its own constitution. By the twelfth century,
there were two institutions that expressed its corporate identity – the popular assembly of the folkmoot and the local court
known as the hustings (held indoors and, from its name,
apparently going back to the time of the ninth-century Danish
invasions). The familiar pattern of medieval London's business
community and municipal government was also beginning to
emerge at this time. The structure of guilds and companies was
in place: chief among them the weavers, bakers, pepperers (i.e.
pepper merchants), butchers, goldsmiths and cloth-dressers as
well as the mysterious 'guilds of the bridge', whose exact
functions are unclear.

Already, the city's militia, ancestor of the famous London
Trained Bands, was a force to be reckoned with. In 1145,

Robert of Gloucester retreated from his new castle at Faringdon before the '*Londonensium terribilium et numerosum exercitum*', 'the large and fearsome army of London', which in this campaign quite probably ensured King Stephen's final success in the civil war. The acclamation of the populace, a vital part in the coronation ceremony of the English kings, in practice generally meant the leading men and the citizenry of London.

When King Aethelred II 'the unready' died, early in the year of 1016, while Cnut of Denmark and his army controlled the greater part of the country, London held firm for Edmund Ironside, Aethelred's handsome and warlike young son. It seemed he was the natural candidate for loyal Englishmen. Together with those members of the Witan (council of the realm) the '*burhwaru*' of London, i.e. the chief citizens, chose him to be king. To complete the formalities, the populace as a whole acclaimed him.

Soon after his coronation at Westminster William the Conqueror granted a charter exclusively to Londoners. His youngest son Henry I courted their favour after his dubious coronation in 1100. Thirty-five years later they made the extraordinary claim that it belonged to them as of right to choose the king of England. On 1 December 1135, King Henry died in Lyons la Forêt in southern Normandy, after days of a lingering death following a hunting accident. Barely three weeks later Stephen of Blois, Count of Boulogne, was crowned his successor and acclaimed by the men of London – just like Edmund Ironside, as Stephen's biographer, the anonymous author of the *Gesta Stephani*, pointed out. At the coronation of Richard I the city rioted when it appeared that its leading citizens had been rebuffed. London's claim to choose England's king was certainly 'over the top': it is equally clear that without its backing no king could hope to be secure.

Some two years before the coronation of Stephen, Henry I had granted London a charter with some notable concessions, including the right to appoint the sheriff of London and the sheriff of the surrounding county of Middlesex. This meant that the king agreed to the exclusion of his own tax-gatherers (for revenue collection was then the sheriff's principal job) from the richest city in northern Europe. The revenues expected from the city were set at the very low figure of £300. Londoners were also allowed to appoint their own justiciar (i.e. law administrator).

Then, in February 1141 King Stephen, the Londoners' favourite, was defeated and captured at the Battle of Lincoln. His rival, the Empress Matilda, was in the ascendant and at Winchester his own brother Henry, the bishop and also papal legate, proclaiming the capture to be the judgment of God, claimed for the assembled clergy the Pope's authority to make Matilda queen. London's representatives at the council had to gather their dignity about them as best they could. Only six years before they had asserted their claim to elect the monarch as of right and had acclaimed Stephen. Now they could merely demand his release.

Matilda had spent her formative years in Germany as the wife of the emperor Henry V and revelled in exacting the honour and obeisance due an empress. Everyone knew that now was the time to woo the Londoners to win their support for her cause. Matilda entered the city like a conqueror in triumph, wore the insignia of an empress, required the leading members of the city's militia to do homage by kissing her stirrup, and then ordered a tax to be levied on the very city her own father had granted should be free of royal revenue officials. Her forces were not sufficient to maintain such arrogance. The citizens first swore to establish a 'commune'. The term should have had an ominous ring for

Matilda; something of a novelty in the English political vo-
cabulary, it was familiar in lands of the empire where the city
communes of north Italy, though nominally subject to the
empire, were burgeoning centres of economic independence
and political self-government. Within weeks of her triumphal
entry the Londoners expelled Matilda. She next fell out with
the Bishop of Winchester and proceeded to besiege him in his
own city. Need one say, she never became queen of England.

The bulk of London's population was English. In their
important book *Medieval Kingship*, Henry A. Myers and
Herwig Wolfram refer to the 'Saxon pre-eminence in the
merchant interest'. The city's immense wealth ensured its
continuing influence in the 1190s during the conflict between
Richard's chancellor William Longchamp and Prince John for
control of the royal government. The prince won the Londoners' support when he agreed to recognize the commune; the
chancellor, as well as accusations of corruption and incompetence, was charged with being a 'foreigner'. It is a telling detail.
No doubt it was because of his loudly expressed contempt for
the English and because of his peasant origins. Prince John, on
the other hand, whatever his ethnicity as a prince of the
Angevin family, was of the royal house of England. For a
time, in the late summer of 1191, the country was paralysed by
the conflict between the chancellor nominated by King
Richard as his 'representative' and his brother John, whom
he had recognized as 'rector of the realm'. London provided
the stage for the resolution of the drama. 'The chronicles of the
day', wrote the Victorian scholar J. H. Round, 'allow us to
picture the scene for ourselves, as the excited citizens, who had
poured forth overnight with lanterns and torches, to welcome
John to the capital, streamed together on the morning of the
eventful 8th October at the well-known sound of the great bell,
swinging from its campanile in St Paul's Churchyard. There

they heard John take the oath to the "Commune".' There were other magnates and also bishops in London at the time who also took the oath. While it suited John's political calculations, none of these great men can have had much choice between discretion and valour. The city was roused, the tocsin had sounded and the populace were ready to stand to arms if need be.

Longchamp was obliged to leave office after two meetings of the citizens' newly acclaimed commune – one in the chapter house of St Paul's, the other on open ground near the Tower. These were stirring times. M. T. Clanchy sees the 'removal of Longchamp [from office] by an association that claimed to speak for the English people and the Londoners in particular' as a 'significant steps towards the articulation of public opinion as a political force'. It would also seem obvious that memories of the oath taken to the London commune of 1191 fed into the events that would lead to the oaths sworn by the opposition barons of 1214–15.

As to the nature of the London commune itself, indeed the precise nature of communes as such in medieval Europe, the matter is still an open debate among historians. But we can say that it was a type of urban community, with an elective council and an elected head. To establish such an institution in a feudal world that recognized only military force or the claims of birth and descent, required the evolution of a novel procedure by townsmen – the taking of a common oath or '*conjuratio*'. On the continent such communes were, to all intents and purposes, subversive institutions standing apart from the established order. The part played by Prince John and those magnates and clerics who joined him in the oath to the London commune must have startled contemporaries. Speaking with cynical detachment, the chronicler Richard of Devizes, who was present in the city during those stirring days, observed: 'A commune is an unnatural growth on the people, a cause of fear to the realm . . . and a matter of indifference to the clergy [*tepor sacerdoti*].'

It was certainly a landmark for London, for at the time of setting up the commune the citizens also established the right to elect a mayor for life as its head. When John acceded to the Crown, a payment of 3,000 marks won the city a further series of charters.

John's London charter, dated 9 May 1215, clearly intended as a bait to lure the city away from the baronial cause, confirmed all existing liberties including annual mayoral elections with the right to re-elect or replace. It also gave guarantees to foreign merchants that they would be tolled only once, by the king's chamberlain. With the provision regarding the mayorality, London reached the mature status of a self-governing municipality. Another document, dating from about this time, is perhaps headings for a petition prepared by a committee of Londoners prior to the May charter. It lists exemption from arbitrary tallage, control of the Thames, the annual election of the mayor in a folkmoot, the right to distrain for debt against the property and persons of debtors, freedom of access for foreign traders and freedom from excessive tolls by the royal government.

The opposition barons were to find firm allies among the capital's leading men of business; the Articles of the Barons contain important clauses to protect London interests, such as exemption from arbitrary tallage, many found, if in modified form, in the Great Charter. However, some were omitted in the final version of that document; most notable was that concerning tallage. This could be levied without appeal, by king or lord from townsman or serf, village or city, and was particularly loathed because it was arbitrary, could be extortionate and was not levied on the nobility. To be subject to tallage was a badge of inferior status. When an aid was levied, in theory at least, the city could offer its own estimate of a reasonable sum to pay, with the prospect that a sensibly generous offer would be accepted. Tallage was fixed by the king's or the lord's officials. Where the aid was paid in a lump sum from the citizens as a body they were responsible for raising it among themselves; tallage was fixed by the revenue officials on the basis of an individual's wealth and levied on him directly. Their Articles show that the barons petitioned the king to exempt their London friends; the relevant clause in the 1215 Charter shows that they did not carry the point. The great city was to be free from feudal aids, from tallage, no.

Perhaps the barons did not press London's cause in this matter over-zealously because they too, as the royal officials no doubt reminded them, were entitled to levy tallage on the boroughs in their lands: if that was so, by what justification could they demand the king surrender the same right with respect to the richest 'borough' in his kingdom? London continued its struggle for exemption. But to no avail. In 1255 Henry III's government imposed a tallage of 3,000 marks upon the city. Perhaps as a concession it was not to be levied directly on individual citizens. The city's first response was to offer an aid of 2,000 marks. This was rejected. The Londoners now denied outright that they were liable to tallage. Forthwith, the mayor and leading citizens were ordered to present themselves at the exchequer, where they were confronted with the entries on the exchequer and chancery rolls demonstrating quite clearly that Londoners had paid tallage on numerous past occasions. The following day they returned with the cash.

Of all the towns and cities in England London is the only one mentioned in the Charter by name, though the clause that guarantees its 'ancient liberties' and customs stipulates that the same is to go for all other cities and towns in the kingdom. The grant of 'liberties and customs' by land and by water made to London was specifically extended. Though it did not win exemption from tallage, London remained a steady ally of the baronial party and its mayor was named as one of the Twenty-five charged with supervising the king's adherence to the terms agreed at Runnymede. At the time it was surely a notable honour and responsibility to be awarded to a mere commoner.

An important source for our knowledge about the selection and resources of that Committee of Twenty-five is the Lambeth manuscript compiled by a Londoner. A man most likely employed in the chamber at Guildhall over ten years from 1206, it is clear that he was interested in political events and was probably close to the councils of the baronial opposition in the weeks running up to Runnymede. The manuscript not only lists the names of the Twenty-five – except strangely the mayor of London – it also adds after each name a quota of knights. Since these quotas correspond neither to the known power of the barons in question nor the knight service they owed on their lands, it has been assumed that the figures indicate the number of retainers each could call upon in the London–Runnymede region at the time the list was drawn up. Among other things this important manuscript also contains the supposed 'Laws of Edward the Confessor' and the customs of London.

The early thirteenth century witnessed the growth of new towns, many of them today major cities, such as Liverpool founded by John himself. They could be highly profitable for the lord of the land if the site was well chosen. In August 1207 the king wrote a letter patent to the prospective townsfolk of the green-field site by the Mersey. It was divided into plots of land, known as burgages. Burgage tenure brought with it privileges known as liberties; the settlers were to be free of customs, free from servile dues or obligations to do labour services. By 1210 the place was paying an annual farm, set at £10, in exchange for rights to administer the place and collect market and other dues. This was more than double what the land would have raised in agriculture. Between 1180 and 1230 some fifty-seven towns had been founded in England, among them Stratford–upon-Avon by the Bishop of Worcester.

Bristol, thanks to a monopoly of the trade with Ireland awarded to it by John's father, was rising to match the capital itself and like it would soon achieve full county status. Centres such as York and Norwich were coming to prominence as England's wool trade grew ever more prosperous. Work during the 1970s on the archaeology of standing buildings in Chester has led to a reassessment of the age of the structures in the famous 'Rows' of that city and dated some of the shops back to the thirteenth century. The finds confirm admiring passages in the panegyric on the city written around the year 1200 by a monk from the nearby monastery of St Werburgha.

Returning to the south of England, we find that in 1191, the year of London's commune, Oxford issued its own charter with its own seal. It was a flourishing trading centre with a population of 5,000, large by English standards. It had emerged from a prolonged struggle over market rights with nearby Abingdon and Wallingford and, besides a thriving commercial community, it had a growing weaving industry. This was governed by its own guild under royal charter, handsomely paid for, and meant it had a monopoly of cloth production within a radius of 5 leagues (approximately 15 miles) from the town centre. In that same year of 1191 the royal exchequer held its accounting sessions at Oxford. It also enjoyed a nationwide reputation as an academic centre.

During the twelfth century numerous towns, among them
Exeter, Northampton and Lincoln, had notable cathedral or
monastic schools and attracted masters in various faculties.
But law was the academic discipline preferred by the ambitious
and, outside London, there were few places more suited than
Oxford for the study of this passport to the royal service. With
a court continually on the move and Oxford but a day's march
from Windsor, the town was often on the itinerary. Nearby,
the royal hunting lodge of Woodstock was a favourite with
both Henry I and Henry II. King Stephen had held his first
council at Oxford and the empress Matilda had made it her
base when she lost London. Henry II held two great councils
there and his sons John and Richard were born at Beaumont
Palace, just outside the city's west gate.

Among the cluster of royal camp-followers and hopeful
courtiers were ambitious clerks looking for permanent employment and in need of the increasingly vital qualifications in
civil or canon (i.e. Church) law, keys to promotion in Church
and state. Graduates in law from Paris or Bologna, the original
home of the new discipline, had long found Oxford a profitable base in which to set up a teaching practice. Masters in
other faculties followed, so that by the early 1200s the place
was becoming recognized as a *studium generale* for the study
of the liberal arts, with a combined master and student
population, said one contemporary, of some 3,000. But in
1209 'town–gown' relations, always uneasy, exploded when a
student murdered a townswoman. Acting with the king's
authority, the city authorities hanged three students by way
of reprisal. They probably were not involved in the crime,
and they certainly should not have been hanged since as
'clerks' they were subject to the ecclesiastical courts which
did not dispense capital punishment. The academic body
decamped en masse, some moving to the township of Reading

in the lee of its great Benedictine Abbey, others to Cambridge in the Fens, where nearby Stourbridge was host to a famous international commercial fair. The continued absence of the student body brutally exposed how dependent on it Oxford's economy had become. After five years the two sides came to an agreement. The academic body was to form itself into a legal corporation with legal privileges but also liabilities – a 'university' – and the town guilds agreed to control rents and food prices. In the year of Runnymede the clerks of Oxford had been back in residence for a year; the academic settlement at Cambridge had taken root and was to seed a new university; and Reading Abbey probably expanded as a centre of learning.

Higher education at the time consisted of studying the seven liberal arts, divided into the *trivium* (grammar, rhetoric and logic), the lesser or 'trivial' course, and the *quadrivium* (arithmetic, geometry, music and astronomy). Mastery took up to nine years and entitled one to be called Master of Arts. Law teachers, as noted, also set up shop in university towns. Many students might study elements of the *trivium*, particularly logic, improve their Latin and take a course in some aspect of the law and leave the university after two or three years. Many a student, perhaps the son of a rich peasant eager for him to advance in the world by becoming a cleric, would have begun his career in a local school. By the year of Magna Carta most English towns had a school of some sort. A higher degree in law or theology meant Mastery in the Arts; then three or four further years of study were necessary to complete the course.

In 1235, some forty years after its dispute with the city authorities, Oxford became the focus in the conflict between King Henry III and opposition in the baronage led by Simon de Montfort, Earl of Leicester, once called 'the struggle for the charters'. On 12 April 1258, Simon and six other magnates swore an oath of common purpose (one thinks of those 'conjurations' made at the time of the London commune and the Articles of the Barons). Others joined them and three weeks later, at a confrontation in Westminster Hall, they forced King Henry and his son, the Lord Edward (later King Edward I), to take an oath on the Gospels to follow their rulings.

The king issued letters that announced his agreement to a reform of the realm and convened a general meeting to be held at Oxford in June. By now it was a natural venue for such a conference. The university was winning a European reputation, especially in sciences such as optics, under its first, great chancellor Robert Grosseteste, Bishop of Lincoln, who counted de Montfort among his friends, while one of his successors in the post, the canon lawyer Thomas Cantilupe, was an adviser of the baronial opposition.

Assembling on 9 June 1258, many of them armed, the delegates to this constitutional assembly, the king and his son and leading advisers among them, all swore oaths in the name of '*le commun de Engleterre*', the 'commune/community of England' echoing the '*communa tocius terre*' of Magna Carta Clause 61. As we know, the oath was the cement of medieval society, the most common being the oath of homage sworn by a man to his lord. The bond that this established was one of dependency and subordination in exchange for protection and favours granted. The oath to the 'commune', on the other hand, was one in which members, considered equal for the purposes of the oath, swore to work together for the common good. In these Oxford oaths the king with his son and heir joined together as partners with nobles subject to them in a common purpose.

The Oxford meeting next went on to frame the conditions for the reorganization of the governance of the kingdom known as the Provisions of Oxford. Like the Great Charter, they provided for a monitoring body, in this case numbering twenty-four and not twenty-five, with twelve from the king's side and twelve from the opposition. The daily business of government was to be conducted by the king in consultation with a council of fifteen; and there were to be discussions or '*parlemenz*' (the first record of the word 'parliament') three times a year between the council and twelve appointees of the 'commune'.

Altogether, the Provisions of Oxford appear to have been more stringent and carefully thought out than the arrangements for Magna Carta. Like that document they were promulgated nationwide, in the English language as well as French, its first and very significant deployment in the political arena.

7

COMMUNITIES OF THE FOREST

Even though only three of its clauses dealt with forest matters Magna Carta made a definitive break with past practice. Until then, afforestation and all matters relating to it had been at the will of the king without consultation. Clause 48 of the Charter provided that twelve knights of the shire, chosen by 'worthy men of the shire', should at once investigate evil customs and practices. In other words, the local community was to be allowed to probe the acts of the royal officers, regulate boundaries and amend regulations. It was a massive intrusion into the Crown's powers. Two years later it was secured 'in perpetuity' (*in perpetuum*) by the 'Charter of the Forest' charter, issued in November 1217.

Not so long ago, the idea of the forest conjured up images of quiet leafy glades, animal sounds, bird calls, the idea of a nature sanctuary, stories of gamekeepers and poachers and tales of Robin Hood and the greenwood. These were part of the medieval experience, though one feels it must have been much noisier, more densely populated at least – for just one year's Christmas feasting in the mid-thirteenth century the royal huntsmen supplied the royal kitchens with 830 deer of various types, 200 wild boar, 1,300 hare and much lesser game, not to mention hundreds of swans and other game birds. But more important were utilitarian connotations associated for us with the work of the forestry commission, for the wastes and forests of medieval Europe were a prime source of food, animal feed and raw materials – and of course of royal and baronial sport.

The word 'forest' derives from the Latin *foris*, 'outside', and was used to designate any area, woodland or not, that was barred to common use and reserved for the king or a great baron, above all for hunting and 'the chase' (from French, '*la chasse*'). The mainly heathland area known as Cannock Chase in Staffordshire, for example, was in legal terminology within a royal forest. The wooded forests resembled the sacred groves of the Germanic ancestors of the Anglo-Saxon kings; the royal hunt once had religious and mythological associations and the woodlands had their own ceremonies and services. Echoes of these ancient traditions and still older ones, dating back to Iron Age times, linger in the services and dues recorded in Domesday Book. Legends of wood spirits and mystic huntsmen survived long into Elizabethan times so that Herne the Huntsman, a spirit of Windsor Forest, could terrorize Falstaff at the end of Shakespeare's play *The Merry Wives of Windsor*. But such folk memories played little part in the calculations of the royal foresters of the Norman and Angevin kings of England. For them the forest lands they inherited from their Anglo-Saxon predecessors and the large new areas of land they 'afforested' for themselves were for exploitation, profit and above all else for sport.

Modern commercial woodlands are mainly managed by monoculture for timber. The medieval forest was a diverse ecosystem whose animals and fruits were all carefully husbanded. In his book *Des arbres et des hommes: La Forêt au moyen-age*, the French scholar Roland Bechmann gives a vivid account of the diverse nature of forest resources in the Middle Ages. Berries and mushrooms provided foods, and in addition there were medicinal plants and poisons; bee products such as honey and candle wax; oil from walnuts and beechnuts; forage, such as the salt-rich compost of fallen leaves, for farm and draught animals; mast, such as acorns or beech nuts for pigs; wood resins for torches, pitch and glue; leaves for mattress-stuffing for cottage households (beech leaves were called 'wood feathers'); bark for tiles and roofing shingles, boats and baskets; wood ash for fertilizer and washing lye for use in soap-making; leather and furs from wild animals; horn for drinking-vessels, hunting horns and knife handles. Even so, the principal forest resource, then as now, was wood.

Timber was a prime material in the building industry. All but the grandest town houses were built of wood, while church construction consumed vast quantities in scaffolding and 'centring' to support masonry vaults and arches during the building process. Timber went to John's new shipyards by the ton, as expanding trade was carried in ever more merchant shipping. Then there was the increasing range of industrial users such as glass-makers (who preferred beech wood) and ironmasters, whose industry demanded large supplies of charcoal for smelting the ores in their super-heated furnaces – 1,766 cubic feet (50 cubic metres) of wood fuel to make 220 lbs (100 kg) of iron. The charcoal-burners were a skilled somewhat reclusive workforce of forest-dwellers, who tended to live in hut settlements round their turf stacks and move on to a new site of operations when the wood in one part of the forest had been used up by their activities. There were basket-weavers exploiting the pliable twigs of the osier willow; some-what sturdier rods were harvested every two or three years by 'coppicing' (cutting back the sturdy shoots to ground level) to make hurdles. To this day there are coppice plantations still in exploitation, notably in French woodlands, that have been in cultivation since medieval times.

Hardwood was used among other things for 'blades' for spades and hoes (iron was used only for the highest quality of tool). Softwood saplings might be bent and tied so as to grow to the shape required for scythe handles and other specialized applications. And of course, in times of war such as the civil conflict of the Magna Carta years, timber was in heavy demand for war machines and castle works – repairs or replacements of portcullis, postern gates or drawbridge. Clause 31 of Magna Carta pledged that in future royal officers would not take 'other people's timber for castles or other works' except by agreement of the owners.

The law of the forest

The busy pageant of life in the scattered communities seemed a secret world to outsiders and over all loomed the sinister presence of the forest laws: laws absolute and binding on all who lived or owned land within the forest boundary. A juridical rather than a topographical concept, this boundary was widely drawn and could embrace not only woodland and heaths but also upland wastes which on their lower margins could include cultivated lands, villages and even towns. Henley-in-Arden, set in the enchanted forest of Arden, would have been such a township. Nor was the royal forest boundary confined to royal properties as their game runs might cross into neighbouring estates.

Kings might 'afforest' lands, i.e. enclose as forest, at their pleasure, without deigning to consult the common people or any but the most powerful barons. Land and resources until then belonging to a local lord or tenant farmers became subject to a royal monopoly. Forest law was at the disposition of the unfettered will of the king. The year before his death, Richard I authorized blinding and castration as the penalty for the killing of a royal deer. A senior minister of Henry II had conceded that 'justice' as commonly understood had nothing to do with forest law. The system rested on the twin principles of 'venison' and 'vert'. The one prohibited not only the killing but even the disturbing of game animals; the second forbade the cutting of timber or the cultivation of further land as it would damage the animals' habitat. Such regulations could apply to private land skirting the royal forest. Not content with robbing private landowners of the profitable exploitation of their own forest land, the Crown insisted that owners of land within the forest boundary maintain at their own expense full-time wood-wards with the duty to protect the king's interests in their masters' lands – notably the prevention of damage to trees so as to preserve animal habitats outside the actual lands of the king that might be sought as refuge by animals pursued by the royal hunt.

Even before the Conquest, England's kings had jealously guarded the hunting within their own domains. Cnut forbade trespassing on the royal hunt 'wherever I wish to have it preserved', but the Normans afforested huge areas where before the land had been free of restriction. The very name of William I's 'New Forest' in Hampshire proclaimed the change brought in by the Conquest settlers.

Royal prerogatives in the forest lands had been infringed during the time of King Stephen – Henry II more than restored the status quo ante-bellum. He reinforced royal rights and privileges; he appointed itinerant forest justices; he re-established previous forest boundaries; and, John's opposition barons were to claim, he brought yet more tracts of land within the royal forest. It has been estimated that by the end of his reign a third of England, including the entire county of Essex, was forest in the legal sense. One acre (0.4 hectares) in every three, whether waste, arable or tree-covered, came under a jurisdiction which, to quote the words of the king's treasurer, Richard FitzNeal, rested 'not on the common law of the realm but on the will of the ruler'. In fact forest-dwellers were absolutely excluded from the normal laws of England as administered in the shire courts and subjected to a separate jurisdiction with its own courts and with its own repertoire of harshly restrictive and punitive sanctions.

The Angevin kings exploited the system for their own pleasure in the hunt but also for profit. A Forest Commission sent round the country to ensure that all regulations were being properly enforced was a guaranteed fundraiser – regulations were not always precisely defined, 'evidence' depended on the word of a royal official, penalties were exorbitant. The financial proceeds could amount to as much as half of the Crown's annual revenue. Richard and John cynically profited from their father's unjust appropriations by magnanimously disafforesting huge areas, perhaps an entire county – in exchange for substantial payments.

Law officers, courts and penalties

Each 'forest county' had its own set of law officers. Twelve knights were appointed as 'regarders'; their job was to make tours of inspection every third year to report any encroachments on forest lands and to ensure that the prohibitions against carrying arms, particularly bows and arrows, were strictly enforced. They also had to see that any hunting dog, mastiff or greyhound kept by a forest-dweller was 'lawed', that is, that it had three claws cut from the paws of each front foot. Four other knights called 'agistors' were appointed to protect the king's interests in matters pertaining to the pasturage of pigs ('pannage') and cattle. The proprietor of land within the royal forest boundary was not allowed to turn his own live-stock loose in the forest, or rent out the grazing until thirty days after Michaelmas (29 September) when the best season for mast was reckoned to be over.

At the head of the forest administration stood the forest justiciar, or chief forester (after 1238 the country was to be divided between two forest justiciars, one north and the other south of the River Trent). Under him came the wardens, men of great power in the land, each having one or more forests under his control. Directly answerable to them, an army of foresters and under-foresters combined the functions of a gamekeeper with the powers of a magistrate. Next came the 'verderers', men of knightly status elected in the shire court, with the job of assessing the evidence against a man charged with an offence under the forest laws to determine whether there was a case to answer. If there was, it was for them to produce the culprit for trial by the forester, or in more serious cases the warden.

Many quite minor offenders found themselves at the mercy of the courts and it is easy to see why. This was a world in which hunting was almost an obsession with many monarchs (the saintly King Edward the Confessor had been a notorious devotee): it was a world in which a knight-verderer charged with deciding whether the prisoner before him was or was not guilty of spoiling the royal sport would take lot of convincing that the poor wretch should be released without charge.

The warden, who in many cases was also the constable of
the principal royal castle in the district, was answerable only to
the king. He derived his income, sufficient to ensure him a
handsome living, from the exercise of rights and perquisites
that enabled him not only to live well but also to pay his
foresters who were thus, in theory, salaried officials. A warden
paid handsomely for his appointment, in anticipation of the
immense private fortune his powers would enable him to
accumulate. The system ensured corruption and extortion.
The appointee began to recoup his outlay the moment he
was installed in office by selling off under-forestships to the
highest bidders. No warden, of course, actually paid his
underlings. They were expected, to use the expressive phrase
of the time, to 'live upon the country'. For the average forest-
dweller, one imagines, the resulting state of affairs can rarely
have been little better than a reign of terror.

The hierarchy of officials was matched by a hierarchy of
courts. At the lowest level, the investigatory tribunals held
every six weeks took evidence for cases to be tried, usually
before the itinerant forest justices. Since these higher courts
were held at wide intervals, offenders might have the
prospect of conviction hanging over them for years. The
multifarious offences under the forest law were a rich source
of profit to the Crown and could reduce the forest-dweller
to abject poverty. If he failed to serve on a court inquisition
or, if serving, failed to produce a culprit, he was liable to a
fine. If he gave, or was judged to have given, false informa-
tion he was fined. If he sold or gave away timber, if a bow
and arrow were found in his keeping, if he kept greyhounds
or mastiffs which had not been lawed (i.e. their claws
clipped), he paid a fine.

The actual penalties were draconian. By the terms of the
1217 Charter of the Forest possession of an unlawed dog

carried a fine of three shillings (15p) – the best part of a
month's pay for a skilled master-huntsman. And yet this was
regarded as a reform. Up to that time, a peasant caught with
a hunt-ready dog in the king's forest was required to hand
over an ox, without which he could not hope to plough his
land. Penalties were often arbitrary – especially in the event
of a 'serious trespass'. If one of the royal beasts of the chase
was found dead in the forest, an extraordinary 'court of
inquisition' was convened; all the men of the nearest settlements were liable to attend. In the summer of 1209, the town
of Maidford in Northamptonshire, together with the profits
of its traders, the proceeds of its farms, the wealth of its
inhabitants, the value of its livestock, in short 'the whole of
the aforesaid town of Maidford, was seized into the king's
hand'. This fearful vengeance was, the records tell us,
wreaked in retribution for the death of a hart in the wood
of Henry Dawney and the failure of the court inquisition to
find the guilty party. The king's foresters had discovered the
severed head of the animal on Dawney's land. The landowner's forester had recently died while Dawney himself
disclaimed any knowledge of the matter. When the townsmen refused to finger a culprit they were summarily dealt
with. Evidently the punishment was less for the death of the
venison than for the dumb insolence of these rustics in the
face of outraged majesty.

The term 'serious trespass' could be elastic, and if it misfired
there was bound to be some other offence that could be made
to serve. When the king's official in the Forest of Somerton
found the corpse of a hare, which he deemed to be a beast of
the chase, he had men representing the four townships of the
forest sit in solemn judgment on the body. They duly found
that the said hare had 'died of a murrain'. Since the deposition
contains no reference to any trap, and since it is clear that a

poacher would have removed his booty from the scene of the crime, it would seem fairly obvious that the creature met its end by natural causes. The forester did not question the finding but got his money nevertheless, fining all four townships on the pretext that they had not sent a sufficient number of representatives to the inquiry.

Attendance at the court was an onerous duty. Travel, by foot of course for most jurors, plus the day or two of the session itself, could mean the best part of a week knocked out of one's schedule and there was no question of expenses or attendance allowance! When the king's justices of the forest made their appearance in a district, the entire population, whether living within the forest boundary or in adjacent outlying districts, had been due to attend according the laws of Henry II. The 1215 Charter at last brought them some relief as Clause 44 exempted them from this obligation. They were still required to attend the shire court, of course.

A list of the things that a man might not do on his own land, if it fell within the boundaries of the forest, makes impressive reading. He might not uproot trees and clear land for cultivation, for that was to commit an assart which robbed the animals of cover; the lopping or pruning of branches without due permission attracted its own fine. Outside the coverts the landowner was forbidden to put waste or pasture land under the plough, to exploit natural deposits of marl or lime, to enclose any area by hedge or paling, to dig fish ponds or to build water-mills or channel rivers into millstreams. All these encroached on the king's rights. Such restrictions inevitably meant that any land within the 'forest boundary' tended to revert to scrub and woodland cover. Thus the word 'forest' developed the meaning we understand by it today.

Hunting, the sport of kings . . . and barons

A king's determination to have good hunting wherever he might be in his kingdom lay at the root of the system. The beasts of the chase – red deer, fallow deer, roe deer and wild boar – could be taken only by the king himself and his men or by the express authorization of a royal warrant. Anyone might hunt small animals such as hares, foxes, badgers, wolves or wild cats, though even these might not be taken without formal notification to the forester. Peter of Liddington was held in chains for forty-eight hours in a flooded subterranean cell on the suspicion of having taken a rabbit in Eastwood, Leicestershire. Many a prosperous peasant arrested within the forest boundaries on such pretexts found himself tortured until he bought his release. Hunting was exceedingly popular with all ranks of society. At the lowest level that rabbit in the pot was a valuable addition to the daily diet. Higher up the social scale the prosperous citizens of London claimed an ancient right to hunt the woodlands of Middlesex. Of course, the most coveted of all game were the 'royal beasts', and these remained in the gift of the king.

Clause 11 of the Charter of the Forest made a concession to the baronial love of the hunt with the provision that a magnate passing through a forest might take two royal beasts. By this time King John was dead and the charter itself was drawn up under the supervision of the barons loyal to the ten-year-old Henry III. Perhaps this in part explains the 'royal' generosity. Even so, there were conditions: the would-be hunter must notify a royal forester and if one could not be found must signal his presence in the woodland by sounding a blast on his horn. In any case two animals was a modest enough allowance. Years later the king's brother, Richard, Earl of Cornwall, in nine days of hunting in the Forest of Rockingham in Northamptonshire took more than thirty buck. In the civil war of the 1260s, with royal authority at a low ebb, a baronial hunting party took their sport in the royal forest of the Peak in Derbyshire and made a bag of fifty deer of various types.

A great landowner within the forest boundaries might be allowed to buy grants of 'vert and venison' over his own land and favoured nobles might be given the franchise to hunt over a tract of royal forest. Such land, technically known as a 'chase', was not formally disafforested but here the forest law was administered, generally in a modified form, by officials appointed by the franchise. In any case kings made such grants very selectively and to be sure of his hunting the landowner was best advised to create his own deer park, if at all possible, by enclosing land outside the forest boundaries. This would be stocked by purchase or, if he was favoured, by a gift from the king.

Statute law would require such deer parks to be fenced securely so that there might be no confusion with the beasts of the neighbouring royal forest. The newly enclosed hunting ground, its livestock and the maintenance of the boundary fence, were the responsibility of a 'parker'. The lord of the park might have the right of 'free warren', that is, to kill lesser game such as foxes, badgers, squirrels and so forth. Not being able to appeal to royal forest law to protect his preserve, he had to rely instead on strong boundary fencing and the common law of theft and trespass. This soon acquired a specialist branch, which by the nineteenth century had evolved into a code of game laws almost as vicious as the medieval law of the forest.

Deer parks were to be found all over the country (there may have been as many as 3,000 in England at the time of Magna Carta); some were a modest 70 acres (28.3 hectares), others, like Wiscomb Park in east Devon, extensive estates. First made about the year 1200, it had a 4-mile (6.4 kilometres) boundary fence enclosing 640 acres (259 hectares) of well-watered pastures and woodlands rich in wild fruits such as strawberries and raspberries, well-stocked trout streams and, of course, game.

The typical park enclosure was an earthen bank with a ditch inside the boundary, topped with a paling fence or quickset hedge. Despite the huge extent of the forests, royal beasts did stray from time to time and encouraging them to do so was an art all its own. Favourite was the concealed deer leap, a wide ditch that was inviting to jump but impossible to recross. Once the animal was outside the forest boundaries it would be outside the forest law and could be taken legitimately.

But the same principle also applied in reverse. One autumn day in 1251 the 29-year-old Richard de Clare, Earl of Gloucester, took a party of guests into his chase at Micklewood. The earl's dogs started a hart and finally brought it down in a covert in the neighbouring royal forest. As an earl, Richard was answerable only to the king; his friends were summoned to appear before the justices of the forest. Some years after the Micklewood chase incident, Prince Llywelyn of Wales was hunting along the River Dyfi in Merionydd when a stag ran out of a brake in front of his party and plunged across the river to the king's forest. The Welshmen followed it and ran it down. Then, as Giraldus Cambrensis relates, 'the king's officers of those parts and others came to the huntsmen with horns and cries just as is done in times of war'. The Welsh prince looked on, outraged, as the English foresters took charge of the animal and jostled and ill-treated his huntsmen.

Given the tensions of the border territories in the Welsh Marches, the mention of war is telling. Like the tournament and most activities associated with horsemanship, hunting was closely connected with the ethos of war (in the contemporary Mongol empire the royal hunt, which involved coordinating thousands of horsemen over hundreds of square miles of steppe, was recognized as part of the training in wartime manoeuvres). At the courts of medieval Europe, the mysteries of the hunt were served by large establishments of skilled men to train and care for the hounds and draw the coverts and a multitude of other tasks. Among this band of professionals incompetence or any breach of the code was not to be tolerated. Early in the fourteenth century William Twici, chief huntsman to King Edward II, summed up the state of the sport in his *L'art de Vénerie*, one of the earliest treatises on hunting. His salary matched what Edward's father had paid the architect-mason of Caernarvon Castle. The repertoire of horn calls still heard in the hunting field in England or France today was already well developed and must have been the favourite music of many a nobleman and his lady.

The Charter of the Forest

Restrictions on their freedom to hunt were irksome, but it was the restrictions imposed on their rights as landowners which the baronial opposition at Runnymede had in mind when they had the king swear to institute committees of enquiry and to abolish all 'evil customs' within forty days of the completion of the enquiries. The twelve knights from each shire charged with this task (Clause 48) presumably made some progress before the disruptions caused by months of civil war.

Their investigations, in their turn, seem to have disturbed developing customs and rights. Indeed in some parts of the country these investigations provoked outbreaks of lawlessness which threatened to undermine forest administration and settle nothing. They were among the causes that led to the framing of the Charter of the Forest.

By an order of June 1209 John had ordered that hedges should be burned and ditches levelled so that, in the words of a contemporary, 'beasts might fatten upon the crops . . . while men starved'. But evil customs like these had been part of the standard conduct of public life in England since the time of the Norman Conquest: even when not abused by royal forest officials, they constituted gross limitations on the freedom of the landowner.

In November 1217 the short clauses of 1215 relating to the forest were replaced by the new document known as the Charter of the Forest. It was infinitely wider in extent than the clauses it superseded. In so far as it related to the access of forest communities to the resources of the forest, the Charter of the Forest had far-reaching significance for the ordinary English man and woman. But while its main aim was to force the king to disafforest, the areas removed from the royal domain more usually fell into the hands of some local baronial lordship than reverted to common ownership. In the late seventeenth century the Earl of Aylesbury and Lord Rivers were able to invoke the charter to enforce their rights in Savernake Forest. Perversely in later ages commoners would appeal for their rights not to the Charter of the Forest, which often provided pretext for private landlords to seize forest lands, but to the Great Charter, as for instance did the protesters in the anti-enclosure riots of the 1830s.

In fact even before 1215 many local communities had obtained various exemptions from the forest regulations. Richard and John had sold off Crown rights in much land afforested by their father. John, needing funds for his campaigns in Normandy, authorized his chief forester Hugh de Neville to sell charters of disafforestation to a greater or lesser extent in Devon, Cornwall, Essex, Shropshire and Staffordshire. Only local vigilance could ensure that privileges were respected, even though Henry III insisted that the barons, who had received new liberties from him, should grant the same to their men. An investigation of forest conditions in 1225 found that William of Lancaster, Lord of Kendal, had kept certain woods and moors afforested to himself 'to the damage of the . . . honest men of the neighbourhood'.

Unfortunately the Charter of the Forest stipulated that the extent of royal forest and the customs within it should be determined by reference to the coronation of Henry II. But did this mean the forest that Henry II could claim at his accession or the forest that he actually owned at that time? Since Henry I had afforested at will and Henry II had claimed the same right, and since the chaotic reign of King Stephen during which vast areas of royal forest had been 'annexed' by the turbulent baronage lay between the two, the door was open to endless dispute throughout the thirteenth century. This in part explains the frequent demands for the confirmation of the charters. Some would argue that the motor for the reissues of Magna Carta was in fact concern about the Charter of the Forest.

It was a smaller document (in 1218 we begin to hear of 'Magna Carta' or 'large charter' to distinguish the 1215 from the 1217 version) but it was detailed and practical and greatly expands the treatment of forest matters. Probably it drew on work of the commissions of knights set up by Clause 48 in 1215. Its aim was to regulate the forest boundaries, to investigate further the royal officials of the forest and to make changes in the administration of the forest regulations.

The first clause rescinded all new afforestations made by Henry II, and with the third the boy king Henry III is made to rescind all similar additions to the royal forest by 'King Richard our uncle' and 'King John our father'. It went on to make comprehensive provisions over a wide range of grievances; it came to be recognized as on a par with the 'great' Charter (Magna Carta) as one of the chief sureties of the liberties of England. Some of its provisions made important ameliorations in the day-to-day life of the average forest-dweller, though others made valuable concessions to land-owners. Clauses 1 and 3 meant that much land illegally appropriated to the royal forest over the previous sixty years was returned to baronial landlords. With their wrongs righted, the barons proved as keen as the king had been to enforce their newly acquired forest rights, to the disadvantage of their neighbours and tenants.

On the other hand, the rural economy was benefited in many parts of England where the king's forest writ ceased to run. Landowners were now permitted to put up mills on their own property, to develop fish ponds, to dig drainage ditches and bring land into cultivation so long as they did not damage the coverts of the royal game on their property – previously cultivation of all kinds had been banned on these lands. The landowner had even been barred from harvesting wild honey from bees in his own trees. On his tour of France in the 1780s Arthur Young stood amazed at the backward state of agri-culture in large tracts of the country where royal and many aristocratic estates were arrested in medieval conditions – much attributable to the preservation of the rural landscape in the interests of *la chasse*.

The lot of the ordinary forest-dweller must have been much improved by a reform in the conduct of the forest courts. With Clause 16 the charter banned the former practice whereby the wardens held the pleas of the forest: since it was they who had most probably brought the case in the first place they had been able to act as judge in their own cause. Commoners were, of course, still banned from taking game in the forest; even the gathering of winter firewood, a 'perk' of life within the forest, was subject to stringent rules and payments to the forester. In any case, the power of the forest official on the ground was a local reality and his abuse of his authority was unlikely to be curbed for long by any charter, unless that charter was rigorously enforced.

A classic instance was the practice known as 'scot [i.e. 'tax'] ales' ('*scot allas*') forbidden in Clause 7 of the Charter of the Forest; a description from a petition of complaint from Somerset in the 1270s reveals the abuse banned by the 1217 charter. At harvest time the forester and his men 'came with horses to [plunder] sheaves of every kind of corn within the bounds of the forest as well as from fields bordering the boundaries and brewed their ale from the plunder'. The peasant faced a choice: he could drink the ale brewed from his own barley and pay for the privilege – or else be refused permission to gather his winter fuel within the forest boundaries. Even those fortunate to escape pillage by the foresters' marauding bands suffered; for no one 'dared brew when the foresters brewed nor sell ale so long as the foresters had ale to sell'.

Forest-dwellers and miners

Farming communities that happened to lie within the forest boundaries, although they faced hazards and hardships outside the common experience of rural life and might enjoy, if lucky, perks such as winter firewood, shared the basic rhythms of the farming year with villagers in the manorial economy of the arable countryside. But forest life also embraced various lifestyles and communities not found in the world outside. The life of the charcoal-burner is one such, the woodsman with his axe and the travelling sawyer teams other examples. Skilled craftsmen and artisans, they were outside the craft guilds to be found in the little towns that dotted the country, but some of them, such as the charcoal-burners, might be members of or associated with the organization of 'free miners'.

The Royal Forest of Dean in Gloucestershire, running northwards from the rivers Severn and Wye, rich in coal and iron ore, and a centre for ironworking, had long been home to such crafts. Its self-contained woodland community retained much of its private and withdrawn character down to the twentieth century. In the Middle Ages, in most other areas of the country mine-workers ranked as ordinary labourers; in the Forest of Dean, despite its remote location in the unstable world of the border territories between England and Wales, thanks in large measure to the extreme richness of the lodes, its mining community enjoyed a status rare outside the feudal hierarchy or the town guilds.

The aristocrats of this 'forest' world of the free miners, whose privileges were rooted in ancient traditions and officially recognized in government prescripts of Henry III, were the iron ore miners. The actual ironworkers followed in the ranking. Every forge made work for a given number of charcoal-burners and miners and forgehands. The value of the extractive industries to the growing tradition of medieval technology is demonstrated by the wide terms of the privileges granted the free miners, outside the regulations governing ordinary forest-dwellers.

First, the customs assured the miners of their monopoly. The right to mine in the region was restricted to men resident within the bounds of the forest and members of the free miners. They controlled not only extraction of the ore but also any exports out of the region along the River Severn; carriers were bound to pay dues to the miners on penalty of having their boats confiscated. By contrast with the stringent limitations on land development usual in forest law, the free miners were permitted to prospect and dig anywhere, except in gardens and orchards. Prospecting teams or partnerships comprised four 'verns', or partners. In addition to the carte blanche to open mines as and where they saw fit, the verns were entitled to free access for their wagons and sumpter horses to the pit head from the highway; in other words they were exempt from the levy of 'chiminage' (French, '*chemin*') allowed by the Charter of the Forest to certain foresters. They were also permitted to take timber necessary for shoring. In return, however, the miners were required to incorporate the lord of the soil, whether king or private landowner, as one of the verns, with a partner's share in the proceeds. Laying siege to the town of Meaux in Normandy, Henry V recruited the cream of his sapper corps in the Forest of Dean. Each miner raising more than three loads of ore per week paid a penny levy to an official known as the gaveller every Tuesday morning. From the records it seems that in addition to forges within the forest, the Forest of Dean was exporting about 10,000 loads of ore annually.

Rights in a mine could be bequeathed. To prevent trespass on a neighbour's claim and lessen disputes, it was stipulated that no man could start a working near another man's adit (i.e. access tunnel) within so much space that 'the miner may stand and cast ridding and stones so far from him with a bale, as the manner is'. Disputes were settled at the miners' court at St Briavels, under the presidency of the constable, by a jury of twelve miners; appeal was permitted to further jury judgment. The penalty for perjury was the heaviest possible for a skilled artisan, namely the destruction of his working tools and kit. The list is instructive: the tools and 'habit', which were to be burnt 'before his face', comprised his miner's cap and his leather breaches 'tied below the knee', the wooden mine hod (for carrying out the ore), his mattock for working the seam, and the candlestick held between the teeth to light him at his work.

The president at the court at St Briavels was the constable of the royal castle there, as often as not the warden of the forest. Like other forest-dwellers, the denizens of the Forest of Dean were governed by many of the provisions of forest law and liable to the draconian penalties infringements such as killing the royal game animals could incur. The Forest of Dean seems to have been particularly noted for its wild boar.

Rebels, outlaws and Robin Hood

Despite the harshness of its laws, criminals, vagabonds and vagrants of all kinds looked for refuge in forest land. It was in this context that the legends of Robin Hood were born. The oral tradition was well established by the fourteenth century and the rhymes about the outlaw yeoman Robin rivalled the popularity of those about the noble ruffian Earl Ranulf of Chester (d.1232) who was active in the north of England and the north midlands in the 1220s.

The Yorkshire pipe roll for 1226 records a charge imposed on the chattels of one 'Robert Hod', fugitive. He may have been a common debtor on the run from his creditors, or had perhaps, like the Robin of the stories, fallen foul of corrupt forest officials and rather than submit to their extortions voluntarily become an outlaw. As to the notorious 'Sheriff of Nottingham', it is true that King John appointed a Ralph FitzStephen as forester of Sherwood with the right to seize for himself the goods and chattels of robbers and poachers taken within the forest bounds. Somewhat later we find three royal officials of the period have been suggested as candidates: Philip Marc, sheriff of Nottinghamshire and Derbyshire, who certainly had custody of Sherwood Forest; Brian de Lisle, chief forester of Nottinghamshire and Derbyshire, chief justice of the forest in the early 1220s, and sheriff of Yorkshire in the

1230s; and Reginald De Grey, the sheriff of Nottinghamshire, who was pursuing rebels against Henry III's government in 1266–7.

Whether or not Hod the Yorkshire fugitive was the original inspiration for the Robin Hood ballads and stories, the period immediately following the royalist victory in the baronial wars of Henry III's reign would have provided fertile soil in which such stories could proliferate. After the defeat and death of Simon de Montfort, Earl of Leicester, and leader of the rebel cause at the Battle of Evesham in August 1265, the forests of England seem to have been congested with a distinctly better class of outlaw as the disinherited rebels sought refuge in the greenwood. Here was the ambience in which Robert of Loxley, the disposed English lord, might be expected to thrive as Robin by fanciful balladeers. Perhaps David of Uffington, whose company of outlaws roamed the Forest of Epping, or Adam Gurdon, flushed out from the woods around Alton in Hampshire in the spring of 1266 by the Lord Edward (later King Edward I) inspired them. Although he had started his career as a royal forester, an aroma of the chivalry of the greenwood does linger round Gurdon's name. According to one tradition, when the royal troopers caught up with Gurdon's band, the Lord Edward himself took on the outlaw captain in single combat and was so impressed by the man's courage that he spared his life. Lastly we can perhaps note that for six years following Evesham, the shires of Leicester, Derby and Nottingham were harried by a band of outlaws led by a certain Robert Godberd (a name to remind people of the folk legendary Robin Goodfellow, as did Robin Hood's). He was finally run down in the early weeks of 1272 by Reginald De Grey, who may have been involved in a personal vendetta.

None of these speculations, of course, fits the tradition that links Robin with King Richard the Lionheart, but then this particular fiction first surfaces in the sixteenth century to be 'confirmed' in the writings of the eighteenth-century antiquarian William Stukeley. Robin Hood is first mentioned in literature in William Langland's allegorical poem *Piers Plowman* in the 1370s, though by this time he had been part of the folk tradition for at least a century. Langland did not in fact greatly approve of the greenwood hero. Castigating the vices of his time, he personifies Sloth as an idle priest who knows no Latin but is fully versed in the rhymes of Ranulf of Chester and Robin.

And, truth to tell, the Robin Hood of those days was no Douglas Fairbanks Junior. One ballad tells how he hacked off the head of an enemy and speared it on the end of his bowstave, the better to reshape its features with his knife. The heroic figure of the benign, sporting, and chivalrous Hollywood variety seems to have emerged in the broadsheet ballads popular in the Elizabethan age, and the idea of Robin as an English champion against Norman oppression later yet.

The outlaw was not a glamorous figure for the prosperous classes of thirteenth-century society, but rather a threatening one which they viewed much as the average citizen today views the urban terrorist. The transformation of Robin the bandit into Robin the merry outlaw would mirror the contracting role of the forest in English life over the centuries.

Yet there was an underlying appeal which ensured the survival of the legends. From another perspective we can see Robin Hood as the first in the line of English criminal heroes stretching through Dick Turpin and the eighteenth-century highwaymen to the great train robbers of the 1960s. The lower orders of medieval England may well have seen Robin as the embattled hero against the brutal establishment that administered the forest law, and he had an appeal to the lower gentry and to a latent mood of anticlericalism. For while

he waged war on prosperous landowners, wealthy Church
landowners were particularly favoured.

'The struggle for the charters'

From 1217 on the struggle to ensure that kings respected the
Great Charter included the struggle for the observance of
the forest clauses of the smaller Charter of the Forest. In
fact the boundary issue was bitterly fought between Crown
and barons for the rest of the century. Periodically, attempts
were made to define the proper limits of the royal forests by
perambulations and enquiries along the boundaries. There were
repeated findings against the Crown – to little effect. At the
Parliament of Lincoln in 1301 the baronial opposition forced
King Edward I to agree a reduction in the boundaries. The
strongest of all medieval England's kings, he was not about to
comply but quickly petitioned for and received a special bull
from Pope Clement V which revoked the concessions on the
grounds that they had been granted under duress.

But this was the last royal victory in the struggle over forest
boundaries. Edward's son, Edward II, was forced to restore the
Lincoln settlement and it was never reversed. When, two
hundred years later, Henry VIII took a fancy to enlarge the
forest land around Hampton Court, he not only made sure of
Parliament's consent but paid compensation to all the landowners affected. A century later, King Charles I, always on the
lookout for ways of raising money without calling Parliament,
did for a time restore certain long-forgotten levies of medieval
forest law and aimed to extend the boundaries of the forest.
When he was eventually forced to recall Parliament, it passed a
statute ordaining that the forest should be 'as in the time of
King Edward I'. (Presumably they were thinking of the Lincoln
settlement.) At this time also there were appeals to the Great

Charter on the wider constitutional front (see page 280). Thus, for a moment, 'the struggle for the charters' played out a final brief episode, the liberties of the forest featuring along with the liberties of the community of England as the country girded itself for the historic struggle of the English Civil War.

Today, the acres of forest still remaining in Crown ownership are administered by the Forestry Commission. In the 1980s, however, as more and more of Britain's woodlands were turned over to the private sector, oak and ash, beech and hornbeam found themselves outnumbered by mercenary regiments of monotonous conifer. The cruel regime of forest law is long past, but so is the colourful tapestry of forest life and lore. While Robin Hood leads his merry men across the film and television screen, today the villains of the piece out there in what remains of the greenwood seem to have an uncanny resemblance to city accountants and their clients.

The dawning of the 1990s brought hopes that England might once more boast extensive woodlands of beauty and ecological diversity, with the news that the Countryside Commission was planning to develop a new national forest in the midlands. It seemed possible that the realization that exploitative monocultures practised at the scale and intensity demanded by modern technology would be damaging as well as monotonous might lead to policy decisions which would restore sizeable tracts of England's landscape to an appearance and condition they had not known since the Middle Ages. In 2008 the alarming predictions of the impact of global warming and the expected consequences of climate change seem to suggest we should look forward to future forest landscapes remote from anything known in old Sherwood.

8

THE COMMUNITY OF JEWRY

English Jewry was largely self-governing. For the draftsmen of the 1215 Charter the Jews were of interest only in relation to their business as money men. In 1210 John, we are told, demanded the improbable sum of £44,000 from England's Jewry, an idea of the wealth it was thought to have at its disposal. Any who refused the royal officers were liable to extreme torture. Jewish money seems to have been considered an extension of the royal treasury. Jews are mentioned in Clauses 10 and 11 where the concern is the plight of heirs and widows encumbered by debts to Jewish moneylenders at the death of the head of the family. In Clause 10 we read that if anyone owes a debt to the Jews and dies before it is repaid, it shall not bear interest while the heir is under age and that if the debt falls into the king's hands he is not to take anything more than the principal mentioned in the original bond. Clause 11 provides that in the case of a man who dies indebted to the

Jews his widow shall receive back her dower and pay nothing of the debt; furthermore, if the debtor leaves any under-age children, they shall be provided with 'necessaries' – presumably the basic necessities of food and clothing – in keeping with the holding of the deceased tenant. In other words, the widow and heirs of a debtor were not to be left destitute and their needs were to be attended to before the debt. This seems particularly hard on the moneylender – until we remember that in the last resort the Crown stood behind the Jews. These clauses, with their possibly damaging consequences for the royal government, were dropped from the 1216 reissue and never reappeared in any subsequent version of the Charter.

Cultural traditions and cultural divides

In the early 1200s, England's Jewish community probably amounted to no more than 5,000 and like the rest of Europe's Jews they were victims of severe legal discrimination. Justinian, the great sixth-century Byzantine emperor whose codification of Roman law formed the basis for Roman law studies in medieval Europe, had prohibited the study of Jewish holy texts. The prohibition had little impact in the long term as the great series of commentaries on these texts would show. In the short run it may even have benefited synagogue worship, since some Jewish communities in the Byzantine empire responded by creating special types of the metrical hymns known as piyyutim (Greek *poietes*, 'poet') as a means of teaching the faith and these became popular with worshippers.

Such melodic embellishments of the Jewish liturgy spread from the Mediterranean into northern Europe. Popular with synagogue congregations, though frowned on by strict traditionalists, they seem to have attracted Christians – a ninth-century bishop complained that some of the parishioners in his diocese were trying to learn Jewish melodies. The earliest piyyutim melodies to have survived are to be found in a manuscript written for a Norman nobleman about the year 1100. Then in the 1190s we find another episcopal directive, this time against clergy themselves, banning the study of Jewish doctrine or melodies. A generation later orthodox Jews in Germany were forbidding the teaching of synagogue melodies to Christian clergy. Both the interest of these way-ward priests and the fact they were able to find willing teachers confirms hints from other sources that relations across the religious divide could, despite horrific outbursts of anti-Semitic violence, sometimes be friendly. Just how Christians came to know these Jewish melodies is in itself intriguing. Did perhaps performances by Jewish travelling musicians (*joculatores*) prompt open-minded music enthusiasts to explore the alien world of synagogue worship?

The official stance of both Church and state to Jews was bound to be ambivalent. Following the Gospel account of the crucifixion, which attributes the blame for the death of Jesus Christ to the Jerusalem mob primed by the chief priests, Church teaching held all Jews guilty – had not that mob shouted, 'his blood be upon us and on our children'? Equally, the Church could not, nor did it wish to, deny the origins of Christianity in Judaism. Christ and his disciples were Jews, as was St Paul, originator of much Christian doctrine. The books of the Jewish scriptures, the 'Old' Testament, were almost as important in the theology of the Church as the New Testament of Christ and his teaching. King David's Psalms, in their Latin Vulgate version, constituted one of the most beloved treasures of medieval churchmen.

A common image of 'Synagogue', the emblem for Judaism, was depicted as a beautiful woman blindfolded, so as to symbolize a tradition rich in the beauty of Truth which had

wilfully closed its eyes to the fulfilment of that Truth in the
coming of Jesus. For the state the position was simple. To
most kings the enemies of Christ were no more and no less
than a necessary part of the economic management of the
state. But there could be ambivalent attitudes in the upper
reaches of educated society. People recognized that Jewish
culture represented by the city of Jerusalem was ancient. An
early tradition concerning the Roman persecution of the
Christians in Britain gives one of the most revered martyrs,
a native of Carlisle, the name of Aaron – a classic 'Jewish'
name during the Middle Ages. The city itself, according to
the *History of the Kings of Britain* by Geoffrey of Monmouth, was built by King Leil at the same time as Solomon
was beginning to build the kingdom of Jerusalem, and the
Queen of Sheba came to listen to his wisdom. Such ideas
seem to make some attempt to accommodate the enemies of
Christ into the world of Christendom.

Pride and prejudice

Suspicion and dislike verging on hatred were of course more
general sentiments across the religious divide. During the
boyhood of King John, the people of Arles in southern France
commissioned the building of a fine stone bridge across the
River Rhône. It was to be financed with Jewish money, but
bridge-building was considered a work of piety. The idea may
have had its origins in Roman times when it seems that the
activity was thought to desecrate the domain of the Naiads –
the local nature spirits (*genii loci*) of the river – and a 'bridge
priest' was assigned to conduct a ceremonial designed to
placate them. The chief priest of Rome, charged with the
administration of religious law, was the senior member of a
college of bridge priests with the title Pontifex Maximus

(literally, 'principal bridge builder'), a title adopted by the popes and as 'Supreme Pontiff' still in use today.

Something of the mystic aura of the pagan era lingered over the activity of bridge-building well into medieval times. Vital to royal communications as well as to trade, expensive, expert and laborious, it was also considered a work of charity to wayfarers. Many bridges paid for by a rich benefactor or group of benefactors had little chapels built on them in which travellers were invited to pray for the soul(s) of the builder(s). In most cases the local inhabitants or town community were charged with giving their labour or raising the funds. At Arles the Jews, being among the richest groups in the city, were natural 'volunteers' for the fundraiser. Equally, it seems that their participation was considered tainted for this semi-sacred public enterprise. A nasty little arrangement was reached whereby the city's Christian authorities received the cash without having to accept charity from the 'enemies of Christ'. To avert the hostility and retain the custom of their fellow citizens, the Jewry of Arles agreed to a document which bound them to a hundred years of forced building labour, to be done on the Sabbath. It was of course profane – an impossible obligation. So they were permitted to buy themselves out of it with a suitable down payment and an agreement to an annual levy.

By such fictions, historical, legal and financial, and at the additional cost of sporadic pogroms, Europe's Jews were bitterly accustomed to collaborating in their status of non-citizens. King Philip of France opened his reign by confiscating the property of the Jews of Paris and expelling them. In times of unrest the underlying context of humiliation was punctuated by disaster, but in 'normal' times they could be reasonably assured of the practice of their religion and customs within their own closely knit communities.

The Jews in England

An incident involving William II of England (d.1100), who spent long periods as acting ruler of Normandy while his brother Duke Robert was on crusade, illustrates a particularly ingenious fiction. The story is found in the *Historia Novorum in Anglie* ('New History in England') written about 1115 by Eadmer, historian and monk of noble Anglo-Saxon birth. He recalls how, in the 1090s (a period of anti-Semitic outburst in the wake of the First Crusade) when a number of Jews from Rouen converted to Christianity, a group of their co-religionists approached the king to use his influence to persuade them to return to the faith. The father of one of the converts offered 60 marks, sufficient to support fifty fully armed mercenaries for a month, if William would intervene and talk the young man out of his apostasy. The offender was duly summoned to the royal presence and told to obey his father, 'or by the image of the Blessed Virgin I will have your eyes put out'. He flatly refused, and then went on to accuse the Christian king of unchristian sympathies. William was notoriously hot-tempered but the Jewish would-be martyr was simply dismissed from the royal presence in disgrace. His father paid half the agreed fee even though the royal conversion attempt had failed. Since Eadmer intended the story as an instance of William's shameful irreligion and blasphemies we must suppose that the setting would have been quite credible to contemporaries. Some of the Rouenais Jews may have been genuine converts; others were no doubt calculating time-servers and still others perhaps cowardly traitors to their faith. Whatever may have been their motivations, Eadmer's story would hardly have carried conviction with his readers had not the leading members of the Jewish community of Rouen had standing in the city and felt free to

speak on terms amounting to familiarity with the local
Christian potentate.

There had been Jews in Gaul in the late Roman period and
the Rouenais may have been a continuous settlement from that
time. The first Jewish settlement in England came after the
Conquest when, according to the chronicler William of Mal-
mesbury, the Conqueror brought a number of families over
from Rouen to London. By the early 1200s it seems there were
about twenty towns with a Jewish community. York, one of
the larger, may have amounted to some 250 people to judge
from excavations (1980s) at the medieval Jewish cemetery
there.

The first written notice of the condition of the Jews in
England comes in the 1130s from the document known as
'The Laws of King Edward'. As a matter of historical fact its
mention of Jews in England is one proof that it is not from the
reign of the Anglo-Saxon king; it also means that for contemporaries Jews held residency status of longer standing than
the Norman barons themselves. The author tells us that they
and all their possessions belonged to the king though with his
licence they might put themselves under the protection of a
lord. Wherever they might be, it was the duty of the king's liege
subjects to guard and protect them. This has nothing to do
with philanthropy, everything to do with economics. From the
same document we learn that the king had the right to demand
the return of any Jew and of his money.

Henry II, who legislated to allow the creation of Jewish
cemeteries outside the walls of any city where there was a
community, also granted a special charter to the Jews, though
it has not survived, which authorized the terms on which they
might do business and provided for sons to succeed to their
fathers' estates on payment of a swingeing estate duty. This
was much heavier than the relief paid by the heir to a barony

and, unlike a baronial heir, the Jew was not guaranteed the right of succession. At law, the king was heir to every Jew in the kingdom. When, in 1186, the renowned merchant and financier Aaron of Lincoln died, neither his sons nor his nephew were granted leave to succeed to the vast estate. It was so large that the exchequer set up a special department to deal with it.

The Jewish community was in the last resort at the king's mercy, liable to arbitrary and punitive levies, to confiscations and to fines. But there could be benefits. A papal ruling of 1215 ordained that Jews should wear some form of distinguishing badge; but the king might excuse those of 'our Jews' who paid for an exemption. In general, however, John's exactions must have been exceptional even by the standards of the times. According to chronicle sources it would seem that his favourite pastime was torturing rich Jews to learn the whereabouts of their cash. As confirmatory evidence of John's reputation for cruelty, this is telling. After all, as a group Jews were usually considered fair game, almost proper victims for Christian oppression.

In his own self-interest, however, a king was also the Jews' protector against other men. Christian plaintiffs claimed that John's Crown officials favoured Jews when it came to litigation. In a civil case between Jew and Christian, oaths and evidence of witnesses of both religions were to be taken according to their respective customs. Whereas a Christian wishing to clear himself on oath might, as the law then stood, have to find eleven 'oath helpers' to swear with him, a Jewish defendant was allowed to make his oath 'single-handed' on a book of the Jewish Law. The courts grasped that perjury was more likely if the litigant was taking an oath that he did not consider binding. The Book of the Law was an object of deep reverence to all Jews, for whom the business of the oath helper

no doubt seemed a primitive rigmarole. The Christian in court
merely observed that while he had to find a body of neighbours
to vouchsafe for him, a man whom he regarded as an enemy of
Christ could 'get away with' a simple oath on a strange book
written in strange script.

Thus Christians objected that in a civil case a Jew could
defend himself 'contrary to the custom of the realm'. Moreover
(as explained by McKechnie) by the terms of the charter John
granted in 1201 to the Jewish community in England, confirming the existing rights it enjoyed, it was provided that if a
Christian brought a charge against a Jew, it was to be adjudged by *'pares Judei'* ('peers of the Jews'). This seems to
mean men of their own race, though it was once argued that
the phrase could refer to the specialist officials of the exchequer, headed by 'the king's justices at London assigned to have
custody of the Jews' set up in the 1190s. Either way, it is not
about 'positive discrimination'. 'Human rights' are not the
issue – merely the efficient administration of the king's business and concern for some of the king's most valuable property. In addition to special procedures in the law courts, the
Jew was also under the special protection of the sheriffs and
royal castellans and his well-being was their responsibility
throughout their jurisdictions.

'Bishops' and cantors

The royal justices or 'custodians of the Jews' had their
opposite number elected by the Jewish community, the
'archpriest of the commune of the Jews of England' and
considered far more important there than the king's men.
One such *'archipresbyter Iudeorum'* (the origin of the term is
uncertain) boasted of his responsibility for the 'great' debts of
the English Jewry; the smaller debts such as individual fines

were recorded by his clerk, subject to the control of one of the minor royal officials.

Despite the churchy sound of his title, the Archpriest seems to have been concerned exclusively with secular duties. In the Christian Church hierarchy there was also the title of 'archpriest' for a functionary who discharged various administrative duties today associated with the president of the local ecclesiastical court or rural chapter. Titles such as 'priest' ('*presbyter*') 'bishop' and even 'archbishop' were accorded to other Jewish functionaries. Jews themselves applied the term priest to an officer of the synagogue (most likely the *chazzanim* or cantor). Such words were probably first coined in the Jewish context to explain the workings of their society to Christian officials and neighbours in terms they would understand. We find Jewish 'bishops' at Exeter, Hereford, London and York; occasionally they functioned as bailiffs. The term *episcopus* was, it is true, sometimes used as an equivalent of '*cohen*' (Hebrew, 'priest') but such men held some form of public office within the local Jewish communities, chosen to act as intermediaries in their dealings with the Crown and other Jewries.

Many Jews seem to have left the country to avoid the harsh regime operated by King John; more still during the months of the Magna Carta civil war. After the king's death and as the situation began to normalize some of the refugees returned. But they found that conditions had changed. The self-regulating communities of the old days were giving way to direct rule (as well as protection) by sheriffs and royal castle constables. As the thirteenth century advanced and Christian banking expanded and became ever more sophisticated, conditions for Jews in the community of England worsened. Prejudice and the resultant hostility increased as the royal government became less concerned with protecting 'the king's Jews' as it became less and less dependent on them.

Not that moneylending was the only business conducted by Jews. Pawnbroking called for the skills of jeweller and metalworker in the repair and refurbishment of plate, armour and jewellery to make unredeemed pledges saleable. As well as Jewish goldsmiths, there were physicians, soldiers, vintners, fishmongers and cheesemongers. Aaron of Lincoln, twelfth-century England's wealthiest commoner, dealt extensively in corn and probably wool too. However, being automatically excluded by his religion from membership of the monopolistic craft guilds, it was virtually impossible for a Jew to make a full career in the major urban trades and crafts.

Occasional references in government records indicate a steady trickle of converts to Christianity. The pressure on the smaller communities that had spread outwards from London to most of the major towns was constant. Suspicion and hatred and the sense of ostracism from the normal con-course of human society were hard enough to bear. Add to this the standing discrimination against Jewish endeavour in all fields of skilled or professional employment, and it is clear that many must have been sorely tempted to abandon the faith. But the convention that a Jew's property belonged to the king meant that any rich convert would have to surrender all his wealth to the Crown. So it seems likely that most converts were poor men. Of little economic value to the king, they were liable to expulsion from the kingdom. Conversion might save them from forced exile, which could hardly be imposed on a Christian without cause.

Anti-Semitic violence as such was generally the work of the mob. The upper social orders, both religious and lay, indivi-duals and institutions, often found association with the en-emies of Christ profitable. In the 1180s five prosperous London merchants combined in a property development in Old Jewry, near the site of the Mansion House, and close to the

London house of Aaron of Lincoln – who financed the deal. More than once, Jewish finance was instrumental in facilitating the pious benefactions by which many a religious house extended its landed possessions. A Jew might be outside the feudal network, but land could be pledged to him as security for a loan. In case of a default by the debtor the Jew could not enter on the land, but he could acquire the deeds and arrange the conveyance of the land to an individual or institution with sufficient funds to pay the debt. Many debt-encumbered properties passed to religious houses in this way. More than one monastery archive housed documents concealing outright land purchase in the guise of pious benefactions.

Councils and troubles

Outside the Spain of Alfonso X the Wise (reigned 1252–84), where Jews enjoyed great respect as scholars and physicians, their position deteriorated in the thirteenth century. Crucial was the Fourth Lateran Council, which opened in November 1215. In less than three weeks it passed seventy canons, many of them of major importance in Church doctrine, particularly in relation to the 'Cathar' heretics of Provence. Hunted down in the bloodthirsty campaigns of the Albigensian crusade, they were also harassed by a new body known as the Inquisition dedicated to extirpating heresy. Four of the Council's canons related to Jews. They were henceforward required to pay tithes and other Church dues – for centuries non-Muslims in the Islamic world had been obliged to pay a tax for the practice of their faith. Jews were now banned from intermarrying with Christians – hardly arduous since orthodox Jewish law, then as now, banned mixed marriages. Far more objectionable than either of these was the order that confined Jews to their houses on Passion Sunday and during Holy Week and, most hostile of all was the order that

Jews should wear a distinctive badge or some other distinguishing item of dress.

The decrees reached England early in 1216. John may have noticed the opportunity for money-raising that the dress regulation might offer, but he was preoccupied with the more pressing business of bringing his rebellious barons to heel. After his death, when the civil administration of the country began to return to its normal rhythms, the council of regency regulated the position of England's Jews. Their chief concern seems to have been to reassure those who had remained in England during the troubles of the past few years and to encourage those who had emigrated to return. Those who did so had only to register with the justice of the Jews, while local authorities were to ensure their protection, especially against any 'crusaders' who had taken the cross in accordance with another decree of the Lateran Council.

Early in 1218, William Marshal, now regent, personally saw to it that committees of burgesses were set up in various towns – Lincoln, Bristol and Oxford among them. A government wishing to woo the return of valued money men would have no desire to see them slaughtered by self-styled soldiers of God; so a papal order that ensured these valuable citizens would be publicly humiliated and marked out by unmistakable identification must have been distinctly unwelcome. Even so, since the regency council numbered among its members the Pope's personal representative, Legate Guala, in March 1218 a decree ordered that all Jews in England should wear a white 'tabula' or badge. It does not at first appear to have been rigorously enforced, but then the regulation gradually tightened. A series of statutes of 1253 concerning Jewish matters restated the dress requirement; but they also governed intermarriage, regulated the construction of new synagogues, and the employment of Jewish servants by Christians and the engagement

The Angevin kings: Henry II; Richard I, with the leopards of England; John; and his son Henry III, who built a shrine for Edward the Confessor. Matthew Paris (d.1259) who painted this as one of the illustrations for his Chronicle had little time for King John. Alone of the four monarchs he is depicted sitting not on a throne but on a folding campaign chair. Half-blocking our view of the church and with crown precariously perched over one ear, he looks an altogether shifty and disreputable figure.

The ruins of Château Gaillard overlooking the Lower Seine in Normandy; the sweep of the cliff-like escarpment of the river valley can just be seen in the background. At the time of King John, the valley was covered by a complex of causeways, river barrages and defensive towers. The loss of the great castle in 1204 hung like a doom over the rest of the king's reign.

By his own wish, King John was buried in Worcester Cathedral before the altar of St Wulfstan, the last Anglo-Saxon bishop in England (placed here at the king's left shoulder). At John's right is St Oswald (d.992), an earlier bishop of Worcester. Burial at Westminster Abbey would no doubt have been uncomfortable for John, considering the trouble the memory of its patron, St Edward the Confessor, had caused him. Even so, this tomb slab is an indication that the king may have shared his subjects' growing fascination with the old English past. With his son it became something of a mania.

This document, known as the Articles of the Barons, is a schedule of demands and grievances drawn up by the barons, no doubt in consultation with Archbishop Stephen Langton, for presentation to the king prior to the definitive discussions that led to Magna Carta itself. On the king's orders, his seal was attached on a parchment tag or 'queue' threaded through a slit at the foot of the document. Unlike the Great Charter itself, the Articles are presented in separate paragraphs.

'King John and the barons at Runnymede'. This mural, done for the Royal Exchange London, perfectly captures the classic mythology of Magna Carta. An uneasy King John, seated in all the panoply of state and prompted by Archbishop Langton, is confronted by the wise and freedom-loving leaders of the barons. In the right foreground the officer of the seal operates the press to produce the wax seal from its metal matrix, ready for its attachment to the document. In fact, this was almost certainly done elsewhere.

Magna Carta 1225. This is the version of the Charter revised and amended from 1215 and issued by John's son Henry III. It is the version of the text that was confirmed in 1297 by King Edward I after an inspection (*inspeximus*) and entered the statute law of England. Copies of this 'Inspeximus' text – one in Canberra, the other in Washington – are the only ones of the seventeen versions of the Charter surviving from the thirteenth century held outside England. This particular copy, or 'exemplification', now in the British Library, is the one that was sent to the sheriff of Wiltshire and subsequently held at Lacock Abbey until 1945.

We see here the awful majesty of the King's Bench in the fourteenth century, complete with shackled criminals at the bar. Behind the judges hang, from right to left, the royal arms of England, the king's arms of France and England and the (in fact fictional) arms of the old English royal house of Wessex for Edward the Confessor, who it was supposed had issued a Code of Laws that embodied the justice and age-old liberties of England.

Edward Coke
Lord Chief Justice
B. 1552
D. 1633

Sir Edward Coke (1548–1632), King James I's chief justice of the common pleas and then of the King's Bench (1606–16) and, from 1620, MP. His writings and his championship of the supremacy of the rule of law, even above the king, made Magna Carta central to the parliamentary struggle leading to the English Civil War, and later to the struggle of the American colonies against the imperial Parliament in London.

The impact of Magna Carta worldwide in subsequent centuries is testified by the commemorative oak tree planted at Runnymede on 16 March 1994 by Prime Minister Narasimha Rao of the Republic of India: 'As a tribute to the historic Magna Carta, a source of inspiration throughout the world, and as an affirmation of the values of freedom, democracy and the rule of law which the people of India cherish and have enshrined in their constitution.'

The Magna Carta Memorial erected by the American Bar Association in 1957. Nearby is the memorial to President John F. Kennedy and the Commonwealth War Memorial.

of Jewish nurses in Christian families. (At about this time *The Book of the Pious*, issued for the guidance of Rhineland Jewry, deplored the singing of gentile melodies to babies.)

For the ambitious, wealth and power were, as always, the objectives, though they came differently packaged. To win the grant of a fief in the king's gift – the constableship of a castle, the wardenship of a forest – to have justice, sometimes even to have the king's good will, all demanded money. And in an economy based on land money was short. Cash flow was the problem so it was necessarily a seller's market for money-lenders. Rates of interest were startling. Payment of the relief to enter into one's own inheritance was a special harassment: 'there is no fixed amount which the heir must pay to the king, he must make what terms he can', a treasury expert had written in the last century.

To be in debt to the king was to be in the king's power – it was the king who determined terms and payments. John enjoyed the power he held over his debtors and demanded they put their lands in pledge; this opened them to the threat of forfeiture. One way out was to borrow from a Jew. But, as W. L. Warren pointed out, not only was the interest heavy but a debt to a Jew was an indirect debt to the king, who regularly raided Jews' profits by taking arbitrary tallages. And since the king was every Jew's heir, on his death the king could take not only his chattels and cash, but also his credit notes. 'Thus the baron after years of paying heavy interest to a Jew might find himself still the king's debtor for the principal.'

It is not surprising if wealthy Jews sometimes attracted hostility from great men. Inexhaustibly rich, it seemed, in the one thing the barons were perennially short of – money; spared the strictures of moralizing priests; favourites of the king's laws; and at the same time heirs to the murderers of

Christ: they do not seem to have been ideally placed to win friends and influence people.

As the thirteenth century advanced and other sources of money became available, the Jews became less relevant to the requirements of royal finance. Royal protection became less forthcoming when in the 1260s a series of sensational child killings was blamed on the Jewish community who, it was claimed, ritually killed Christian children for their blood. (Such charges were still being brought in rural communities in nineteenth-century French murder trials.) But these thirteenth-century scandals suited government intentions. In 1290 Edward I ordered the expulsion of all Jews, confiscating much of their wealth but impoverishing the diversity of national life in the process. In the 1650s, Lord Protector Cromwell opened England once more to Jewish immigrants. Thus the community of Jewry, part of the community of England in the year of Magna Carta, would be welcomed back to the realm in the century that had seen the greatest triumphs of the Charter since its granting.

9

THE COMMUNITY OF WOMEN

The subordination of women to men seemed to be justified by the Bible. The Old Testament, that part of their holy book that the dominant Christian culture shared with the despised and oppressed minority, the Jews, taught that God had created man in his own image, that woman had, in one version of the creation story, been created from Adam's rib, and that by yielding to the temptation of the serpent she had been the cause of sin in the world. But for Christians the New Testament introduced a new and liberating possibility which gave a potently ambivalent colouration to the Genesis story. For while Eve caused man's fall from God's grace, the Virgin Mary, by giving birth to Jesus Christ, the second Adam, had brought into the world the possibility of redemption from that original sin.

During the twelfth century, the idea that, in theology at least, women shared with men the working out of divine purpose in the world was emphasized with the growth in the cult of the Blessed Virgin in popular devotion. At the same time, the southern poetic tradition of the troubadours, possibly to some degree thanks to contacts with the courtly poetry of the Arab world, was prompting secular society to accord a new respect to women among the laity with the burgeoning cult of courtly love. These two ideas would help initiate an evolution in the whole concept of women's rights, to be pioneered by western civilization in later centuries. John's own mother, the fabled Eleanor of Aquitaine, had presided over the most brilliant manifestations of the chivalric code of women in her court at Poitiers.

In the 1140s, a lifetime before Magna Carta, reports of Eleanor's amazonian entourage at the time of the Second Crusade had mesmerized European society. Travelling the coasts of Palestine with ladies tricked out in armour and, it was said, flirting – and one knew not what else, many said worse – with her uncle the crusade leader in the Holy Land Count Raymond of Toulouse and Antioch, she had delighted and scandalized the court gossips from Jerusalem to Paris; some even said she had born a child to the chivalrous Muslim warrior, Saladin. It was telling evidence of the kind of culture shock that the southern, fiery beauty of Eleanor represented.

The French King Louis VII, her husband, was both scanda-lized by her reputation and worried by her inability to bear sons. With papal cooperation he had the marriage declared null. While he sought a more compliant and fecund partner, Eleanor wedded the dashing young Henry Plantagenet for whom almost at once she began to breed sons and with whom she lived in turbulent disharmony for the rest of his life. As much at home in the saddle as in the solar (upper chamber), a schemer and a revenger, Eleanor recruited her sons in the quarrel with her husband and was imprisoned by him for her pains. Released by her eldest surviving son Richard I when he became king, she outlived her husband by more than a dozen years, dying in 1204.

For her admirers, Eleanor of Aquitaine ranks ahead of Helen of Troy. She was surely as beautiful – the troubadour Bertran de Born sighed to have the queen of England in his arms – and whereas Helen was content to play the *femme fatale* in besieged Troy, Eleanor would no doubt have taken charge of the city's defences and driven the Greeks back to their ships.

Eleanor's century had had its share of warrior women. Stephen owed his continued tenure of the English throne in large measure thanks to his soldier-like queen, Matilda of Boulogne, while the career of Nicholaa de la Haye, castellan of Lincoln, spanned the turn of the century to the benefit of the royal cause. A favourite image of medieval secular art is of women playing chess, an arena of skill where they might confront men on more or less equal terms. At the time, the board was also a place for betting and a metaphor of battle. Demure ladies such as we see depicted in the miniatures could play the role of silken dalliance but could, too, when occasion demanded ride to the wars or direct a garrison's defence.

A woman not inclined to marriage or not placed on the marriage market might find, in today's terms, distinct career opportunities within the convent. The running of a large religious community was a complex administrative affair and in a world which rated the life of religion extremely highly, it was a prestigious one too. At this period women who, like Hildegard of Bingen or Héloïse, achieved distinction in the intellectual life were a rarity but the *Ancrene Wisse* of about 1200, written in Old English as a spiritual guide for women, reminds us of the cohorts of sisters engaged in the day-to-day campaign of the most important army in medieval life – the army of God.

For Magna Carta women are of interest as wives and widows. Here the lady had great opportunities for responsibility. The running of a large household was a large undertaking which in time of war could involve deputizing for her husband in his military function. In the world of the peasant a wife was a still more important member in the family team: poverty recruited all hands to the common enterprise. And there was one female service, virtually unknown today, where a peasant woman might be recruited. Few society women breastfed their children, most engaged a wet nurse. It seems the child in her care might sometimes bond with her rather than with a remote natural mother – Richard the Lionheart's foster-mother Hodierna became a woman of some social standing thanks to a generous land endowment from her charge.

By and large, however, social conventions and the natural physical superiority of the average man to his wife buttressed the fabric of patriarchal society and, sadly enough, Church teaching concurred with a doctrine that sanctioned male mastery, often brutish and loutish. But besides bearing the children and preparing the food, women commonly worked alongside their menfolk in the field, as fisher wives or, in the productive industries as spinners ('spinsters') or even as foundry hands. Whatever the sanctions of society or the rulings of theology, affection, together with the qualities of intelligence and strength of character, shaped relations within the home.

The draftsmen of the Charter were not concerned with such matters: they addressed the legal position of women in feudal society as affected by marriage and widowhood, both matters where property rights and obligations were of vital interest and of financial concern to their menfolk, and to the king. Land was the basis of wealth and marriage was a vital mechanism in the transfer of land between kin groups. The fact that the king had rights in the choice of a marriage partner for an heir or a new partner for a widow should she decide to remarry affected family politics among the nobility; and the fact that John was liable to abuse his privileges here meant that both matters came high on the Charter's agenda. The relevant texts come in Clauses 6 and 8: they stipulate that heirs shall be married without loss of status (John was liable to marry off rich heiresses in his wardship to mercenary captains he wished to reward) and that their next of kin were to be informed before the marriage took place. Clause 8 provided that a widow could not be compelled to marry against her will, with the proviso that she give a guarantee not to remarry at all without the consent of the king, if she held her land from him, or otherwise of the lord from whom she held her land.

The death of a landowner before his heir had come of age meant, in the case of a male heir, problems over the discharge of the land's military dues. If the heir was a woman there was the possibility that the land could be lost to another overlord by her marriage out of her own lord's domain; worse still, the land might go to an enemy. To use the language of anthropology, in a society where men and land provided the basis of society, women and kinship posed the problem. Sandwiched between the rights of heirs and the remarriage of widows comes a clause of direct personal interest to a widow whether she were to remarry or not. It concerns her personal rights in her dower – that portion of her husband's lands specifically set aside for her widowhood; her marriage portion – that portion of his lands that her father had made over to her at the time of her marriage; and any lands that may have been bequeathed to her personally during the marriage. In addition it guaranteed her the right to remain in her husband's house for forty days after his death in order to settle her affairs, and receive her dower. It is a measure of the injustices a widow might be liable to that such provisions had to be made, but attention to the rights of women in any context was unusual for the period.

Put crudely, an heiress was a valuable property. Henry II's court records kept a 'Roll of ladies, youths and girls in the king's gift'. When Richard I awarded William Marshal the hand of Isabelle, heiress of the last Earl of Pembroke with lands in Wales, England and Ireland, he transformed the champion jouster and respected royal servant into one of the greatest landowners in Europe. The lord who had the right to determine a woman's marriage had valuable patronage in his gift. The affections of the girl need not enter into the case, though according to the law of the Church she had to give her consent. If she refused it the Church had to support her right of refusal. Young women courageous enough to stand out were rare indeed. The whole weight of social convention was against them.

They ran the risk of virtual pauperdom. The records of John are as rich in detail as any in Europe at the time. It has been said that the papal chancery itself could not match the royal chancery of England in the ordering of its archives, but even these do not hint at the personal drama that must have lain behind the decision of a certain Alice Bertram to refuse to marry at the summons of the king. They record merely the fact that all her chattels were sold.

Love may have had little to do with decisions as to a marriage partner but, as in any society where arranged marriage is the norm, it could obviously develop. The clerical chronicler Matthew Paris wrote of the married couple enjoying the harmony of the marital bed, and in the passionate poetry of Marie de France, who had connections with the court of Henry II, we can see that sexual love could blossom between married couples as well as in extra-marital sex. The Church condemned adulterous liaisons – one confessor thought it permissible for a husband to castrate his wife's lover, though another considered some form of extra-marital sex 'the vice of all'. It seems safe to suppose that sex was as prevalent in all ranks of society, outside the Church, as it is today. One lay writer considered it entirely natural and some doctors apparently reckoned regular sex a necessary part of a healthy regime (in fact, the highest rates of longevity seem to have been enjoyed by the monastic population). Inevitably, in a male-dominated society where women were blamed for everything, they were held to blame for the evils, if such they were, of promiscuity. It was 'well known' that a woman could resist no man. Court gossip told of a harassed courtier claiming homosexuality to fend off an importunate great lady.

There were options open to women determined to avoid forced marriage at all costs. They could take the life of religion, in other words enter a nunnery and thus become dead in the eyes of the law, the most effective way; or they could attempt to outbid objectionable suitors making application to the king for their hand. When Godfrey, Count of Louvain, set his cap at the wealthy widow of Ralph of Cornhill, he made an offer to the king of 400 marks for the lady, should she be unable to prove any just cause or impediment against his suit. Perhaps the king took pity, perhaps the lady in question had winning ways, but for some reason her counter-offer outweighed Godfrey's. At any rate she was able to fight off the unwanted applicant with a bid of just 200 marks plus three palfreys (pedigree saddle horses) and two hawks. In the end these may have tipped the balance: John was addicted to hawking and a pair of top-quality birds could well have decided the issue. Generally, however, an heiress could be married at the wish of her feudal overlord to any man willing to pay the going rate.

At the time of Magna Carta the term 'the marriage market' could be taken quite literally.

Not only were the heiresses up for sale, so too was the feudal right to decide their marriage. Three years after the case of Godfrey, Count of Louvain, we find a certain Bartholomew of Muleton receiving the 'marriage' of the Widow Lambert, together with the wardship of her heir and his lands for the sum of 400 marks. As a condition he was required to marry her off *absque disparagacione*, literally 'without disparagement', that is, not beneath her social standing. Twelve years later, Magna Carta used exactly the same turn of phrase in the clause on widows' marriages.

The barons did not object to the principle of wardships and the sale of heiresses' marriages: they too found them a valuable source of revenue in their own domains. But they did object to John's penchant for marrying ladies of great families to low-born 'new men' or even mercenary captains, either because they simply had the money or as a reward for military services.

It is difficult to offer an exact translation of 'without disparagement'; though the sense is clear, the Charter made no attempt to define its own term. In the 1230s, the Statute of Merton gave marriage to a villein or a burgess (a rustic or a townsman) as examples. Still later a legal commentary specified marriage to anyone, no matter what their social status, who was maimed or deformed as disparaging. In the Runnymede settlement the chief objection was based on social status or ethnicity – especially if the foreigner in question was one of those hated mercenaries. In a petition of 1258 the barons gave their opinion that an heiress was 'disparaged' if married to anyone not English born. Maybe 'loss of status' is the nearest we can get, though it probably does not convey the sense of outrage that must have been felt for the fate of women such as Margaret Redvers, widow of Baldwin de Redvers, Earl of

Devon, at the hands of King John. In fact, baronial indignation was probably more through sympathy for the nobility of the family than because of personal feelings for the women themselves.

Margaret's first husband, the young and sickly Baldwin de Redvers, had been the son of an officer of the royal household, and died barely three years after the marriage. He left a widow with large estates in Devon and the Isle of Wight and family connections with the upper ranks of the Anglo-Norman establishment. She came into the king's power during the unsettled months of the civil war following Runnymede. Convention dictated that in the troubled times her large estates required the protection and direction of a man, while she needed a husband for the sake of social propriety. In fact John was desperately short of funds and had many loyal servants long overdue reward. He married Margaret off to Faulkes de Bréauté, a man of obscure Norman origins, but above all an outstanding commander who was unswervingly loyal to the king. Faulkes was to be one of the witnesses of the king's will and a major factor in the survival of the royalist struggle against the rebels and Prince Louis of France. But as a mercenary he was heartily despised by the barons even in the loyalist camp. When the rebel cause was finally lost and the French bought off, Faulkes was stripped of his honours and forced to leave England. Margaret took the opportunity to abandon her husband, claiming that she had married him under duress.

With the king who had forced the marriage dead, that was her right – but she may not have convinced contemporaries. As we have seen, widows could buy their way out of unwanted unions. In the very year of the Charter another Margaret, the widow of Roger FitzRoger, had paid the immense sum of £1,000 for the Crown's rights in her marriage. Lesser women bargained smaller sums or offered hawks or hunting dogs or

whatever they could 'if they preferred to live without a husband'. Margaret de Redvers had married Faulkes when he was
in the king's favour and deserted him when the king was dead
and he was disgraced. That at least is how it could have been
seen by hostile contemporaries. In any event, she ended her life
in a convent and apparently friendless.

In 1205 Alice, Countess of Warwick, paid handsomely for a
charter certifying that she would not be forced to marry; that
she should retain sole guardianship of her sons; that she should
enjoy a third of her late husband's lands in dower; and that she
should be free of the duty of attending the local shire and
hundred courts as well as of paying certain dues to the sheriff –
so long as she remained unmarried. The Great Charter made
only one stipulation in such cases: that the lady give a guarantee (*securitatem*, i.e. 'security') that if she did decide to
marry she would not do so without the consent of her feudal
lord.

Depending on the settlements her husband had made for
her, a widow might find herself a prosperous dowager, or she
might find herself a poor relation to her own sons and
daughters. Before the provision of the Charter (Clause 7)
she had no automatic right of continuing residence in the
family home – even her sleeping arrangements on the night
after the funeral could be in doubt. The same clause guaranteed that she would pay no relief (succession duty) on the
dower set aside by her husband at the time of the marriage to
support her should he die first. The dower was very often made
on the day of the wedding, when the act of transfer was
performed in a colourful ceremony at the church door. The
ceremony was considered a form of contract and was so well
established a part of tradition that if the husband omitted it
and left his widow undowered she was entitled to a third of his
lands. The simple guarantee of 1215 that 'the widow shall

have her dower land' was made in the context of this convention. The 1217 reissue was to go further, but not to the widow's advantage.

If a man chose to endow his widow with less than a third of his estate, then this actual endowment rather than the conventional 'legal minimum' would be awarded to her. It is this that the 1217 text makes explicit, stating: 'The widow shall have for her dower the third part of all her husband's land . . . unless a smaller share was assigned to her at the church door.' The church door ceremony rather than being an instance of colourful tradition could thus sometimes be a fraudulent sham. By 1215 charters were well established as a tool of administration. That the greater magnates had officers equivalent to the royal chancellor and were increasingly used to attesting charters for their own tenants no doubt contributed to the impact the Great Charter made on the public mind. The brief clauses that deal with marriage law and rights reflect a number of important points. First, proffers for the wardship of the marriage of heiresses and rights in widows' marriages had by the time of John become frequent, and the objective, to exclude the king from a transaction so closely connected with the territorial interests and dynastic policies of the kin, was explicitly stated. Such applications had become increasingly successful on mutually agreeable terms so that, to some extent, the principles applied by the draftsmen of the Charter largely confirm existing trends. In this matter as in so many others the Charter's innovation was not so much to introduce new principles as to set down existing conventions within a legal context.

A tailpiece to the story of Magna Carta and women's rights is provided by the sad case of Eleanor Cobham reported in the rolls of Parliament for the year 1442. Along with Thomas Southwell and Roger Bolingbroke, graduates of Oxford and

her supposed accomplices, she was found guilty in an ecclesiastical court of planning the death of the king, Henry VI, by
witchcraft and sentenced to the final penalty of treason (burning in the case of a woman) on the authority of the king but
without a trial in a duly constituted secular court of law. At the
next Parliament, 'a petition introduced into the Commons
House appealed to Magna Carta on behalf of such defenceless
women [i.e. women charged with witchcraft in the ecclesiastical courts]'. This appeal to the Great Charter was to ensure
that in future, peeresses, whether in their own right, or as
wives, were to be guaranteed the same trial 'by their peerage',
for charges of felony, 'as was enjoyed by their husbands'. Thus
in at least one respect, though for them a very important one,
women won equality at law with men.

   It is difficult to place the Charter's dealings with women on a
scale in the history of the emancipation of women, the very
idea of which evolved exclusively in western Christian society.
The patterns of male domination in medieval England were so
oppressive when compared with modern practice and expectations that to discuss conditions then with a view to identify-
ing possible signs of hope for the future would seem to be
fanciful. Nevertheless, in comparison with other societies,
medieval European attitudes to women must seem extravagantly enlightened. Writing in the 1160s, the Syrian gentleman
Prince Usamah of Shaizar records with unconcealed amaze-
ment the freedom that the Franks of the crusader kingdom of
Jerusalem allowed their womenfolk. Not only were they
permitted to walk openly in the streets with their husbands,
but if one happened to meet a friend, man or woman, the
husband might stand patiently by while the friends had their
chat. If the conversation dragged on, the Frank thought
nothing of leaving his wife with the man while he went about
his own business. Of course, like their Muslim counterparts,

western women of social standing were constrained in the world of the arranged marriage. Had freedom of choice been allowed to them there Usamah, who refers the extraordinary behaviour of the Franks to the mysterious ways of Allah, whom no man may question, might have found his faith in the divine wisdom under test. One commentator on Magna Carta wrote that one of the great stages in the emancipation of women is to be traced to the Charter's provision that they should not be distrained to marry for a second time without their consent. It seems little enough for a woman to ask and yet, compared with other high cultures, it was indeed a step forward.

Slow though the process may have been, the emancipation of the individual, whether male or female, has been the theme in western civilization that distinguishes it from all others. Inevitably, the process started at the top of the social pyramid. The rights or disabilities of rich heiresses in early thirteenth-century society had little bearing on the lot of their peasant contemporaries. Yet the fact that women of any rank could gain at law the right to marry at will, no matter how circumscribed the circumstances, was a notable advance in principle of interest to all women.

10

LORDSHIPS, CHARTERS AND HOSTAGES: JOHN'S DEALINGS WITH THE CELTIC REALMS

Seen from a Celtic perspective events in England in the middle of the 1210s could appear bizarre. To the writer of the Scottish *Chronicle of Melrose* it seemed that 'the body wished to rule the head . . . the people to rule the king'. For England, actions in the Celtic periphery could sometimes be decisive. During John's reign the Welsh prince Llywelyn was an important factor in English politics. To a greater or lesser extent Irish and Scottish players also affected events in their more powerful neighbour's land.

In the year 1209, at the so-called Peace of Norham, King William the 'Lion' of Scotland agreed terms with King John by which he abandoned his dynasty's long-held claim to Northumberland and surrendered the sons of a number of Scottish nobles as hostages. There had been no open war between the two countries, but the 'peace' followed years of strained relations and the king of Scots further agreed to make a payment of 15,000 marks over two years to 'have John's goodwill' and, most serious of all, to make his two daughters, Margaret and Isabella, wards of John and so deprive himself of the diplomatic asset of the choice of their husbands – the girls were still unmarried when John died. Two years after Norham, the powerful Welsh prince Llywelyn ap Iorwerth was obliged to hand over his son Gruffydd as surety for his father's good behaviour.

John's hostage policy soured his dealings with his Celtic neighbours, as with the barons of England, until a resolution was reached in Magna Carta. The Welsh princes, Llywelyn chief among them, disrupted John's plans more than once and their policy of collaboration with the dissident barons brought its rewards with the return of the hostages. The Scots, too, seemed to have won a short-term benefit from the turmoil of 1215, when the barons of Northumberland did homage to their new king, Alexander II, by order of the Twenty-five.

Ireland features in the first line of the Charter where John's regnal title designates him 'king of England and Lord of Ireland'. The title is derived from a still disputed papal letter, 'Laudabiliter', dated 1155 from Pope Adrian (Hadrian) IV, the only Englishman to occupy the chair of St Peter, which placed the see of Dublin under the authority of Canterbury and conferred the 'lordship' of Ireland on Henry II. The exact wording of the document is still disputed but its ostensible aim was that Henry would promote reforms in the Irish Church in line with those introduced in Europe in the eleventh century.

King John and the Irish

Fatefully, in view of his involvement with Irish history, the year of John's birth marked the beginning of Norman baronial intervention in the story of the country's kingships. In 1167 Diarmait Mac Murchada (Dermot MacMurrough), King of Leinster, seeking help against his rivals, visited England, swore fealty to Henry II for his ancestral rights in the province kingdom and returned to the country with members of the Welsh-Norman baronage ('Saxons' so far as the Irish annalists were concerned) he had recruited as mercenary allies to prosecute his claims.

The actual ethnicity of those involved in this first incursion into Ireland was mixed. The leaders were of the Angevin-Norman ruling caste of England who had married into Welsh noble families such as the Geraldines. The composers of the Irish annals might call the newcomers 'Saxons'; the Welsh scholar Giraldus Cambrensis (Gerald of Wales), whose book *Expugnatio Hiberniae* ('The Conquest of Ireland') told the story of the intervention, brother of Robert of Barri and other early settlers and proud that his own people had not been involved in the débâcle of Hastings, had nothing but contempt for the native English, who in his view had submitted themselves to slavery.

Adventurers, like the original companions of William the Conqueror on his triumphant raid into England of 1066, these baronial entrepreneurs hoped to carve out independent domains for themselves across the sea from England. They were so successful that in 1171 King Henry II, fearful they might come to challenge his throne, led an expedition to enforce his authority over them.

Up until that time the island, engrossed in its own inter-necine conflicts, had made little impact on English affairs.

Apart, that is, from a period during the tenth century when (soon after Scandinavian cousins of theirs had founded the duchy of Normandy) the Norse kings of Dublin irrupted successfully into the north of England against yet another Norse lordship, the Viking kingdom of York. The prospect of Ireland serving once again as a power base for independent regimes, ruled by descendants of the warlike Norsemen, looked a disturbing one for London. It was to scotch any such development that Henry, with the eager encouragement of a new pope Alexander III (who issued a bull to the Irish clergy to mend their ways), had sailed for Ireland with an imposing expeditionary force. Landing at Waterford, he was welcomed by the King of Thomond and in a few months' successful campaigning asserted his supremacy over Irish kings and Anglo-Norman barons.

The Pope may have been disappointed: the king's objective was clearly not the reform of the Church. Henry had earmarked the new island province for his youngest, landless son. He wasted no time in establishing his authority in the matters that concerned the Crown. The Irish had no interest in opposing him, since he was there to discipline their Norman rivals; the Normans had no interest in provoking the wrath of a notable soldier who was also their liege lord and master and, in addition, had a sizeable army at his back. After a token resistance they acknowledged his overlordship. The Irish formally did homage as vassals, while Henry asserted the Crown's exclusive interest in the old Viking ports of Dublin, Waterford and Wexford. A viceroy was left in Dublin to hold the ring, while the Irish reverted to their rivalries and the Welsh-Norman incomers quickly learnt the rules and joined in.

At the Treaty of Windsor in 1175, the King of Connacht, the reigning Irish High King, came to an agreement with Henry that seemed to regularize the position of the new barons resident in Ireland. At the council of Oxford two years later, so far as the king of England and the Pope were concerned, Ireland came under a new dispensation. Now in his tenth year, John, Henry's fourth son, was named 'Lord of Ireland' by his father. The origin of the title, as noted, is found in a bull of Pope Adrian IV, but Henry conferred it with a confirmation we are told from Adrian's successor, the former professor of law, Alexander III. The intention was that John should, in due course, become king of this new province of the Angevin empire; few people could have imagined that he would ever be king of England. At the Oxford assembly Henry also assigned various lordships in Ireland to barons such as de Lacy and de Briouze and had them take oaths of allegiance to him and his son.

In 1185, now aged eighteen, John led his first expedition to Ireland as its 'lord', landing at Waterford. He was well funded by his father and well received by the local Irish notables 'as their lord and with the kiss of peace'. Things soon went dreadfully wrong. John mocked the strange 'barbaric' costumes and flowing beards of the Irish nobles and his companions followed suit. Years later, an English chronicler observed that John liked to snigger at those he considered beneath him and encouraged his sycophantic courtiers to do the same. According to Gerald he also distributed lands held by the first settlers to his cronies; he also antagonized many longstanding supporters, among them the King of Thomond.

For John the year had opened on a rather exotic note. In January Heraclius, the Roman Catholic Patriarch of Jerusalem, had arrived at the English court to offer King Henry the crown of the beleaguered crusader kingdom of Jerusalem, its courageous leper king, Baldwin IV, then dying. Henry declined the dubious honour and forbade his youngest son to accept though John, we are told, begged permission on bended knee. But 1185 ended in humiliation. John wasted his war chest in extravagant living rather than paying his soldiers, so that his forces haemorrhaged through desertion as well as death in battle and he was forced to withdraw. It was a political failure because John, building castles in the Norman manner in his new territories, embittered the local population and dispossessed Irish lords. All this subverted any likelihood of Irish participation on an equal footing with the invading elite. The expansionist ambitions of Hugh de Lacy, constable of Dublin, reinforced where they did not lead the policy.

Like the English and the Welsh before them, the native population of Ireland was succumbing to the ripple effect of Hastings. But the Anglo-Saxon nobility, though absolutely dispossessed, ethnically cleansed or bludgeoned into submission, had eventually absorbed the invaders, thanks to the vigour and sophistication of a centuries-old unifying tradition of administration and government. By contrast, pre-Conquest Irish culture and society, separatist by nature, seemed unable to unite against the intruders. So Ireland's clans, tribes and kingdoms survived for centuries apart and ineffectually hostile – excluded from access to the incomers' laws and from a share in the alien government. Unable either to repel the invaders as the Scots did, or to reverse their encroachments by force as the Czechs of Bohemia against the German empire did, they were to become an oppressed majority in their own country.

The papal intention seems to have been to have John crowned king of Ireland and after Christmas in 1186 a papal legate arrived at the court of Henry II, a crown comprising a gold circlet embellished with peacock feathers in his baggage. Presumably the ceremony was to have taken place in the cathedral at Dublin. One can speculate on what the results would have been had it gone ahead, with Ireland's future under a duly anointed king sanctioned and supported by the Pope. It is possible perhaps that such a 'high king' under the aegis of Europe's principal fount of legitimacy might have founded a foreign dynasty, just as the Normans had in England, that could have established a regime to force the warring Irish kings to unite. But the Norman dynasty in England had imposed itself on Europe's most advanced administrative machine and could continue to develop the infant nation state already in the making. By contrast, Ireland comprised a congeries of tribal kingships grinding against one another along unruly frontiers. In fact the death of John's brother Geoffrey, Count of Brittany, caused their father to order John, waiting at Chester for a favourable wind, to return for the obsequies. The moment was lost, the crown never used and Ireland was to remain a kingdom without a king until Henry VIII assumed the title in the sixteenth century. In a letter of 1216 to the Archbishop of Dublin, his legate to Ireland, Pope Innocent III ordered him to put down conspiracies against John 'throughout the *kingdom* of Ireland' [emphasis added]. But John himself used the style of *Dominus Hiberniae* , 'Lord of Ireland', though this was always preceded by his first, French title, *Comes Moretain*, Count of Mortain – evidently the Angevins were first and foremost good Frenchmen.

Ireland is represented in the text of the Charter by William Marshal, one of the top three landowners in the country, and Henry of London, Archbishop of Dublin, along with the archbishops of Canterbury, York and Bordeaux. In 1212 in the build-up to the Charter, thanks to the persuasion of Marshal, most of Ireland's Norman baronage renewed their oaths of allegiance to the king. They were to remain loyal king's men during the struggle for Magna Carta.

It was during his second expedition to Ireland in 1210, when John aimed to enforce his authority as 'Dominus Hiberniae' over the local Norman baronage and the Irish princes, using his preferred policy of enforcing obedience by demanding hostages as pledges of loyalty, that Aodh O Neill, King of Tir Eoghain (i.e. Tyrone), refused point blank to surrender any hostages at John's request. Cathal, King of Connacht, on the other hand, at first agreed to hand over his son but was persuaded by his wife to think again and rejoined the king without the youth. In a fury, John seized four great courtiers of Connacht and took them back with him to England. Hostage-taking was by now John's method for winning loyalty in his own realm – Welsh, Scottish as well as Irish allies were not discriminated against in the matter! Disregard for the sensibilities of such allies was standard. Typical had been the humiliating situation of the Prince of Powys, who after swearing to save the Lord King faithfully in perpetuity was required to find twenty named hostages to be handed over before his release from John's custody and as future guarantee of his word. Hostage-taking had a long and dishonourable history. Back in 1013 Cnut, forced to leave England empty-handed before his final victory in 1017, left horribly mutilated hostages on the beach at Sandwich. By the mid-1100s feudal convention was coming to extend more 'chivalrous' consideration to English or French hostages than to the 'barbarous' Welsh or Irish.

John's father, repulsed from Wales in an abortive campaign in the 1160s, mutilated and then hanged some twenty hostages. His son, forced to abandon his 1212 campaign by reports of baronial conspiracy in England, hanged twenty Welsh hostages in frustrated fury. Presumably he already suspected collaboration between his enemies. Whatever the case, hostages then as now were always at the disposal of the hostage-taker.

Disregard for local sensibilities was standard procedure. When John's minister in Ireland, de Gray, Bishop of

Norwich, followed instructions to raise three new castles in the province he did not hesitate to site one of them at Clonmacnoise, one of the most sacred places in Ireland. De Gray's castle-building programme in the north continued into 1212 but this did not prevent his suffering a defeat by northern kings. John resolved to return to avenge the humiliation but in fact would never return to Ireland as he was overtaken by the developing crisis that led up to Magna Carta. During that period the majority of the barons of Ireland remained loyal to John just as did the Marcher barons of Wales. Almost inevitably therefore the Welsh under Llywelyn aligned themselves with the baronial dissidents. Perhaps the same forces in Ireland tempted the native kings there to stir trouble – the sources are unclear but in May 1214 John wrote to Henry the Archbishop of Dublin, ordering him to send a report on the state of affairs. He had a number of Irish successes to report – a defeat of English forces in Ulster, the burning of the port of Carlingford and attacks on English strongholds among others.

The Normans in Ireland remained loyal to John throughout the 'troubles' in England. We do not know whether they had sight of the Great Charter of Runnymede; after all papal annulment voided the document within weeks. However, when the Charter was reissued in November 1216, following John's death, with a number of significant changes, a copy of this document was forwarded to Ireland on William Marshal's instructions. A copy of this '*Magna Carta Hiberniae*', purporting to be '1216' adapted for Irish conditions, survives. In fact, 'adaptation' meant little more than substituting 'Ireland' for 'England', 'Dublin' for 'London' and 'the Liffey' for 'the Thames' and 'the Medway'.

John, Welsh Wales and the Marches

John encountered different constitutional traditions in his Celtic neighbours. Ireland could be seen as a single lordship expressed in the concept of a 'High King'; apart from the Highlands and Islands whose allegiance was long claimed by the kings of Norway, Scotland under its Anglo-Norman dynasty approached the status of a unitary kingdom, though without the powerful central administration found in England. (In fact, in 1212 the King of the Isles travelled down to Lambeth to swear fealty to John.) Wales was a place apart.

The inhabitants of the country, like the Irish, felt themselves a distinct *nation*; indeed, aggressively so. 'No other people than this Welsh race nor any other language shall answer for this patch of the Earth . . . on the Day of Judgment' wrote Gerald of Wales; though like many a later Welshman, and on his own admission, his command of the language was so slight that when preaching the crusade he fell back from his Church Latin on Norman French and an interpreter, rather than speak Welsh. No doubt then as now there were strong regional differences of the language which presumably matched the regional hegemonies of Gwynedd in the north, Deheubarth in the south and Powys. The princes had something of the aspect of clan chiefs designated by family names rather than territorial designations. Those who did homage to the kings of England regarded it as personal rather than territorial. After their conquest of England, the Normans established independent baronies in Wales by conquest and settlement and by the time of Magna Carta these were known collectively as the Marches or the March – *Marchie Wallie*.

In Wales, wrote Ifor W. Rowlands, John was confronted 'by a duality of authority . . . (Welsh and English) and by two foci of allegiance and obedience (native and settler)'. There was as yet no single 'lordship of Wales' (*dominium Walliae*) to correspond with the 'lordship of Ireland' (*dominium Hiberniae*). Beside these Marcher territories and jurisdictions as the result of castle building, marriage and other events, John held royal authority in various southern regions such as Carmarthen, Pembroke, Glamorgan and Gower – though he gave Pembroke to William Marshal and Gower to William de Briouze. The fractured pattern of lordship in Wales is clearly demonstrated in Clause 56 of Magna Carta which provides that all disputes were to be settled by the judgment of peers, according to English law, Welsh law or the law of the Marches according to the location of the property.

In 1201 John signed a treaty with Llywelyn ap Iorwerth, known also as Llywelyn the Great of Gwynedd. By its terms he came into the king's service and pledged to do homage to him, in England, as his liege lord. Relations between the two seemed to strengthen in 1205 when the prince, who controlled virtually all of north Wales, married John's illegitimate daughter Joan. But five years later, prompted perhaps by John's absence in Ireland, Llywelyn raided southern Wales, threatening English positions there. John counter-attacked and in 1211 forced the Welsh leader to subscribe to a 'charter of security'. By its terms he named John as his heir in Gwynedd if he had no male heirs by Joan. Such charters not only meant humiliation: held in the royal archive, they could be produced as justification for subsequent campaigns of acquisition on the grounds of feudal discipline. In Clause 58 of the Great Charter at Runnymede, John was to promise the return of 'charters made over to us as securities for the peace'. But in 1211, though humiliated, Llywelyn was still very much in contention and in May or June of the following year he was secretly negotiating a treaty with Philip of France, as we know from a sycophantic letter he wrote to the king. In fact John, who had mustered a large force for a planned campaign in France, redirected it to Chester. The additional recruitment of over 8,000 labourers, presumably for castle-building duties, suggests that, making a virtue of necessity, he had decided on a foundational campaign for the final subjugation of the Welsh.

The Welsh venture also had to be aborted when news came through of baronial conspiracies in England. The leading Welsh princes now began to line up with Llywelyn against John. By the spring of 1215 these Welsh allies had made common cause with the dissident barons in England. When Llywelyn seized the English border castle and borough of Shrewsbury at about the same time as the English barons entered London, King John's position in both countries was parlous indeed. Magna Carter (Clauses 56 and 57) indicates the degree of Llywelyn's success. Any Welshmen deprived of lands or liberties or other things without the legal judgment of their peers in England or in Wales were to have their property and rights immediately restored to them. The next Clause went much further, providing that the discontents from Wales should not only have back the lands and liberties taken by John, but also those seized by the king's brother and his father. In the wars of late 1215 to 1216 Llywelyn, with such triumphs as the capture of Cardigan (Ceredigion) and Carmarthen, shook the Marcher position and also reduced the royal territories to a small area in the south-east. In 1211 John had achieved territorial authority in Wales greater than that of any other king of England before him. At his death the Anglo-Norman presence there was weaker than it had been at the end of the reign of King Stephen, and Llywelyn was unmatched by any Welsh ruler since the time of Harold II of England. Even so, according to *The Oxford History of Wales*, the reign of John saw the English monarchy achieve the theoretical pretext from which to convert its acknowledged overlordship to outright lordship should it decide to deploy the military resources required.

The king of England and the king of Scots

By the early thirteenth century the kings of Scots had long preened themselves on their ancestral roots in France though their more recent origins lay in England. In 1174 King William I the 'Lion', who came to the throne in 1165, had been forced to do homage for his kingdom to Henry II of England, but he had bought release from it in 1189 with a handsome contribution to Richard I's crusading fund. William, who held the border lordship of Tynedale and the earldom of Huntingdon, also maintained his family's claim to the earldom of Northumbria, and on John's accession threatened to seize it by force. John refused to concede and eventually King William came south to Lincoln where he did homage for his English titles in an impressive ceremony in November 1200. Contenting himself with Tynedale and the empty title of Earl of Huntingdon, he accepted that John would look into the matter of Northumbria. We have seen William forced to relinquish the claim in 1209; many Scots detested the dynasty's English entanglements. They looked back to the glory days of Malcolm Canmore (d.1093) whose rape of Cumbria was so thorough that barely a Scottish household was without an English slave for years after. In January 1211 an adventurer from Ireland landed in Ross, with support from the local Gaelic notables. Named Guthred and a blood descendant from Canmore, he may have represented a resentful Gaelic reaction to the spreading influence of William's Anglo-Scottish feudatories. But in 1212 William's fourteen-year-old heir Alexander was sent to London to receive the accolade of knighthood from John, and made the king's ward to be married at his discretion.

Historians long debated the nature of William's homage of 1209: did it re-establish the homage for the kingdom acknowledged from 1174 but remitted by Richard I in 1189, or was it merely for the Scottish king's English titles? Most agree the latter was the case. William was the liegeman of John in the same sense as John was the liegeman of the French king for his lordships in Aquitaine.

Aged about seventy, William the 'Lion' died in December 1214, calling on the barons in attendance to swear fealty to his son Alexander II as the next king; the sixteen-year-old succeeded without opposition. The paragraphs of Magna Carta relating to him and his sisters and concerning his franchises stipulate that he is to be treated on the same terms as the barons of England and according to charters which John had received from his father; any disputed questions were to be settled by the judgment of the king's peers in John's court.

The question naturally arose as to how the King of Scots could have peers, or equals in rank. The issue revolved around the question of the homage which the kings of England reckoned was owing to them from the Scots ruler for his holdings in England such as Tynedale – just as the kings of France reckoned the English ruler owed them homage for their French lands. In August 1209 Alexander had done homage on behalf of his father in regard to other castles and lands, while his sisters Margaret and Isabel were handed over as wards of John, being held in close but honourable confinement in Corfe Castle, Dorset. In the 1220s they would marry into the English peerage, Margaret to the Earl of Kent, Isabel to the Earl of Norfolk; meantime they were treated well enough: on 6 July 1213 John instructed the mayor of Winchester to supply them at Corfe, where he was to receive payment, with tunics of dark green, capes of cambric and fur of miniver and light shoes for summer wear. Finally, in October 1213, Pope Innocent ordered both William and Alexander to do homage to King John.

The Scottish king's support for the dissident barons paid off in the short term. In October 1215 the barons of Northumberland did homage to Alexander on the instructions of the Twenty-five. In January 1216 John retaliated with a raid that wrought havoc and seized Berwick and a number of other towns; the first invasion of Scotland by an English king since 1072, it lasted barely a fortnight but briefly repaired John's standing north of the border. However, in August Alexander took Carlisle and marched unopposed through England to London. He came to an agreement with the dissident barons and the city, and went on to Canterbury where he met Prince Louis of France, doing homage to him at Dover. But Louis was now under the ban of excommunication, which was soon to be extended to Scotland and also Wales.

The Scottish claims on Northumberland were of course agreed at Norham. And even after the death of King John in October, they were confirmed at Norham when the dissident Baron de Vescy on behalf of the Twenty-five invested the king with the *comitatus Northumbrie*. Surely a case of the body ruling the head, it was a stark demonstration of the powers the rebels at Runnymede had sought for themselves.

PART III

CRISIS CHARTER
TO LEGAL CHARTER

By the beginning of 1215 the whole community of England, from the Scottish border country to the king's shipyards in the Solent, had long learnt to recognize the firm hand of Angevin government, which to many smacked of tyranny. Nowhere was resentment stronger than in the north where, until King John became more or less resident in England after 1204, the reach of the administration had been less effective. No one was more enthusiastic in the agitation for a charter of liberties than the baronial group dubbed by a chronicler and royal clerk 'the Northerners'. A natural focus for the malcontents was Eustace de Vescy, the lord of Alnwick in Northumberland, and a long-time enemy of the king.

But if the coordinated movement which took the last lap on the road to Runnymede began with the northerners, the leadership was soon taken up by greater men from southern and eastern counties – chief among them Robert Fitzwalter, lord of Dunmow in Essex. Back in 1212 he and Vescy had fled into exile after being denounced, it is said by John's daughter Joan, wife of Prince Llywelyn ap Iorwerth, for conspiring 'to drive the king and his family from the kingdom and choose someone else as king in his place'. Now back in England, they headed a far more formidable combination.

11

TIMETABLE OF A CRISIS

As the month of July 1214 drew to its close, a visitor to Paris would have found the city *en fête*; when news of the French king's victory at Bouvines reached the capital the student quarter broke into a seven-day spree of singing and dancing. The threat to France from the armies of the empire to the north and John of England in the south-west was over.

The French triumph not only shattered John's ambitions to recover his lost lands in France, but his credibility at home. Deserted by his Poitevin barons, John had failed to rally reinforcements from England. Philip August of France, the hero of the hour, made no move against the English army at La Rochelle, correctly calculating that there was nothing to fear from that quarter, at least for the time being. A papal emissary mediated a six-year truce between France and England and on 15 October the royal galley put into harbour at Dartmouth.

John faced a rebellious baronage with his prestige critically weakened. Back in May the group of northern barons had refused even to pay scutage money for the expedition to Poitou, on the highly questionable pretext that their terms of service did not include campaigning outside the kingdom. Now they brazened out royal recriminations while opposition hardened elsewhere in the country. The 1219 exchequer roll for Yorkshire still notes the scutage as outstanding, even though the king was three years dead.

Shortly after the king's return, it appears that magnates from East Anglia and the eastern midlands assembled at Bury St Edmunds to pledge mutual support. According to Roger of Wendover, writing in his chronicle at St Albans more than a decade after the event, the entire baronage of England had assembled to 'confer secretly' about a charter granted more than a century before by King Henry I. The numbers must be exaggerated. Even at the height of the civil war that broke out the following year, the opposition party only slightly outnumbered the loyalist barons. But late in 1214 malcontents were beginning to mobilize; the Bury meeting may have provided a lead for insurgency under the veneer of an ancient royal charter. Henry had seized the throne on the death of his brother William Rufus under suspicious circumstances and despite the claims of his eldest brother, Robert Duke of Normandy. His Coronation Charter had been designed to win friends and influence barons.

Henry's charter had nothing to say on the matter of scutage but it covered a number of other very topical issues – the rate of reliefs, rights of wardship and marriage and debts to the crown. Moreover, it promised to abolish abuses introduced in the reign of Henry's brother, William Rufus, and to restore the laws of King Edward the Confessor. We do not know who suggested its relevance to the current situation. Archbishop

Langton is still the most likely candidate (see above page 60) though a partisan of the northern barons gave them the credit. It was an inspired bit of antiquarianism, whoever was responsible. Such an appeal to past customs chimed perfectly with the mood of John's critics, who dreamed of a return to the good old days before the advent of the Angevin brood in England, and an end to the entire system of government introduced by Henry II and developed by John and his brother Richard. A royal charter, no matter how ancient, indeed the more ancient the better, which coupled repudiation of an Angevin with an appeal to the age of old England's saint-king offered the ideal format to legitimate a protest which was bordering on rebellion.

Thus, at the Christmas court John was confronted by dissidents demanding confirmation of the laws of King Edward and of the charter of Henry I. His first reaction was to promise an enquiry into any abuses that might have developed over the past twenty-five years. Today, a royal commission with carefully restricted terms of reference is the routine response to calls for reforms to which the government is opposed, but John's barons were less easily sidetracked than modern parliamentarians. The opposition claim that the abuses were far more deep-rooted, and their production of a charter to prove it, forced the king and his advisers to rethink their strategy. They proposed a postponement of full negotiations to a London conference set for 6 January.

The baronial dissidents had achieved the basic preconditions for successful opposition – a common purpose, a common loyalty almost certainly based on oaths of solidarity, and a common programme. From now on general discontent and vague if vehement protest gave place to a campaign for a charter of liberties. Discussion within and between the rival groups of court and barons must have kept many a clerk busy noting memoranda of the points agreed or debated. Two documents survive as evidence to this activity, though it is hard to date them precisely.

The first, called the 'Unknown Charter' (because it was not published until the 1860s), may represent the first form of the settlement from which Magna Carta itself was derived. It consists of a version of Henry I's charter with a number of concessions said to be granted by John. Most of them were featured in Magna Carta. The second document, described in detail below, is known as the Articles of the Barons.

The 6 January meeting ended in deadlock. The king might be obliged to enter into formal negotiations with his opponents, but he had no intention as yet of meeting their demands. Having dismissed their representatives with letters of safe conduct for a further meeting on 26 April at which, he promised, their demands would be answered, he briefed envoys to Rome to lobby for legal support at the papal curia. On 13 January another delegation was dispatched with a copy of the charter which John had granted to the Church in England the previous November. The barons too dispatched agents to the curia. In the coming months negotiations would be divided between the English and papal courts. Given that the round trip could take anything up to two months, there were obvious problems of communication – there might also be advantages if papal threats drafted to meet conditions that were in fact out of date could be brandished to cow opponents.

Meanwhile, the aim of both parties was to curry favour with influential members of the curia and to establish their legal credentials. The baronial opposition based their claims on the legally imprecise 'customs of the realm'. Reforms would come only with the agreement of the king, and since the reforms meant curbs on royal powers this would never be given voluntarily. Only by force or by threat of force could they get John to the bargaining table. But an oath given under duress would be worthless and could be repudiated at any time on appeal to the Pope. So long as the king lived, the lives and property of his opponents were in pawn.

In an apparently conciliatory gesture on 19 February, John issued letters of safe conduct to a group of northerners for a meeting with Archbishop Langton and William Marshal at Oxford three days later. The barons did not turn up, either because the notice was unreasonably short or because they distrusted the impartiality of the king's proposed mediators. John kept the initiative with a further offer to redress the more 'burdensome grievances' arising from excesses committed during his reign or that of his brother Richard. But his master-step in the diplomatic minuet came on 4 March when he took the vow of a crusader.

Ever since the débâcle of the Fourth Crusade in 1204, when the army of the cross had sacked the Christian city of Constantinople and left the infidel unscathed, Pope Innocent had had the project of a new crusade very close to his heart. John's pious and public gesture was noted approvingly. It also yielded the 'crusaders' respite', valuable legal immunities until the warrior of God should return from the Holy War. The glow of virtue which now surrounded John can hardly have concealed the grin of the cat who had got the cream. Two years before he had pledged his kingdom to the Holy See, now he was pledged to the Holy War; yet here was this most Christian of kings being harassed by subjects who had already refused dues legally demanded of them. The study of Roman and Church law, revived in Italy fifty years before and now being taught at the studium generale (i.e. the forerunner of the university) of Oxford, was fashionable in intellectual and government circles and legally there was no question who was in the right. John could afford to wait.

He was now so confident that he felt able to economize on his military precautions. Letters dated 13 March order a detachment of mercenaries recruited in Poitou to disperse to their homes 'as the business for which they had been required had been settled'. Although he could not know it, events in Rome were developing still further to the king's advantage. On 19 March the Pope drew up a group of letters which he regarded as a threefold form of peace but which, to the baronial agents who were present, must have seemed tantamount to an ultimatum answerable only by war.

The letters, known to historians as the '*triplex forma pacis*' (the threefold form of peace), were addressed to the king, who was asked to hear all just petitions of the barons and to treat them kindly, and to the barons. After condemning all leagues and conspiracies, Innocent ordered them to renounce armed resistance under pain of excommunication and to petition the king with all the reverence due to his honour. Quite simply, they were ordered to approach the king as supplicants, which when the king in question was John of England was as good as to demand that they abandon their petition.

The Pope was simply spelling out the law, and as John was his liege vassal this was perhaps to be expected. But since the king would never voluntarily abandon one jot of the authority enjoyed by the Crown of England it meant that the barons could not act within the law at all. The letters carried a bombshell. It would not reach England for another five or six weeks. When it arrived the explosion would be almost instantaneous.

On 1 April Innocent carried the logic of his case a step further and issued orders that the barons should pay the long-disputed Poitevin scutage, 'lest they hinder the king's good design'. This can only refer to John's crusading vow and reveals the king at his Machiavellian best as a political wheeler-dealer. Perhaps the Pope knew merely that John was contemplating crusader vows – the delegation that left England on 8 January may have been briefed to this effect. But news of the king's intended vows could have reached Rome by 29 or 30 March, even if the decision to make them had been taken only a day or two before the public declaration on 4 March. We know that in the early fourteenth century royal couriers, travelling in summer weather to England from the south of France, could cover the ground at the rate of 90 miles (145 kilometres) a day. Making allowances for the traverse of the Alps and rougher weather earlier in the year, I calculate that John's messengers, riding post haste, could have made the journey by the end of March 1215. As to the Poitevin scutage, the Pope's argument was legally impeccable. The barons' refusal had been arbitrary and unreasonable. How could they ask the king to restore what they considered their rights when they had deprived him of what were undoubtedly his rights? The scutage controversy was two years old, the argument between the king and barons older still. If the Pope believed that negotiations were impossible until the barons capitulated he might have law on his side, but such legality made war and reform inseparable.

Relationships between the two sides were already worsening before the papal letters reached England. As Easter week approached, with their meeting scheduled for 26 April, there was increasing activity in the eastern and northern counties as great men rallied their retainers and fortified their castles. The meeting of king and barons was fixed for Northampton. In fact barons were beginning to muster under arms at Stamford. For the most part, the northerners were in league with malcontents from East Anglia and the east of England and were young men. They no doubt chose Stamford as a convenient venue since it was well known, being one of the four tournament venues stipulated by Richard I. There they were joined by the contingents from East Anglia, Robert Fitzwilliam, lord of Dunmow, and Geoffrey de Mandeville.

On the appointed day the little township below the castle of Northampton was thronging with armed men but the king and the royalists were away to the south, moving between the capital, the castle of Wallingford and the great abbey at Reading. The opposition barons adjourned from Northampton to nearby Brackley where one of their leaders, Saer de Quenci, Earl of Winchester, was lord of the manor. The king reached Wallingford on the last day of April and offered letters of safe conduct up to 28 May for any who wished to discuss matters with his mediators, Archbishop Langton and William Marshal. The exact chronology of events is confused but we know that on 3 May the rebel barons made their *diffidatio* (i.e. formally renounced their allegiance to the king) at Brackley and that at about this time the king was presented with a schedule of their demands, probably while he was at Wallingford. On 9 May John proposed a court of arbitration appointed under the Pope's aegis; meantime he offered to grant trial '*per legem regni nostri vel per judicium parium suorum in curia nostra*', 'by the law of our realm or (*vel*) by the judgment of his peers in our court'. The barons refused the offer.

If he had hoped thereby to divide the opposition, the ruse failed. The schedule of chapters, or capitula, presented, it is presumed, at Wallingford may have been the document now dubbed the 'Unknown Charter'. Be that as it may, the king fell into a fury as it was read out to him. This display of the famous Angevin wrath may have been provoked not so much by the concessions demanded as by the remarkable request that John guarantee his agreement by having his seal attached to the document. It was an unprecedented demand from subjects to a monarch. This was neither a true charter, a grant conceded by the Crown, nor even a record of agreements already reached in negotiations; it was, in effect, merely a baronial 'shopping list'. No doubt the assembly at Brackley stipulated the royal seal to forestall the possibility of the king disclaiming the agreement.

It seems the Pope's letters exploded on the scene shortly after the Wallingford confrontation. His instruction to the barons to petition the king with due reverence to his honour made their demand for the royal seal seem the more out-rageous. To them it was obvious that to observe the papal conditions would rule out meaningful negotiation. On 3 May, at Brackley, they made their feudal renunciation of the king in a formal act of *diffidatio*.

On 6 May John proposed a court of arbitration appointed under the Pope's aegis. The same day he proposed as a compromise to reform any evil customs of his own and his brother's reign. The gesture was too late, and in any case entirely unconvincing. It merely repeated, after all, the very formula rejected by the barons at Christmas. John's closest advisers knew with certainty that he was acting in bad faith, since just two days later he required Langton to ask the Pope to excommunicate his enemies and when the archbishop refused wrote to the Pope himself to reinforce his request.

The country was now technically in a state of civil war, though the king's opponents represented only a minority of the baronage, his active supporters were hardly more numerous, and the remainder of England's magnates held themselves aloof. Continuing his diplomatic manoeuvres, John now is-sued a charter, dated 9 May, which proposed that the 'issues and articles' in dispute be submitted to eight barons, four chosen by himself, four by his opponents, sitting under the Pope as arbiter. He can hardly have been serious. Quite apart from the fact that to convene such an arbitration court at Rome would have taken months, who could suppose the opposition would accept as arbiter a potentate who apparently expected them to negotiate on their knees?

The following day (10 May) royal letters patent affirmed that the king 'would not arrest or disseise his opponents or their men except by the law of the land and by the judgment of their peers in his court'. Judgment by peers was a familiar concept to feudal law. It featured in the Ancient Customs of Normandy, recorded in written form shortly after John became duke, had been the subject of a German edict as long ago as 1037, and in England was guaranteed by the laws of Henry I. No doubt John regarded this promise to return to feudal propriety as the final flourish in his diplomatic offensive.

So far as he was concerned, the 10 May letters patent marked the end of the phoney war. Nottingham and its castle, the strategic key to the midlands, had been systematically reinforced and provisioned since October and for the past several weeks John had been securing strong points throughout the kingdom. New orders had been sent out to Poitevin mercenaries; key northern garrisons such as Scarborough, Doncaster and Skipton had been increased; and huge financial inducements offered to secure the loyalty of doubtful castellans like Robert de Ros at Carlisle and John de Lacy at Chester. On 12 May writs were dispatched to the sheriffs to seize the lands and chattels of the king's enemies and two days later John was assigning rebel territories among his supporters.

Hostilities broke out across the country. Rebel forces laid ineffectual siege to Northampton but seized Bedford. In Wales, Llywelyn ap Iorwerth, opposed by royalist lords such as Walter de Lacy and William Marshal, seized the opportunity for an alliance with Giles de Briouze, Bishop of Hereford. He had been 'given' the see by John to cement connections with his father William, but now burning to avenge the death of his mother and siblings he supported the Welsh to sack Shrewsbury on 15–16 May. Always looking to buy time, John headquartered at Windsor, ordered agents in various parts of the country to accept truce terms if offered. The following day time ran out.

After their success at Bedford, the baronial army heading south for London had been met at Ware in Hertfordshire by a deputation offering to arrange the capital's surrender. On Sunday the 17th, when the bulk of the citizenry were at church, the rebel forces marched through the city's gates virtually unopposed. According to Roger of Wendover, messengers were dispatched throughout England 'to those earls and barons and knights, who appeared to be still faithful to the King (though they only pretended to be so)', urging them with threats to their property and possessions to abandon the king and to form a united front with the rebel barons 'in a fight for liberties and peace'. With London in their hands (and the mayor replaced with their nominee), the opposition barons hoped to force the king to the conference table and to rally support among the undecided. One detects perhaps a note of desperation in the appeal; there were some defections but clearly the barons were not united in their opposition. However the seizure of London gave new vigour to the rebels' cause.

In the words of J. C. Holt in *Magna Carta*, 'if Bouvines brought on a political crisis . . . the baronial seizure of London led directly to Runnymede'. So it seems in the perspective of history. To contemporaries the inevitability of events was less obvious. Many maintained full loyalty to the king, others sent their sons to London so as to have a foot in both camps, while many, particularly those in remoter parts of the kingdom, continued to watch developments from the safe neutrality of their estates. Of England's 197 baronies, it has been estimated that 39 were active for the barons and 39 for the king. On these figures well over half the chief landowners held aloof from the struggle.

Nevertheless the opposition, led by Fitzwalter, who took the grandiose title of 'Marshal of the Army of God', was formidable. A week after the loss of London the king issued letters of safe conduct to Saer de Quenci, Earl of Winchester, to come to his court to discuss terms on the barons' behalf, and two days later to Archbishop Langton and others to attend him at Staines 'to treat concerning peace'. Four royal agents were informed by letter that a truce had been arranged.

On 28 May John received delivery of royal regalia from the custody of the master of the Temple. Generally impatient of ceremonial, the king knew the trappings of monarchy had their uses. At Odiham the following day, in the presence of Saer de Quenci, he gave an audience to a messenger recently arrived from Rome at which he repeated his willingness to submit the dispute to the Pope. Giving a selective account of the past three months, John's statement to the papal emissary portrayed John as a paragon of reasonableness and concluded: 'So, whereas they have refused to humble themselves to us as they should, we have, for the service of God and the relief of the Holy Land, humbled ourselves . . . before them . . . and even offered them full justice by the judgment of their peers.'

John now moved to Windsor, from where he could be kept informed of the discussions and drafting sessions between his and the barons' advisers at Staines. On 5 June he made a rapid progress through friendly territory to Winchester. Returning via Merton, where he issued further safe conducts, he was back in Windsor by the 9th. Days of 'shuttle diplomacy' were beginning to yield tangible results. Whereas on 25 May Saer de Quenci and Langton had been invited to 'treat concerning peace', the Merton safe conducts are for a baronial deputation which is to 'make and secure' peace. Furthermore, the safe conducts are for a limited period – from 9 June to midnight on the 11th. Events were evidently moving to a climax.

On the evening of 9 June Hugh, the newly elected Abbot of Bury St Edmunds, arrived at Windsor to petition royal approval for his election. There he found Archbishop Langton in conference with the king. Even in these stirring times the lordship of East Anglia's richest religious foundation claimed due deliberation and Hugh was told to present himself the following morning in 'the meadow of Staines', known as Runnymede. Clearly a meeting of high importance had been set for the morning of 10 June.

Conveniently situated between London and Windsor, Runnymede was a recognized point of assembly. In June 1215 it met a third requirement, being south of the river from the barons' base at Staines. Lying between marshy ground to the east and south and a stream flowing into the Thames from the west, it was virtually an island with only two easy lines of access, one from the Windsor direction, the other from the Staines direction. We can imagine the two wary and well-armed deputations moving cautiously towards one another in a meadow of pavilions and fluttering pennants. The exact sequence and nature of the events which unfolded is more difficult to determine. Most scholars now assume a timetable of meetings culminating in a ceremonial oath-pledging on Saturday the 19th.

The sequence opens on the morning of 10 June. Among the observers was Abbot Hugh, awaiting his audience with the king. John's first business that morning appears to have been to dictate letters to his military agents in the southern and midland counties informing them that the truce had been extended to the 15th. He and his advisers now turned to the main proceedings of the day.

For the first time since Easter the king was face to face with his opponents, represented by leaders of the baronial force at Staines (a contingent remained in London as a garrison force). Negotiations over the previous two weeks, in which Archbishop Langton had been closely involved, had reached a stage where the points under discussion needed to be consolidated and confirmed. As at Wallingford the month before, the barons were determined to get something in writing, as a hostage of the king's good faith. The Articles of the Barons was, we may assume, the outcome. Drawn up in a royal clerk's hand under the heading 'These are the clauses which the barons seek and the lord concedes', it lists in non-technical language a number of points mostly confirmed by Magna Carta, and it carried the royal seal. It was neither a true charter nor a royal letter patent, it had no legal force, it conveyed and granted nothing, and yet the dramatic break with protocol refused so angrily just weeks before had now been conceded. We can assume that the seal was to reassure the baronial garrison in London, and that their presence in the capital was the sole reason why the king had agreed to append it to such a document.

Everything indicates that the 10th was scheduled as a make-or-break day. Either the basis of a settlement would be agreed or hostilities would resume in full force. The day's business would not have been possible had the principal points for debate not already been decided in previous discussions. The baronial envoys left the meadow at Staines with proof that the king was at last in earnest. When they had gone John could give his attention to the Abbot of Bury St Edmunds. Letters in chancery dated the 11th confirmed him in the enjoyment of the revenues of the abbey.

But if the king was in earnest, neither he nor his opponents were fully committed. The negotiating teams were agreed on the terms of settlement and a truce was set to run to the early morning of the 15th. But over the next four days the baronial delegates would confer with their colleagues at Staines and in London. The outcome of these deliberations would decide whether the 10 June document would become the basis of a full charter in the form of a legal grant. The date 15 June is that actually on the Great Charter. On this day, presumably, the long, tortuous and nervous negotiating process reached a conclusion with confirmation by all interested parties of the terms agreed. Four more days of work by the technical advisers and lawyers prepared the ground for the solemn and ceremonial exchange of oaths, apparently held on 19 June, which would give legal force to the clauses agreed between king and barons.

Elaborate and unprecedented conditions were laid down in an attempt to ensure they were honoured. The barons were to choose twenty-five of their number 'who with all their might are to observe, maintain and cause to be observed the peace and liberties which we have granted and confirmed to them by this our present charter'. To ensure compliance, they were authorized to distrain royal property to make good any breach of the charter by the king or his officers. In the last resort, of course, the sanction relied on force, and it has been called a right to legalized rebellion. But the feudal system already provided for this in the *diffidatio* by which the barons barely a month before had defied the king. The Charter's *'forma securitatis'* ('security clause', Clause 61), adopted the legal sanctions applied by the courts against common defaulters; it was extraordinary in so far as it proposed to levy them against the king, but it was not technically a threat of duress of the kind which would invalidate his oath. The real sanction was a naked piece of such duress, carefully insulated from the grant of liberties in the shape of a treaty, also agreed on the 19th, which laid down that the baronial garrison should remain in control of London until 15 August, Archbishop Langton having custody of the Tower. During the intervening weeks the oaths to the Twenty-five were to be administered throughout the kingdom, and the king was to meet all the claims against him and restore rights and properties. Should he fail to comply, London would still be held against him. This was duress indeed.

'At length they met at Runnymede', wrote the writer of the Dunstable annals, 'and on 19 June peace was made between the king and the barons. And the king received homage, which the barons had withdrawn at the beginning of the civil war.' Only with the renewal of homage was the state of war at an end, only now could the contracting parties pledge their oaths to the confirmation of the terms. Neither the writing of the charter not even the affixing of the king's seal by the royal official operating the seal clamp or 'spigurnel' carried the charisma of authority conferred by the oath-taking. The impression the great ceremony made on contemporaries echoes from the pages of the chronicler Ralph of Coggeshall: 'Peace of a kind ['*quasi*'] was made between the king and the barons and all, even the king, swore on holy relics to observe it inviolate.' After a period of intensive negotiation and what Holt called 'hard committee work' the agreement was ready to be ratified and made secure by the renewal of the barons' homage. On 19 June this ceremony of peace was duly carried out, by a serious and formal act made by each erstwhile rebel individually, in an atmosphere of due solemnity.

According to the Dunstable chronicler, John 'then restored to many of them their castles and other rights, and charters were completed concerning the liberties of the realm of England'. Each of these copy charters, Coggeshall tells us, had the royal seal attached. Four of them survive, but it is unlikely that there ever was one 'original' charter to which the king himself witnessed the affixing of his seal. It was the oath-taking that secured the 'liberties of England'; only later did they become identified with the physical documents.

In June 1215 the important documents were the writs, many dated 19 June, that were drawn up for the enforcement of the various clauses of the agreement. The most important were the letters patent providing for the administration of the oaths to the Committee of Twenty-five. Others dealt with such matters as the release of prisoners and hostages, the surrender of castles and such matters, and the arrangements for the shipping of John's mercenaries, whose contracts were to be terminated by the terms of the Charter, from Dover to France. We know that the Flemish soldiery despised the document as a '*vilain pais*' (i.e. 'a wicked peace') and a shameful surrender and it seems reasonable to suppose that others such as the Poitevins felt the same.

It was with good reason that Ralph of Coggeshall described the arrangement as a quasi-peace for it lasted only for a little time. The writs enforcing the Charter sparked local conflicts between those who claimed the restoration of lands and those in possession. The whole question of interpretation and of who should arbitrate on the king's fulfilment of his obligations and of when London should be returned to him opened new problems. The strongest card of the opposition barons was their hold on the capital, and they were unlikely to relinquish it voluntarily. The terms of the 'quasi-peace' contained the seeds of a new war and by September it was in full swing.

12

THE MAKING OF A CHARTER

> John, by the grace of God, King of England, Lord of Ireland, Duke of Normandy and Aquitaine, and count of Anjou, to the archbishops, bishops, abbots, earls, barons, justiciars, foresters, sheriffs, stewards, servants, and to all his bailiffs and liege subjects, greetings . . .

The formula that opens the most famous document in English history follows the one used in scores of others drawn up by John's chancery, naming first the grantor of the charter and then those to whom it was addressed, for Magna Carta was a bureaucratic document.

The text survives, fully legible, in three documents – a fourth, severely damaged by fire in the early eighteenth century, can no longer be deciphered, except for a few words. The best known is the one on public display in the British Library. It is part of the Cotton collection and was presented to the antiquarian and bibliophile Sir Robert Cotton in January 1629, having been found in the shop of a London tailor. This, one assumes, is the Charter sent to the city of London at the time of the distribution of June 1215. Sir Robert's house in Palace Yard, Westminster, with its extensive private library, was the meeting place for lawyers and parliamentarians such as Sir Edward Coke and John Pym when preparing their research and parliamentarian strategies in opposition to the government of King Charles I. The second most widely known is now in the keeping of Lincoln Castle, having for centuries been held in the cathedral there, and is presumably the one sent to the Bishop of Lincoln at that time. Thirdly, there is the one now in Salisbury Cathedral, presumed to be the one sent to the sheriff of Wiltshire. Finally there is the Charter found among the archives of Dover Castle in 1630 by Sir Edward Dering, then warden of the Cinque Ports, who sent it to Cotton: it is presumed to be the Charter known to have been dispatched to the Cinque Ports in June 1215. It is also in the British Library but because of the fire in the Cotton collection in 1731 is virtually indecipherable in many places. In addition to these 'Runnymede Four', reissues of the Charter were made in 1216, 1217 and 1225 and copies of these are at Durham Cathedral. The 1225 Charter was reissued many times throughout the thirteenth century and was appointed to be read in Latin and also French in England's county courts; many copies were made but we have only a fraction of the total. The reissue enrolled by command of King Edward I in 1297 and author-ized in its opening with the word '*inspeximus*', 'we have inspected', is one of the earliest statutes of the realm. The documents surviving from 1215 are almost square, but not of a uniform size, and not of course in the same hand. The Salisbury Charter, indeed, may not even have been issued by the royal chancery.

The texts on their parchment support were produced using an ink composed of oak-gall sap mixed with soot or lamp-black. Important in the process were the stings of a myriad wasps which punctured the bark of the tree preparatory to laying its eggs. To protect itself from the poison pin-pricks, the oak secretes a sap which forms protective nut-like scabs or galls. These yield a clear, somewhat acidic liquid which, combined with lampblack or, better, certain iron salts pro-duces an ink that bites into the parchment membrane and in effect etches itself into the writing support. Top-quality ink of this type dries to a rich dark, almost black, which over the years fades to a mid-brown or sepia colour. The ink on Magna Carta, very nearly eight centuries old, is still on the dark side of brown. The text, quite dense on the page, runs unbroken in a cursive and somewhat showy hand. The ink was applied with a pen, i.e. a quill selected from the flight feathers of a goose or swan cut into shape perhaps by an apprentice or more likely by the scrivener himself. Every ten lines or so he would have trimmed the nib with his penknife and recharged it with ink.

All this is, of course, distressingly old-fashioned, not to say 'medieval'. Not at all suited to the kind of cutting-edge policy initiatives we of early twenty-first century Britain are fortunate enough to enjoy. On the other hand few records issued by today's government departments will survive for a century – let alone eight. Some forty exemplars of the Charter itself were originated by John's chancery clerks acting under close baronial supervision. It has been calculated that completing a single copy would have taken the best part of a full working day.

We do not know for certain how the work was done nor how many scriveners were employed. The fact that the Latin is in the highly abbreviated form of the royal chancery would suggest that only chancery clerks could have been engaged on the work of transcription. Supposing that the text was delivered by dictation and that ten skilled scriveners were engaged on the work, then four days should have been sufficient time for the job. The authentication of each document was by the attachment of the great seal, which was produced from a mixture of wax and rosin in a screw press operated by the official of the seal and attached to the Charter with twisted cords or ribbons. Of the four documents to survive from 1215 only one retains its seal and that is the one damaged by the fire in the Cotton collection. Not only is the document virtually illegible, the seal is a shapeless lump. Most seals were single-sided; the royal seal of John, some 4 inches (102 mm) in diameter, had an image of the king in majesty on the obverse. The wax mixture was pressed into two metal matrices which were aligned using pins and rings, then the cords or ribbons were laid on the exposed wax of the lower matrix before the two were clamped together.

Needless to say King John did not 'sign' the Charter. He was certainly literate but probably could not write: it was a skill as necessary to a thirteenth-century monarch as familiarity with the typewriter keyboard would have been to Sam Goldwyn – where the mogul had a typing pool, John had his chancery clerks. Among them was also the sealer of the king's writs. It is possible that we know the name of the man in question. Eight years before Runnymede we find mention of a Godefridus Spigurnel in John's service: a somewhat garbled tradition, seen in materials in the archives, seems to suggest that for later generations his name may have become identified with the office.

It must be supposed that the king and his officials scrutinized the finished document. Following Professor Holt, we can suppose that this was then read out, with Anglo-Norman French translation, before king and barons at the ceremony of 19 June, whereupon the barons formally renewed their allegiance. To reiterate, it was the ceremony and the oath-taking that made the agreement and the commitment. The Charter and its copies merely recorded the facts and, through the sheriffs' readings, notified the counties of what had been agreed. The attachment of the royal seal, a serious business indeed, was also routine and was probably completed without either the king or barons present.

John, like his predecessors back to the time of King Henry I, had used a charter to buy something. But whereas the first Henry and Stephen had bought loyalty on trust, John had so conducted his affairs that after reigning for half a man's lifetime he had to purchase the loyalties of liegemen of sixteen years' standing.

Copies of liberty

Great care was taken to see to the Charter's publication to the country at large and to ensure that this was carried out thoroughly. From the first, the dissident barons and their sympathizers took a hand in the proceedings. The clerk who supervised the arrangements, Elias of Dereham, the household steward of Archbishop Langton, had presumably been present when the archbishop revealed the contents of Henry I's charter to the barons, at the meeting in St Paul's the year before Runnymede, reading it first in the original Latin then in French by way of clarification. On 19 June various writs attested in the name of the king at Runnymede were sent out to royal agents and officials in various parts of the country to let them know that peace had been restored between the king and his barons and his freemen.

Among these the most numerous single type was the pro forma directive to sheriffs, and all royal officials with responsibilities to the counties, such as the bailiffs, warreners, foresters and river wardens, as to how the document was to be publicized. In many cases they would have received these instructions before the arrival of their sealed official copy. The officials were directed to ensure that the Charter be read in all the bailiwicks of the county, that all freemen take the oath of loyalty to the Twenty-five, and that twelve knights be sworn in as an official committee of enquiry into all abuses of the king's officials within the county boundaries.

The copy of this pro forma on the Patent Roll (the official royal record of open charters) is followed by a dispatch list of the counties to which the Charter itself had been sent. Unexpectedly, only thirty-three of the then thirty-nine counties of England are listed, yet Ralph Coggeshall, a usually reliable contemporary, states positively that every county received its copy. Moreover the omissions include the great county palatinates of Durham and Chester.

Either we assume that one of the clerks in John's notoriously efficient administration made a colossal yet spasmodic oversight amounting in statistical terms to an error of some 15 per cent; or that large and important areas of the country were left uninformed of the great righting of the wrongs of the community of England; or that the preparation of the official copies was not completed before it became apparent that the clerks had been overtaken by events, and that virtual certainty of civil war made copies for the remaining counties redundant.

There is yet another possibility: that the list is accurate and that all the counties nevertheless received their copy. If the list on the Patent Roll is precisely what it is said to be, a *dispatch* list, then it could be that the copies of the 'missing' counties were taken to their destinations not like the others by official royal messengers but by some personality or official from the region, who happened to be at Runnymede and gave some token of receipt (now lost) to the recording clerk. This too unfortunately presents us with a problem: we know that the writ of instructions for Worcestershire was given to the Bishop of Worcester on 19 June, but then, five days later on the 24th he is listed as receiving *j. cartam* (a charter). Since every attempt to solve this problem involves absurd assumptions, let us now assume that the Bishop of Worcester was a pedant who insisted that the recording clerk put his county down on the 'dispatch' list even though he himself was acting as royal courier.

If all thirty-nine counties did indeed receive their own copy and we add to this number the one held for the royal archive and the one sent to the Cinque Ports, we arrive at the probable total of forty-one copies. Since four are known to be still in existence, this gives a 10 per cent survival rate over a period of 775 years. Taking into account that besides the Charter itself we also have a near-contemporary copy in French translation, the enigmatic 'Unknown Charter', and also the Articles of the Barons, of which probably only one copy was ever made, and that all this material survives from a period when public administration, for all its comparative sophistication, was still in its infancy, historians really should think themselves extremely lucky.

If the four surviving examples of the Runnymede charter are typical, the copies were each on a single parchment sheet measuring 15 by 20 inches (38 x 50 cm). They were written in a clear script, without a break from start to finish; the punctuation, division into paragraphs and numbering of the clauses in modern versions having been introduced by modern commentators.

The first batch of seven copies was sent out on 24 June, that is, five days after the final agreement at Runnymede. Of these four, by royal command, were entrusted to Elias of Dereham, two to Bishop Hugh of Lincoln (he and Elias had long been friends) and one, we have seen, to the Bishop of Worcester. Twelve copies (out of a total of twenty-one) of the royal letters patent announcing the peace between the king and his barons were also assigned to Elias. In the time it took the expert scriveners of the king's chancery to produce – and release, after the payment of due fees and bribes – twenty-one fairly short and standard documents, they were able to prepare one-third that number of charters of a new and comparatively lengthy type. The final dispatch given on the list (six charters) occurred on 22 July, more than a month after the agreement at Runnymede. These copies were also entrusted to Elias, at Oxford. By this time the king and his opponents were already drifting towards civil war; nevertheless Elias continued with the distribution; he, more than anyone else, was responsible for the Charter's circulation. A brilliant administrator, it seems he was also a man of principle.

First heard of in 1188 as a witness to a charter of West Dereham Abbey in Norfolk – the year in which Hubert Walter, also a Dereham man, became Bishop of Salisbury – Elias concluded his career from the 1220s as a canon at Salisbury, where a new cathedral was going up to replace that at Old Sarum. It was to be the last absolutely new cathedral church built in England before Christopher Wren's St Paul's, started in 1675, and it seems that Elias was the architect-designer. He had been a high flyer in the Church civil service. On Hubert Walter's staff by 1197 he served the now justiciar and Archbishop of Canterbury as steward of the properties and assets of the archdiocese. He was named as executor of Walter's will (1205) and soon afterwards was appointed steward of the archdiocese by the new archbishop Stephen Langton, though during the interdict years he necessarily lived in exile in France. Twice he visited England as an envoy to the Church there. This was the man who, after thirty years close to the heart of affairs of state, supervised the preparation and drafting and then distribution

of the great Charter. In fact he was to remain loyal to the
dissidents and even sided with Louis of France during his
brief bid for the English throne, as did Simon Langton, the
archbishop's brother, who became the French pretender's
chancellor. Not only did Elias defy the papal excommunication of the rebels, in the autumn of 1217 when the French
Prince came to terms in the Treaty of Kingston Elias still held
out and was excluded from its terms. In September that year
he returned to voluntary exile in France. One recent commentator suggests that, loyal to the community of England,
he had persuaded himself that the Charter meant that John
had been deposed by the common will. His master Archbishop Stephen had also gone again into exile though he
returned in the spring of 1218 and a year later Elias also
returned. The final testimony to Dereham's great abilities and
integrity came when, following his death in May 1219,
William Marshal, that great servant of the monarchy, was
found to have named Elias his executor. From then on Elias's
career would lie in Salisbury, but for two critical years, 1215
and 1216, this remarkable man was at the heart of events
that for a time threatened revolution.

The style of a charter – and the royal titles

The first thing in the preamble to a royal charter was the title of
the king himself. The style 'King of England' had been standard since the time of Stephen. Henry I had styled himself
'King of the English', the form commonly used by the Anglo-
Saxon kings, in his coronation charter. Later in this clause
John follows more recent precedent when he employs the royal
'we'. His father, the great Henry II, had been willing to settle
for the businesslike and unpretentious first person singular. It
was Richard, possibly influenced by continental practice, who

modified the simple 'I' of ordinary men to the 'we' of kings. The innovation that John did make was the incorporation of 'Lord of Ireland' in the regal title.

As noted in a previous chapter, aged nineteen John had been sent to Ireland with a respectable military force, a sizeable treasure and expert advisers. He was back in a matter of months, having incensed the Irish chieftains by his ill-mannered ribaldry at their expense and offended the Norman lords by slighting their hopes of patronage. His one achievement, an unusual one then as now, was to unite the Irish.

John had mishandled the historic opportunity to assert an Angevin kingship of Ireland, though he did retain a measure of effective power there for the dynasty. He later lost Normandy and, to his even greater shame, was driven out of the ancestral county of the Angevins. Only the extensive but restless lands of Aquitaine remained of the French possessions.

The sense of proprieties

Such was the king who granted the Charter. The beneficiaries – 'the English church' and 'all the freemen of our kingdom' – appear several lines down, after the Charter has enumerated those to whom it is addressed and those to whom the grantor is indebted for their advice in the great matter of state with which it is concerned. These comprise a select body of churchmen, a number of officials and a few noblemen of the royal party with John at Runnymede. Unless the proprieties are properly observed, no public act can be properly conducted.

Magna Carta may not be a good read for the general reader, full, as it is, of arcane terms of feudal law, and it has little to do with political theory as the words are understood today, but since it has for generations of English people seemed the nearest they have ever had to a written constitution, it is surely tempting to compare it with the most famous written constitution in the English language – the Constitution of the United States as ratified by nine states in June 1788.

Of course we cannot know whether anyone will be writing a book about that document 800 years on, in the year 2588: but we can know that such a book will have nothing to say about the Constitution's comments on fish weirs on the Hudson river; the rights of widows in the America of the 1770s; the condition of Jews; or the standing of the mayor of New York at that time. The American document has nothing to say about such details, from its sonorous opening passage proclaiming the purpose of securing the blessings of liberty for the people and their posterity to its end.

The weakness of Magna Carta is that apart from the pious generalities of what we now know as the preamble and the first clause, 'having regard to God and for the salvation of our souls, and the advancement of holy church and for the reform of our realm' etc., it would not, in the immortal words of P. G. Wodehouse, recognize a high-sounding statement of principle or a clearly defined political theory if presented with them laid out 'on a plate surrounded with watercress'.

In the rhetoric and in-fighting that preceded Runnymede, there had been much talk about the laws of King Edward and the charter of Henry I. But when it came to the form of words that would establish their liberties beyond doubt, the barons fell back on the technicalities of the law – whether real or imagined. That, for a thirteenth-century Anglo-Norman baron, was the language of liberties. The modern meaning of the word 'liberty' still had to be conceived, let alone defined. In the meantime, Runnymede laid down a few useful, if primitive, benchmarks for future reference.

At a time when the debate over human rights is centre stage in the political arena and the question appears to be, how best are they to be maintained, it is useful to look back at the struggle of the barons of Magna Carta. Their one strength was self-interest, intelligently if obsessively pursued in the context of the law as it was applied in their own day and in their own affairs. This led them to a respect for the law as it applied to the interests of others. Clause 60 spelt it out in the name of the king: 'All these customs and liberties', it runs, 'which we have granted . . . towards our men, shall be observed by . . . them as far as pertains to them towards their men.' Runnymede undoubtedly has its lessons for us today. Among them are matters so mundane as good government and decent administrative practice. The technicalities of the Charter, fossilized to us, are the rock-hard foundation stones on which it was built.

The beauties of routine

Among the reams of documents from the reign of King John which can still be consulted in the archives of England's public records is a simple formula of agreement or concord between two litigants in a property dispute dated 15 July 1195. It is one of hundreds of such apparently nondescript pieces of bureaucratic parchment, but it has a special interest. On the back it carries a note to the effect that it is the first example of a new system of records instituted by the justiciar Hubert Walter. For a generation and more it had been standard practice in land disputes that the final settlement should be recorded in standard form and in two copies, one for each party to the dispute. In July 1195, it appears, the justiciar ordered that thenceforward a third copy be retained for government records.

By the year 1200 government, both local and central, made regular use of a variety of instruments and documents. It was, if one may use the term, the dawning of the age of bureaucracy, and like anything new it was popular. This may seem a little odd today, when jargon, forms and paperwork are comprehensively deplored. But to a generation that was only just beginning to accept literacy as an accomplishment among educated lay people the developing use of documents signalled a growing sophistication of government.

One of the most popular innovations of Angevin government was the introduction of various types of 'writ', available to anyone who could afford the fee. The writ as such was as old as the early Anglo-Saxon monarchies which had established a system of more or less standard directives, bearing the seal of the king and binding on all who received them. But the writ was expensive and generally confined to the monarch. Henry II introduced a range of standard formula writs drawn up in the royal chancery or exchequer and available to anybody who could afford to pay the fee.

The classic example, and probably the most popular of all these new-style writs, was the writ *praecipe*. This was an instruction to the sheriff that he order the defendant in a case to restore property to the plaintiff – the man drawing the writ – or else appear before a royal justice to give his reasons for not doing so. At the time there were many types of case that were tried in the private courts of feudal lords. The right to hold a court was much valued because the fees and fines made the administration of justice very profitable. Litigants generally preferred royal justice because, at least in theory, it promised a fairer trial if the case were heard in the Lord King's court rather than that of the big man of the local neighbourhood. The writ *praecipe* had the effect of taking a case out of such private jurisdiction, causing the lord 'to lose his court' as the jargon had it. By Clause 34 of the Charter, however, the government of King John agreed that in future the

writ would not be issued to anyone 'regarding any tenement whereby a freeman may lose his court'.

A view as to the origins of the Great Charter itself much
favoured by the Victorians argued that they were to found in the
practices of the Anglo-Saxon kings. One scholar traced it to
the Anglo-Norman writ charter, which he described as
merely the Anglo-Saxon writ translated into Latin. We can
also trace something of the content found in the Charter to pre-
Conquest practice. By the mid-tenth century it had become
standard practice for the archbishop officiating at the coronation to exact from the king an oath of good government. The
oath comprised in essence three promises – to protect the
Church; to ensure the peace and repress violence among men
of all ranks; and to combine justice and mercy in all judgments.

A history of royal obligations

The oath is first known to have been exacted from King Edgar
at his coronation in Bath in the year 975. The first record of the
words used are of the oath administered to the young King
Aethelred II by St Dunstan in 978. William the Bastard of
Normandy, who seized the crown by conquest in 1066,
followed the practice of his English predecessors and thus
gave sanction to a historic practice which would continue to be
appealed to by successive generations.

William Rufus continued the practice and even, we are told,
issued a brief charter of confirmation to reassure his under-
standably sceptical subjects. His brother Henry took the oath
in due form and he too issued a charter (the Coronation
Charter) on the day of his coronation. In surprisingly specific
terms it promised not merely to 'make free the church of God'
and to abolish 'evil customs', but also to permit heirs to
succeed to their fathers' lands by a 'just and lawful relief'

and covered a number of other technical points of feudal custom. Having seized the kingdom following the suspicious death of his elder brother William and from under the nose of his eldest brother Robert, King Henry I needed all the support he could get from the English, of whom the charter proclaims him king. The charter ends with a promise to restore the laws of King Edward, together, be it noted, 'with such emendations as my father made with the counsel of his barons'. A surviving copy is addressed to 'Samson the bishop . . . and all [the king's] barons and faithful vassals, both French and English, in Worcestershire'. A chronicler reports that 'as many charters were made as there are counties in England, and by the king's command they were deposited in the abbeys of every county as a memorial'. King Henry II also granted a charter at the time of his accession. King Stephen, his predecessor, had granted two. The entire sequence of twelfth-century coronation charters provides an informative set of precedents for the historian.

King Stephen's first was a general charter of liberties; it was combined with a solemn oath securing generous liberties to the Church. The two combined were granted as the price of support for his seizure of the crown and his consecration by the Church. It was a good bargain. For the rest of his reign, no matter how parlous the state of his cause might become, no one could seriously contest his claim to the title of king; he, after all, really was the Lord's anointed, whereas his rival Matilda never received that recognition.

We next find Stephen conceding a charter some four months later, at Oxford. Again something had to be bought, this time the collaboration of Matilda's leading supporter, Geoffrey, Earl of Gloucester. The rights were still more handsomely confirmed. The charter not only made a general reaffirmation, but also made numerous specific concessions, notably that the Crown would not claim rights of wardship of abbey lands during vacancies in the headship of the houses. In fact the chief provisions were of interest to the Church; a general clause promised to observe good ancient customs and to do justice. There was one specially valuable concession to the baronial interest – the renunciation of all land afforested since the death of William II. Otherwise the chief concession was the understanding that the barons' loyalty would be conditional on the king's good future treatment of them; and there was a group of charters to individual barons, granting specific rights.

With King Henry II's coronation charter we come to the first in the sequence not granted to buy the support of any specific individual or interest lobby. It was brief and vague. His succession had been secured by arrangements made with his predecessor. The country, if not so ruined by anarchy as once thought, was nevertheless glad of a smooth handover of power after the death of Stephen in December 1154. It might seem, then, as though the eighteen-year-old Henry issued the charter merely as a gesture to tradition.

But there was more to it than that. A few years into the reign one of Henry's admiring officers of state described his policy as 'renewing the golden days of his grandfather' (Henry I), while a chronicler spoke of 'the restoration of ancestral times'. From the outset of his reign Henry made it clear that all grants made by the 'usurper', as he termed his predecessor, were considered invalid. In practice of course many had to be allowed to stand if the kingdom were not to be reduced to a worse state of anarchy than that which he had replaced. But the principle, clearly established, gave the new king almost complete latitude as to what he would and what would not confirm. The omission of all reference to the 'usurper' in the coronation charter was eloquent. It was reinforced by what the charter actually did say.

To the Church and the barons the new king conceded only what his grandfather had conceded. And here lay the second reason for his granting any charter. Stephen's concessions to the Church had been lavish to the point of excessiveness. By declaring the reign of his predecessor null and void as to precedent, Henry recovered the position of the monarchy vis-à-vis the Church at a stroke. It was also strong if blatant propaganda. Since he had been crowned, consecrated and anointed by the Church, Stephen could in no sense be termed a usurper. Indeed, since Henry had embarked on his English venture in the name of his mother and she was still alive at the time of his accession, he, if anyone, might be considered the usurper.

The little charter of Henry 'Curtmantle' had the dash and swing of his stylish short cape: it swept his predecessor from consideration and with the same gesture dismissed much of the mystique claimed by the Church. Small wonder that when Langton began talking charters to the barons, he drew their attention to the grant made by the *first* Henry. Why, it might be asked, did he not look at the coronation charters of John or Richard? The reason is simple; neither issued one. After almost a hundred years of struggle since the dubious accession of Henry I, the succession to the throne of England was so certain that the mere formality of the coronation oath was all the Church could do in its own favour before discharging its duty and consecrating the king.

Nothing could more graphically demonstrate how far the question of the kingship of England had travelled than a quick survey of the titles borne by successive monarchs. Henry I terms himself merely 'Henry, king of the English' and then explains, 'Know that by the mercy of God and by the common counsel of the barons of the whole kingdom of England I have been crowned king of this realm.' The wording tells it all. This is no assertion of divine grace upon the person of the monarch. It is, rather, a news report that a crowning has taken place with the agreement of the baronage. The fact that the 'mercy of God' received first mention tends to expose the conventional nature of the invocation. The whole tenor of the announcement seems to be 'Take note, I have been crowned', with a barely suppressed 'Thank God' thrown in.

When we come to the second charter of Stephen insecurity is the keynote, so anxious does it seem to justify the event. He declares himself king 'by appointment of the clergy and people, by the consecration of the archbishop and papal legate, and by the pope's confirmation'. This sounds like special pleading for the defence rather than an assertion of authority. In any case the last claim was unjustified; the Pope had not given his formal confirmation. However, the Church in England undoubtedly had, and this is what chiefly mattered to Stephen.

What a contrast with the giant self-assurance of Henry II, who called himself 'King by the grace of God'. So we find that when King John does, belatedly it must be said, come to grant his Charter it is as 'John, by the grace of God, King of England, Lord of Ireland . . .' that his clerks entitle him in the opening words.

One of the puzzles about the events of John's reign is why it took so long for the barons to raise the standard of revolt, if their wrongs were so great. Part of the answer lies in this high-sounding title. It was not that men were notably more religious than they are today, but they did tend to believe in God, and in such a thought-world it was difficult to shake off entirely the feeling that a duly consecrated king was someone special – perhaps as special as he claimed.

The history of the royal title, as we have briefly traced it, helps explain the awe in which even a monarch such as King John was held. The development of the Charter as an instrument of government accounts in some measure for why the opposition barons, whether at the prompting of the archbishop or not, adopted it as their tool to tame the king. The coronation charter was only a special case of this development.

The routine of rights

It has been argued that the Angevin system of government was not so much an innovation as the codification and fossilization of existing practice thanks to the universal adoption of the technology of writing in secular administration. By the nature of the thesis it is almost impossible to put it to the test, but there are indications in the records that support it.

First, the bulk of those records themselves is much greater from the time of John onwards. Although his father reigned twice as long, John can show more than twice as many documents. The reforms of Hubert Walter played an important part, but thanks to the prompting by Henry II's legal reforms, 'paper' (i.e. of course, 'parchment') was simply becoming more popular. And men's attitudes were changing.

Earlier charters, from Henry's time for example, reveal the unlettered society they were drawn up for in their wording. They refer to grants already made which the charter merely confirms. The legal deed of transfer would be some public ceremony before witnesses, marked no doubt by the handing over of some token such as a hunting-dog or a knife to lodge it in the memory of those present. This had been the pattern for centuries. It was only at the period we are concerned with that the document itself, instead of being regarded merely as a record of an event, came to be seen as the actual deed of conveyance itself. Hence title 'deeds', once physical acts, would in the course of the development of the English language become merely pieces of paper.

The further back in time one goes, the more common it is to find charters that are undated. Validation of the deed came not from them but, if necessary, the convening of a jury or inquest of men of the neighbourhood able to testify from their own memory that such a deed of transfer had once been made in such a year and on such a day. The bulk of property titles had long rested on foundations such as this; many a cathedral chapter or monastic estates office could do little better if challenged than claim to have held land in question, as the saying goes, 'from a time when the memory of man runneth not to the contrary', track down some aged estate worker or member of the community, or point to its own chronicle or list of founders, and hope to be believed.

From the twelfth century onwards the forgery of documents became more frequent. Sometimes this was for the obvious reasons, but very often it was because ownership of property which had been in the community's possession literally since time immemorial was now being questioned. It was an age when literacy was leading to the expectation of memorials. At a time when the royal government was issuing charters merely as written records of arrangements which had been made orally months, perhaps years before, pious churchmen connived at creative recording in the form of documents produced generations after the event, rather than lose valuable endowments that were undoubtedly theirs by right.

Nor was it merely that writing was becoming the guarantee of what had actually taken place that made John's barons favour the form of the charter. Such documents were the common currency of baronial as well as royal administration. A charter issued by the royal administration some three–and-a-half months before the events at Runnymede is a case in point. On 1 March 1215 King John is recorded as granting to the abbey of Holmultram in Cumberland the hermitage of St Kilda along with its clearing in the royal forest of Inglewood, for the monks to cultivate or keep pasture as they pleased. It was issued because the hermit of St Kilda had died and the abbey wished to be sure that it had the title as his successors. Without a specific grant to cultivate, the pastureland of the clearing within the bounds of the royal forest would come under the rules of 'vert' (see page 125) and cultivation would be an encroachment of the royal rights of the forest.

This was just one of hundreds of such charters issued during the reign to confirm grants to all kinds of petitioners. Like the king, barons, lords, churchmen and monasteries all issued charters for dozens of purposes. In the next century there would be teachers of business studies at Oxford giving instruction in the drafting of such charters to budding estate managers and estate stewards. The Charter was in a recognized bureaucratic tradition. Its contents, however, were not. From the care that was taken over its distribution across the country and the detailed instructions given to sheriffs and bailiffs for its publication, we can see just how important this particular charter was considered to be by John and his contemporaries.

A copy of the Latin text was dispatched to each county and, as noted, accompanied (in some cases preceded) by a writ dated 19 June that enjoined the sheriff to ensure the Charter was given a public reading. The first writ to arrive at its destination was the one to Yorkshire, where it was delivered to a liegeman of one of the leaders of the opposition. Another messenger took charge of the writs for Warwickshire and Leicestershire; thirteen of the Charters were delivered for distribution to the steward of the Bishop of Durham. Chancery records indicate that writs requiring the enforcement of the oath to the Twenty-five and the reading of the Charter in public throughout the country were drawn up by 19 June. They were sent out ahead of the Charter copies and it seems that twenty-one counties had received their copy of the writ by

24 June. On that day, two copies of the Charter itself, the first such to be mentioned in the distribution, were handed over to the Bishop of Lincoln: they were destined, it seems, for the counties of Bedfordshire and Oxfordshire, both in his huge diocese. The delivery of the Charter copies seems to have been completed by late July. Today, it is difficult for a British citizen to imagine any department of government acting with such electric speed and thoroughness, even in pursuit of a policy of which its civil servants approved, let alone a measure so hostile to government as was Magna Carta.

A triumph of medieval PR

One chronicler tells us that the Charter was carried round through towns and villages and all swore to observe the king's instructions. In that summer of 1215, the sweltering roads and lanes of England, the market places and parish churchyards, must have been sporadically abustle with un-familiar business or thronging with gatherings of neigh-bours, so that all might swear to observe the Charter's terms. In some places the reading of the Latin text would have been followed by a version in French for the benefit of local landowners.

The reading out of the screed of legal Latin would have meant little even to educated laymen at the county court. It is tempting to suppose that the barons ensured that French copies were made as a matter of course. At least one such French version has survived. But England was a country of three languages and numerous dialects and skilled officials were probably capable of delivering a translated version in French extemporare from the Latin, or possibly in English from a French 'stage script' of the kind travelling *jongleurs* used as prompts. Leading members of the village community may have been helped with a spoken commentary in English. It seems probable that a full English version would have been made for London. The mayor was one of the witnesses of the document and English was very much the Londoners' language. Twenty-odd years earlier, the people had protested when William Longchamp addressed them in French. On 24 August Pope Innocent would solemnly annul the Charter, as an outrage against King John his loyal liegeman and pledged crusader, but before the news of this reached England many people had taken the oath to the Twenty-five or heard of localities where it had been administered. Presumably many were confused by the revolutionary proceedings; but all were surely aware that in some important way authority had been humbled and the head of government had been forced to rein back his plans.

It would seem that by early July or within a fortnight of the delivery of the Latin Charter to his county, Hampshire's sheriff, William Briwerre, had a French translation made for use in his county. Only days later, it seems, a copy crossed the Channel to Normandy. Another copy, made from it for some reason, turned up in France. It can be seen in the Municipal Library of Rouen where it is known as *La Grande Charte de Jean sans Terre* (the French designation for King John). It is written in a clear hand and is faithful to the Latin, though an engaging alternative spelling for Runnymede, 'Roueninkmede', indicates that this transcription was the work of a French scribe. He records that his model is the one addressed '*al visconte de Suthantesire*' – i.e. 'to the sheriff of Southamptonshire'. This French text of the Charter is immediately followed by a vernacular French text of the royal letter of 27 June issued at Odiham in Hampshire that instructed sheriffs to enforce the taking of the oath to the Committee of Twenty-five.

The beautiful Rouen parchment is part of a leather-bound cartulary of documents relating to Anglo-Norman affairs. For centuries it was held in the archive of the Leper Hospital of St Giles at Pont Audemer to the west of Rouen in southern Normandy. I would like to think that it was made from the Hampshire French version by the hospital's archivist before that document was carried on elsewhere. But why was the document, specifically made for the elucidation of the English baronage at the reading of the Latin text in the English shire courts, taken over to France at all? To me it seems very much like a recruiting 'flyer' – perhaps taken over by a rebel baron hoping to rally support on the south side of the Channel? True they had been subject to the French king since 1204, but the English opposition, now in armed rebellion against John, had had words of support from Prince Louis of France. In the fullness of time they would even offer him the crown of England. The Charter was a startling proof of their success to date. Its very layout suggests it was produced to baronial requirements. Unlike the Latin original, but like the Articles of the Barons, it has been drawn up in separate paragraphs. With a document that recorded their triumph over the king, in the language of their class and presented according to their specifications, the dissident barons had a fine PR tool in their hands with which to recruit allies in the forthcoming conflict with the king. Their cousins in Normandy did not, in fact, rally to the cause but for a time a prince of the French blood royal did.

13

A CHARTER FOR WAR

As we saw in the last chapter, six of England's thirty-nine counties are unaccounted for in the list recording the copies dispatched, and it was suggested that one possible explanation lay in the sheer workload of producing so many fair copies at such a high standard of penmanship in the time available. The last charters are recorded as having been sent out on 22 July, just over a month since the formal delivery of the document and the renewal of their allegiance by the opposition barons. John was still instructing his sheriffs and other officials to carry out the terms of the Charter and a great show was being made of restoring traditional liberties claimed by the more obstreperous of the barons. For example, in Durham royal foresters were instructed to restore his hunting rights in the royal forest to Eustace de Vescy. But these acts of compliance were probably intended to gain time while the king regrouped for a renewed confrontation.

On 20 June, the day after the solemn ceremony, John had written post-haste to the Pope with his own account of the events that had led to his predicament. On the baronial side, too, it seems there was less than straightforward dealing. We learn from a letter of protest by the leading churchmen that 'when the peace had been made between the Lord King John and the barons of England . . . those same barons promised the Lord King in our presence and in our hearing that they would let him have whatever guarantee he required of them, except their castles or the giving of hostages'. What in fact John asked for was the issue of a personal charter by each baron, confirming his oath, whereupon, we are told by the bishops, the barons reneged on their promise.

Maybe the king had never intended to abide by the terms of the Charter; it seems equally clear that the more extreme of the opposition barons were equally unreliable. One or two, according to a contemporary account, even left Runnymede before the 19th so that they would be able to dissociate themselves from whatever was agreed, on the grounds that it did not bind them since the terms had been settled in their absence. No names are named, but it is obvious from their subsequent behaviour that neither Eustace de Vescy nor Robert Fitzwalter, who was still vaunting himself as the 'Marshal of the Army of God', considered themselves obliged to observe the terms of the Charter until the king had discharged every last jot and tittle of his obligations. Others still more extreme had been bitterly frustrated by the decision of their colleagues to come to terms with the king at all. They had all along wished to carry the struggle on to the death.

In a sense they were right, for no matter how often the barons brought John to his knees he remained king and, as events were to show, could find a king's party willing and able to help his cause triumph over the opposition. In 1215 the argument was never followed through to its logical conclusion. The wild men on the baronial side merely wished to see the end of the enemy.

It is doubtful whether they saw the constitutional implications. Some four hundred years later, however, this precise question was debated in a discussion on Parliament's military strategy during the Civil War when the army's fortunes were at a low ebb. The Earl of Manchester lamented ruefully: 'Let us beat the king ninety and nine times, yet is he king still.' Such defeatism had to be nipped in the bud, and Cromwell put his case in a nutshell. 'My lord,' he replied, 'if this be so, why did we take arms at first? This is against fighting ever hereafter. If so, let us make peace be it never so base.'

At the end of the Great Argument of the seventeenth century, Parliament followed the logic of the case and beheaded King Charles. In the civil war over the Charter the opposition barons were to prove as logical when they made Louis of France the offer of England's crown. They had to. There was no way in which they could win the argument: unless they could establish an alternative monarch in John's place theirs was by definition a lost cause. Oaths given under duress were not binding. No king, certainly not John, would willingly surrender powers: any forced concession would necessarily be merely a tactical withdrawal.

The struggle for Magna Carta was a classic example of the eternal problem of how to replace an established system. When the aim is to overthrow the law and the lawmaker himself, the traditional injunction of every establishment in history, 'Act within the law', becomes not only disingenuous but pointless. In the run-up to Runnymede, the barons had found their alternative law in precedents drawn from the ancient past and the reassuringly normal conventions of charter bureaucracy. During the months following the humiliation of John they found themselves, willy-nilly, in a fight to the death. In his *The Governance of Norman and Angevin England 1086–1272*, W. L. Warren argued that Magna Carta was not a programme imposed on a reluctant king brought to bay in 1215 by the united opposition of the overwhelming majority of his barons. It was, rather, 'an attempt to find a formula for peace between the king and those of his subjects who had taken up arms against him made by those who wished to avert a civil war.' Yet it is surely significant that, as A. L. Poole pointed out, not one of the notorious Committee of Twenty-five came from the 'loyalist' group of barons. And the critical clause that established their role, could be seen, to all intents and purposes, as a sentence of deposition. In the words of John Speed in the early seventeenth century, it made the king of England but the twenty-sixth petty monarch in his own dominions.

The Twenty-five

As we have seen above, the famous *forma securitatis* was in the form of a standard legal sanction for enforcement of a contract upon a defaulter. The wording would not have been strange to any of the barons who attended the drafting session. Yet they may have been astonished at their own temerity when they considered that these words were being used against a king. The Clause (61) provided for:

> five and twenty barons of the kingdom . . . who shall be bound with all their might, to . . . cause to be observed the peace and liberties we have granted . . . by this our present charter, so that if we . . . or any one of our officers, shall in anything be at fault toward anyone, or shall have broken any one of the articles of the peace or of this security . . . those Twenty-five barons shall

together with the community of the whole land, distrain and
distress us in all possible ways . . .

So the king was to be penalized not merely for the breach of the
Charter he had just 'granted and confirmed' but for anything
in which he might be at fault towards anyone. There was
nothing general about the clause, in fact it was so precise in its
provisions that all except the most hostile of John's opponents
must surely have had doubts about its propriety. The procedures to be followed by any complainant are laid down in such
detail that there was no loophole for compromise or adjust-
ment on either side.

What is best described as a sub-committee of four was to be
appointed by the Twenty-five. Anyone with a grievance
against the king was to notify the Four; who in their turn,
supposing they reckoned the complaint justified, should go to
the king, or to the justiciar if the king was out of the realm, and
petition him to have that 'transgression' rectified with all
possible speed. Should the royal government fail to redress
the injustice within forty days, the Four were then duty bound
to lay the matter before the full Committee of Twenty-five who
would proceed about the business of distraining the king 'in all
possible ways', ways which are spelt out in pitiless detail. With
all the community of the realm they were authorized to seize
royal castles, lands and possessions and to act generally as they
saw fit with respect only to the person of the king, the queen
and their children. 'And when the redress has been obtained,'
the text blandly continues, 'they shall resume their old relations towards us.'

It has been called a licence to civil war: better call it a licence
for mayhem. For these astonishing reprisals were to be levied
on the king not only for his own misdemeanours or oppressions but for those of any of his bailiffs or officers anywhere in

the country. Nothing is said about how serious must be the offence to set this awesome machinery in motion. As worded, the Charter left it open to any mischief-maker to raise any complaint, however trivial, if it was technically a breach of the Charter or an injustice, with the aim of raising the realm against the king. Nor does the Charter specify who was to adjudicate as to whether a wrong had been redressed or not. Given the creditworthiness of John's regime at the time, it could hardly have been left to the royal justices to determine that the plaintiff's case had been satisfied, should he himself not feel appeased. And if not the justices or the courts, who?

The only answer must be the Twenty-five, perhaps more aptly termed the Committee of Public Safety on the model of the French revolutionary committee of that name. For its powers were not merely conferred by the Charter, they were intended to be confirmed and buttressed by an oath of loyalty from every freeman in the land. And 'all those . . . unwilling to swear to the effect aforesaid'. This one provision is more radical than anything else in the Charter and can properly be called revolutionary. The oath it called for was of a kind never before heard of, though it had points of similarity with other types of allegiance.

Men were familiar with the idea of something higher than their feudal allegiances to lord or king. While kings and emperors claimed to be the vicars of Christ upon earth, they were also thought to hold their kingdoms from him just as men below the king held their tenure from him. Christ was the ultimate liege lord and, as such, in the last resort could demand service against the king. During the years of interdict and royal excommunication Englishmen had been reminded of this more forcibly than most people in Christendom. And, if it came to that, by John's own act of some two years back Englishmen quite literally acknowledged that their king had a feudal superior, namely the see of St Peter as embodied in the person of Pope Innocent III.

The idea of an oath levied on every man in the kingdom was also not new; John himself had used the device after the fall of Normandy. Nor yet was the idea of an oath jointly sworn against the authority of the king. The London commune of 1191 had called for such an oath, even if only for a short term and for a clearly defined purpose. What is so startling about the oath of Magna Carta's Clause 61 is the combination of all these elements to produce an oath which bound all the king's free subjects in allegiance to a *secular* authority which, given the range of its power as also specified in the clause, was higher than he.

This authority was not an abstract notion nor yet a person embodying an abstract notion. Before John had given his kingdom into the hands of the Pope and received it back from him as liege lord, Richard I had surrendered it to the emperor and received it back at *his* hands. Thus, feudal Europe could conceive of the possibility of an oath to lay a ruler higher even than one's king. What would have seemed inconceivable before June 1215 would have been an oath of ultimate allegiance, the highest bond known to society, given not to a liege lord but to a body of lords, all of whom were subjects of the king but who collectively were supposed to exercise authority above the king. To the people of the time it must surely have seemed as startling and revolutionary as if today the Queen were to demand an oath from every man and woman on the electoral roll to uphold her authority against that of Parliament.

As if all this were not enough, the Charter provided for the continuance of the Twenty-five as a self-perpetuating oligarchy. Should their number be depleted by death or by the prolonged absence of one of them from the kingdom, the vacant place was to be filled not by canvassing the opinions of the baronage as a whole but by mere co-option by the existing members. It seems as though there was an absolute determination to make the new regime for the governance of England work if it were at all possible.

Given the diverse interests and opinions of those opposed to the king, it must have seemed more or less certain to most participants in the drafting sessions that the Twenty-five would be stopped in their tracks at the very first judgment they were called upon to render, simply by disagreement among the members. It was a world where community decisions were still expected to be unanimous. The supposition was that in any important matter there would be a right judgment revealed by God to the community through the deliberations of its representatives. At a less exalted level the very idea of majority voting, if considered at all, was seen as divisive. Unless those who held the minority view could be persuaded to agree with the general opinion, they would form a faction of discontent and, still more serious, the pattern of the divine or universal will would be frustrated. Until a few years back English and American juries were required to render a unanimous verdict, for reasons that stretched back to ancient tradition based on similar grounds.

With the development of workaday bureaucracy, where decisions had to be made if work were to proceed, the idea of decision by the will of the majority began to gain adherents during the twelfth century, and the first example of an institution regulating its affairs in this way appears to be, somewhat unexpectedly, the Roman conclave of the 1170s for the election of new popes by a bull. The first time we find the proposal described in an English source is at Clause 61 in the Great Charter. The relevant passage may be rendered thus:

Furthermore, in all maters entrusted to these Twenty-five barons for action, if by any chance when the Twenty-five have been summoned and all being present are unable to agree on any matter, or if some of them even though summoned fail to attend, whether because they will not or cannot, that shall be held to be fixed and established which the greater part of those present ordain or command.

The selection of the Twenty-five seems already to have ensured that the 'greater part' were extremely hostile to the king; this provision was meant to ensure that the extremists should always have the upper hand and dictate the policy of the group, and through them the actions of the king. No monarch could accept as conditions of office such terms as the Charter sought to impose on John. If Magna Carta, including the *forma securitatis*, seemed like a formula for peace to those in the realm 'who wished to avert a civil war', they must, one feels, have been excessively simple-minded. This one clause may have scuttled the Charter; it has been suggested that it was the sight of the *forma securitatis* that led Pope Innocent to absolve John from the obligations of his oath.

The tournament, banned by more than one king because it provided ideal camouflage for raising armed rebellion, was in vogue in the summer of 1215. But the barons were nervous of the direction their actions were leading and fully aware of the importance of their hold on London in strategic terms. A tournament, scheduled to be held at Stamford, was moved at the last moment to Hounslow so as to be nearer the capital. The occasional meetings with the king were prickly affairs; the barons denied him the ordinary courtesies and absolutely refused to surrender London on one pretext or another. At length it was agreed that the Archbishop of Canterbury should be given custody of the Tower of London and the baronial leaders could hold the city itself, on the understanding that their conditions would be met by the middle of August when they would return it to the king. If their conditions were not met, they should be allowed to retain the city until such time as they should be.

This compromise in fact confirmed the barons in possession of what one of them had described as 'our refuge', while giving control of the Tower to the very man who was known to sympathize with them. Langton's position was ambivalent. If, as seems probable, it was he who had prompted the opposition to adopt the idea of a charter, it is unlikely that he was any more confident of the king's honesty of purpose than the barons themselves. Nevertheless, as John's right-hand man according to the conventions of the time, and the Pope's senior representative in the English Church according to the facts of the case, he was obliged to accept at its face value the king's sworn oath to observe the Charter.

Reactions from Rome

For the time being, perhaps, he tended to agree with his fellow bishops that the barons in fact were in the wrong. Certainly the archbishop joined in the letter of protest against them referred to above. But if there was the beginning of a shift in his sympathies towards the king, it must have been badly jolted by the arrival of a papal letter based on Rome's understanding of events in England, which roundly condemned opposition to the king and upbraided the very bishops who had in fact been working to keep the peace and help the reconciliation between king and barons for having shown him no favour against the disturbers of the realm.

So far as Innocent was concerned, John was not only a crusader but a crusader-king who had surrendered his realm to

St Peter, and the very king who, 'it was especially hoped, would succour the Holy Land'. But Innocent must fully have recognized the advantages which his crusader vows would mean to a hard-pressed king. For John's oath to take the cross, made back in March at a time when the baronial opposition was building up unpleasantly, was very clever politics indeed. From the moment he took his vows, any crusader was considered to be under the special protection of the Church – both his person and his property. Furthermore, he was allowed three years in which to meet all his secular obligations – which in the king's case could be taken to mean any commitments he might make to his barons.

Innocent was absorbed in his dreams for a crusade, and of all Europe's crowned heads John was so far the best bet for its leadership. His letter went on to proclaim excommunication as the penalty for any who still opposed the king and ordered the bishops, on pain of being suspended from office, to enforce the decree. Written at a time before the meeting of Runnymede and the mutual undertakings there between John and his barons, the papal letter was long out of date. Accordingly, Langton refused to carry out the Pope's instructions. Elias of Dereham preached a sermon at St Paul's Cross to the effect that the papal initiative was invalid because the Pope was unaware of the true situation. But the legate Pandulf and the Bishop of Winchester, together with the Abbot of Reading Abbey whom the Pope had also nominated as commissioner for the execution of his orders, pointed out that they had also been given the power to enforce the sentences on the express authority of the bull: 'that Our mandate be not impeded by anyone's evasion'.

In any case, even though the letter had been overtaken by events, the opposition barons were still occupying the chief city of the realm in defiance of the king and they could be convincingly argued to be, in the Pope's words, 'worse than Saracens' and 'trying to unseat' a king who had pledged himself to full support for the cause of Christ and his apostles.

Acting on the authority conferred on them by the bull, Innocent's commissioners declared the offending barons excommunicate, imposed the same sentence on all their supporters, naming the citizens of London especially, and went on to announce the suspension of the Archbishop of Canterbury himself from his office. Langton's appointment had caused a six-year interdict and his own exile; his intervention had prompted the imposition of the most humiliating charter upon the king; and now his resistance to a direct papal instruction had caused his removal from office barely two years after his return to England.

With their most distinguished champion humiliated, the barons' cause was far more seriously compromised than it would have been by his removal from the scene. John had no desire for any loyal supporters to murder the archbishop and so produce a martyr in the mould of St Thomas Becket. Outraged by what he considered the Pope's ill-advised policy, Langton wearily took a ship across the Channel, en route for Rome where he would put his case to the Pope himself. As he made his way southwards, couriers were already on the road for England with letters of still heavier import for the baronial cause. In terms both outraged and explicit, they released the king from his oath to the barons and declared the Great Charter 'null and void of all validity for ever'.

If the proposers of Magna Carta seem a trifle simple-minded in expecting that John would accept a new-model monarchy which made him little better than the executive officer for a baronial cabal headed by his principal opponents, their ecclesiastical advisers (Langton included), who seem to have supposed that Innocent III, the most jealous advocate of papal monarchy to sit on the throne of St Peter for more than a century, would consent to the emasculation of his candidate, crusader, and liegeman John of England, must have taken leave of their minds. The king, wrote the Pope, had been forced into an agreement that was 'not only shameful and base, but illegal and unjust'. If it were allowed to stand, not only would the king's legitimate interests be injured, but the apostolic see would be dishonoured and the crusade endangered. Church-men in the opposition camp must have been brought rudely to their senses. It was now obvious that King John had a special place in the spiritual politics of Rome.

The document revealed John's skill in surrendering England to the Pope and then taking his vows as a crusader. He had won absolution from the interdicts on very modest terms of compensation to the Church in England; now it appeared he had won the Pope's unswerving support in perpetuity. Even if, continued Innocent, the king wished to honour the obligations incurred in such a way, he would have to abandon them on behalf of Almighty God and the Apostles St Peter and St Paul. John was not *permitted* to ignore the Charter, he was *ordered* to ignore it on pain of excommunication, and on the same sanction his baronial opponents were forbidden to insist on the fulfilment of its terms.

There was a large king's party with its own interests to defend, who rallied to John's cause over the ensuing months and so ensured that his child heir could secure the throne, but more than that, the common code of the great majority of the ordinary baronage would have been affronted by the proceed-ings at Runnymede. The most elementary convention recog-nized that oaths given under duress were not binding, irrespective of paper rhetoric. Given the expectations and assumptions of their times, the barons could not hope to win the argument; accordingly they had to win the war.

Civil war

Hostilities had already begun when the Pope's letters arrived. Stephen Langton, though far from England by this time, was in spirit at least in the thick of it. Rochester, the second strongest castle in Kent after Dover, was part of the military responsibilities of the diocese of Canterbury and its castellan was one of Langton's appointees. When, in September, the baronial 'Army of God', commanded by Robert Fitzwalter, appeared before the walls of the castle and demanded it surrender he opened the gates with alacrity. Robert installed a garrison before himself falling back on London.

John was furious. It may be that his hatred for Langton dated from this event. Granted, the archbishop had been opposed to him more or less since the moment he returned to England. Even John, however, could recognize that in the early days this had been to be expected, given his obligations as a servant of the Church. But since then he had obstructed the king's will over the Charter and now his castellan had surrendered one of the key points on the approach to London to the rebels. However, the king was not over-impressed by the military capabilities of Fitzwalter's garrison. The idea was that Rochester should hold out until the arrival of Prince Louis, the barons' candidate for the crown from France. John forced the surrender of the garrison in a matter of weeks.

Meanwhile, the rebels in London were playing at government. In conformity with Clause 61 they called upon the kingdom as a whole to distrain upon the king's property; they called certain northern landholders to conference in London; they sent hopeful messages to Llywellyn ap Iorwerth and the King of Scotland; above all, they awaited news from France.

While his enemies passed the winter 'in camp' in traditional fashion, awaiting the advent of spring and with it the campaigning season, John led his army on a fearful punitive raid of waste and pillage through the lands of the hostile barons. He reached as far north as the then Scottish town of Berwick-upon-Tweed, which he captured and sacked before pushing on into the Scottish lowlands, Alexander II the new King of Scotland having retreated pell-mell from his own harrying raids into Northumberland on the approach of the royal army.

It was a terrible winter for the north country. Towns paid handsomely to avoid the fate of Berwick, rebels begged mercy – even the once arrogant Eustace de Vescy turned petitioner. Turning south again, the king meted out like vengeance on the rebel strongholds in the south and East Anglia until only London remained. But, of course, London was the key to England, and the reinforcements of French troops had arrived early in 1216. The arrival of their leader Prince Louis could only be a matter of time. In May, the prince set sail for England.

Following in the tradition of Stephen, Matilda and Henry II, Louis (later Louis VIII of France) was the fourth adventurer to bid for the English throne since the Conquest. Between 1216 and 1688, the year in which William of Orange frightened King James II out of his kingdom, there would be five more attempts backed with foreign money; in 1327, Queen Isabella overthrew her husband Edward II; in 1470 Henry VI and his French Queen Margaret of Anjou, financed by French gold, briefly recovered the Lancastrian crown; in 1485 Henry Tudor, another client of the French king, defeated the Yorkist Richard III to become Henry VII; only the Duke of Monmouth's rebellion of 1686 failed. It is one of the many myths entertained by the English about their history that the country has been free of invasion since the Conquest. In fact there have been at least nine, six of which succeeded.

Statistically, and in the historical perspective, Louis had a good chance. Like William of Orange he was invading at the invitation of a significant proportion of the disaffected English baronage. Louis's landing on the south coast late in May was the signal for a revival of the turmoil which John's terror tactics had so recently quelled. The Scots invaded once more, while Louis swept through the south winning support from defectors as important as John's half-brother William, Earl of Salisbury. However, Dover, under Hubert de Burgh, held firm, while John's mercenary captains such as Faulkes de Bréauté in the midlands and Engelard de Cigogné at Windsor, and his trusted liegemen, such as William Marshal and Ranulf of Chester, remained loyal.

As summer turned into autumn, the rebel camp began to be embarrassed by its early success. The Frenchmen in Louis's train had come over in the expectation of rich pickings from the lands of the English baronage ranged against him. As more joined their prince's cause, so their prospective victims decreased. And now events began to run in John's favour. The Scots were defeated once again; William of Salisbury returned to the royalist camp, as did a number of other important lords. At the end of September John was able to bring relief to the loyal lady castellan of Lincoln, the redoubtable Nicholaa de la Haye. From there he went on to a royal welcome from the prosperous port of Lynn (now King's Lynn) on the north Norfolk coast to arrange for victuals to be sent to various royal strongholds.

Between 11 and 17 October, in extreme pain from dysentery probably brought on by food poisoning, John made slow and painful progress to the castle of Newark. On 12 October the lumbering royal baggage train, apparently trying to catch up with the king by taking a short cut through the treacherous lands skirting The Wash, lost a large number, possibly the bulk, of its packhorses and wagons in the quicksands of the Wellstream estuary. According to tradition it was a disaster which took the crown jewels with it. Certainly one set of regalia, that of John's grandmother the empress Matilda, which he is known to have had in his possession, is never heard of again. But it is also the case that in the early hours of 19 October the king passed on from the realm of this world to that of the next, where one cannot lay up treasures. Wayfarers on the roads around Newark reported men and packhorses leaving the city loaded with loot over the following twenty-four hours.

As a postscript to the king's life we can note that his queen, Isabella, though she continued to style herself Queen of England for the rest of her life, quit the country at the earliest opportunity in 1217, never to see four of her five children by John again.

14

CHARTERS, LIBERTIES AND POWER

The death of King John of England on 19 October 1216 is one
of those events in history that seem as important to posterity as
they did to contemporaries. Roger of Wendover, the St Albans
chronicler, welcomed England's deliverance from a monster of
depravity; the Barnwell annalist mused on the passing of a
great if unhappy prince. If we now incline to Barnwell rather
than to Wendover, we share with both the conviction that
John's death was a major event. In fact, it was more important
than either of them could have imagined.

Despite the death of the king, and despite the fact that his
son Henry was still only a boy, the royalist cause had underlying strength. The west country was solidly for Henry and his
advisers, while King John's last campaign in the east midlands
had prepared the foundations of royalist supremacy there. The
Charter, which had seemed to set the seal on the rebel cause,
was legally a dead letter since Pope Innocent had pronounced

it null and absolved John and his successors from his oath. True, the rebel barons had required Louis of France to uphold its clauses; but the excommunication of Louis and the high-handed behaviour of the Committee of Twenty-five weakened support for the rebels. Had John lived only a few years longer the affair at Runnymede might well have become one of the half-forgotten curiosities of history. Secure in papal support, backed by a large part of the baronage and a wily operator when his back was to the wall, John could no doubt have buried the Charter. His death made it once more live politics.

While Louis besieged Dover, the gateway to England, and his allies roamed the south-eastern counties and East Anglia, the royalists prevailed in the north and west. They were led by William Marshal, the papal legate Guala and a small group of powerful nobles and churchmen. These hardened and wealthy men of affairs owed their allegiance to a nine-year-old boy and their futures were dependent on his success. Now he was brought to Gloucester where, on 28 October, he was made king as Henry III.

Westminster, since the time of Harold II the traditional coronation church for kings of England, was held by the rebels, but St Peter's, the abbey church at Gloucester, had venerable royal associations, being one of the three traditional venues for the crown-wearings of the Anglo-Saxon kings. The young King Henry was focus for a modest yet, according to witnesses, a moving affair. First the 'pretty little knight' was given the accolade of knighthood; next he took the usual coronation oaths to maintain the honour of the Church and to administer justice; then he did homage to the legate as the Pope's representative for a kingdom which his father had surrendered to the see of St Peter. He was crowned by that worldly churchman and his father's friend, Peter des Roches, Bishop of Winchester. Together with Legate Guala and

William Marshal, the bishop made up the regency triumvirate that would secure the boy king on his throne. At fifty-six years his was to be one of the longest reigns in English history.

Unconventional though it might be, the coronation was undoubtedly valid and opposition to Henry was now opposition to the Lord's anointed. The following day, by the acclamation of his peers, William Marshal accepted the post of regent. A fortnight later, on the day following the ceremony in which bishops and magnates pledged their formal oath of allegiance to the boy king, the regent and his advisers played a trump card. At Bristol, on 12 November they solemnly reissued the Charter of Liberties in the new king's name.

Everything possible was done to give weight to the event. Each of the great lords and churchmen present was named separately as party to the act. Not only Marshal, but also, surprisingly, the legate attached their seals. Guala's decision to do so, which reversed the papal annulment of the document only the year before, cannot have been lightly taken, though some have seen it as a cynical piece of politics. But this Charter differed in one vital respect from the document anathematized by Pope Innocent, who had died three months earlier. The *forma securitatis* had been dropped. Since the king, a minor, was for the time being no longer a factor in government and the running of the kingdom was in the hands of a group, albeit a loyal group of barons, the Committee of Twenty-five was, inevitably, dropped. Guala no doubt considered this sufficient justification for giving his assent. He had hardly had time to consult the new Pope, but the cardinal priest Cencio Savelli, who now occupied the papal throne as Honorius III, came from a dynasty of Roman aristocrats well attuned to political realities and, like Guala, would have seen that this gesture of what one might call 'Charter politics' was a powerful move in maintaining the integrity and allegiance of Rome's new client state. What had begun life as a manifesto of rebellion was being transmuted into a government policy document.

The reissue would encourage waverers to return to their allegiance. In fact one may doubt whether Henry's cause would have had a chance had the Charter not been confirmed. It had addressed real abuses and all freemen whether barons or no would have been hostile to any attempt to return to the previous status quo. But, no doubt, there was more than an element of self-interest among the loyalist leaders. Men such as Ranulf of Chester and William de Warenne were fighting King John's war for his son as much to ensure the continuance of their own grip on public affairs as to support any notion of constitutional rectitude, or to help the 'pretty little knight'. Nor was it merely cynics who observed that the king in whose name the charter was now being promulgated was a minor. Who could know what he might not do when he reached his majority?

In any case, this Charter differed from Runnymede in other important respects. It was above all concerned with the practicalities of the current situation. Significantly Clauses 50 and 51, with their demands for the expulsion of foreign advisers and mercenaries, were dropped. The country was in turmoil and the regency council was not so well blessed with capable professional soldiers or administrators to drive out even unpopular foreign mercenaries – time enough for that once things were settling back to normal. The advisers of Henry III seem to have had a firmer grip on the realities of war and government than those in charge of the fate of post-war Iraq in 2004. The Charter clauses ruling against living off the country and commandeering livestock and pack animals, practices almost unavoidable in time of war, were relaxed and other clauses were either changed or omitted altogether. But the loyalist party now had a king who actually had reissued the Charter, even if with modifications, while the rebels merely had a foreign pretender who had promised so to do if he should become king. The loyalists also had a papal bull of excommunication against those infringing the Charter promulgated both in English (*Anglicana*) and in French (*Gallicana*) as well as Latin.

Even so, the winter of 1216–17 saw various advances by Louis. Local truces gave him local advantages, while concentration of forces in the east midlands brought him the surrender of numerous royalist castles outside the radius of relief forces from the west country. But time was on the side of the loyalists. The boy king had no political or personal enemies; and he undoubtedly represented the legitimate royal line. When, in February 1217, William Marshal led his forces to the south-east, allegiances began to shift back to the king's cause. It was now that Louis returned to France for consultations with his father. Back in England, while royalist partisans in the Weald of Kent harried the rebel armies, loyalist regulars forces retook south coast ports and a number of important castles such as Bedford, which fell to John's chief mercenary captain Faulkes de Bréauté who was effectively commander-in-chief of loyalist forces from the Thames Valley to the east midlands. (Once the rebels had come to terms, this loyal king's man became an undesirable alien and was forced to surrender his command and leave the country.) While the loyalists were now guaranteed papal support, Prince Louis had been excommunicated for making war on a loyal son of the Church – and even his own father, keen to mend bridges with Rome, was cool and unsupportive. When, in April 1217, the prince returned to England to pursue his claims he found himself playing the role of adventurer supported only by rebels and malcontents.

He also found his position further weakened by the divisions within these supporters. While he continued the siege of

Dover, a number of his English baronial party riotously set up their garrison in London; and his chief French lieutenant, the constable of Arras, continued a desultory siege against the castle of Lincoln, once again held for the Angevin king by Nicholaa de la Haye. The lady, as we have seen, was a stalwart soldier; but her position was not very secure, so that when the French besiegers were reinforced from London by troops under the Count of Perche she and her garrison seemed under real threat. But the rebel troops surrounding Lincoln and roaming the country to the south comprised mostly English northerners and French freebooters, both equally hostile to the southern English. Feeling themselves on foreign territory they looted and pillaged at will and so lost their own cause such support as it may have enjoyed, as the general mood of the country at large was swinging back the royalists' way.

William Marshal had left his west country base at the head of a sizeable force and was now marching northwards towards Northampton, calling on loyalists in the rebel territories to declare themselves and march to meet him at Newark. There, on 19 May Legate Guala donned his white robes and, in the company of all the clergy present, solemnly repeated the excommunication of Prince Louis and the rebels. By this time, Pope Honorius III, viewing the rebels against the loyalists as rebels against the Holy See, acknowledged Marshal's army as soldiers of the Church. They were permitted to wear the cross of crusaders and their opponents were classed as infidels – no quarter need be given.

On 20 May they pitched camp before the walls of Lincoln, ready to besiege the rebel force within as it besieged the castle. Their ranks were swelled by the warlike Bishop Peter des Roches of Winchester and Faulkes de Bréauté, the Norman mercenary captain, at the head of a corps of hardened professional soldiers, skilled fighting men though disdained by the barons. The rebel force far outnumbered the royalists and had the young Count of Perche, their commander, chosen to fight in the open country around the city he could have expected victory. Instead, he continued the siege, hoping to take the castle before his enemies could breach the city walls.

In fact, the loyalist army, finding it difficult to make a breach, did seem set for a long and tedious siege of the besiegers. But then a weakness was found, probably a badly secured postern-gate, and royalist troops were able to force an entry. Fighting in the narrow streets of the city robbed the French of their advantage in numbers while in the open space of the market place the combat looked more like a tournament than a battlefield as, no doubt to the amusement of the mercenaries, rival knights jousted in 'gentlemanly' style. Young Perche was slain in one such encounter and his forces were scattered. The aged Marshal, the renowned paladin of chivalry, was in his element and apparently made his first charge into the mêlée forgetting his helmet and had to return for it. There were few battlefield casualties in the 'Fair of Lincoln', as it came to be known. For all its festive tournament quality, it was a royalist triumph of great importance. The strategically vital fortress and city of Lincoln was secured for the royalist cause. And the victory was followed by a flood of *reversi*, former rebels anxious to return to the king's colours, among them several of the Committee of Twenty-five.

London still held for the rebels and Prince Louis, who had now raised his siege of Dover and led his forces to the capital. In June members of his council met royal representatives with a view to exploring peace terms. When these broke down, Louis's hopes rested with an invasion fleet mobilized off the coast of Artois by his wife Blanche of Castile which was expected to come up the Thames to join him in London. It was headed by a large transport vessel carrying a trebuchet, the last word in siege artillery, which was so heavy that the ship's deck was almost awash. As the flotilla, sailing easily on a steady following wind, approached the port of Sandwich, it encountered the English vessels sailing close to the wind; these evaded action and manoeuvred round to windward of the French. In fact, they were equipped with pots of pulverized lime. Having achieved the wind gage they bore down on their enemies, scattering the lime at close range. The burning dust cloud blinded the French sailors and the English boarding parties were virtually unopposed. The great French ship capsized under the weight of the trebuchet; those who were not captured made it back to France. The French expedition, the last serious foreign attack on England before the Spanish armada of 1588, was over. On 12 September Louis made peace with the royalists on an island in the Thames, at the so-called Treaty of Kingston.

By its terms the French prince was not only allowed to leave England unmolested, he was even paid a handsome subsidy for doing so. Years later these generous terms would be heavily criticized. It is true that in return for his 'pay-off' Louis had promised to endeavour to persuade his father, King Philip, to return the lands King John had lost in France; but since Philip would never have agreed it was a meaningless undertaking. It also stipulated the return of the 1215 Charter and other government records in the possession of the French. It is doubtful whether even this was done since there are still documents relating to the Charter in the French state archives. The treaty was indeed well overpriced in money and concessions but the country was at least free of foreign armies and rebellious magnates. With young Henry secure on his father's throne the Angevin succession was assured and, it seemed, the *ancien régime* fully restored.

In reality things were very different. The departure of the French was followed by the issue that year of another version of the Charter. Once more there were changes. It would appear that men with legal experience had been enlisted to look through the original text with a view to reducing the costs to government resulting from certain clauses by cutting them to manageable dimensions. The clauses on debts, for instance, were modified or omitted. The opportunity was also taken to remove the clauses relating to the forest and to consolidate them with new provisos on forest matters into a separate Charter of the Forest (see pages 134–8). For the rest of the thirteenth century, which would see numerous baronial 'protest movements', risings and periods of civil war, there would be numerous calls for the confirmation of the Charters.

This 1217 Charter, like the one of 1216, was more like an act of hope than an act of government. Grants made during the minority of a king could only be provisional since there was no way to guarantee that he would confirm them when he came of age. The version of the Charter that would eventually be lodged in the statutes of England was the one which, along with its accompanying Charter of the Forest, was issued by Henry III in 1225 by the king's own spontaneous good will and confirmed in 1227.

The changes were not substantial alterations to the intentions of the original text, for that document, far from being a list of radical rebel demands, represented what most reasonable men reckoned was wrong with the way the Angevin kings had conducted the government of the realm. The fact that its reissue, accompanied by formulaic guarantees of observance by successive royal 'governments', came to be almost a convention of thirteenth-century politics, indicates the determination of the more articulate opposition among the leaders of society to hold the regime to this reasonable practice. Though, as Robert of Gloucester observed in his chronicle, the Charter was 'as often granted as it was undone'. Nevertheless, it became accepted as the legal yardstick in many areas of good government.

Central was the concept that the law of England protected rather than restricted the liberties of the subject. For 'liberties of the subject' it is tempting to read 'freedom of the individual'. In fact, the differences, distinctions and discrepancies between the meanings of these two vibrant phrases occupy much of this book. Nevertheless, the equation of law and liberty, the idea that the man-made common law of England could bind even a king, that it was the champion of personal interests rather than the embodiment of government pronouncements, an ally rather than enemy of the subject, was central to the Charter and lay at the heart of English political thought until very recent times.

The fact that the Charter concerned itself with laws governing social conditions quite irrelevant to later generations was of far less importance than the fact that it was framed as a legal document. It was this that gave it its importance for centuries to come. Feudal society was based on the idea of contract. Kings and lords held power and authority because they had received the homage of their vassals in return for the promise to lead them in times of war. Land was held in return for actual military service or agreement to supply fighting men. Both obligations were hedged about by conditions, customary rights and obligations which could be expressed only in the language of contract. This is the language behind the Charter. It aimed to summarize the traditional and accepted obligations and duties which made the society of its own day function but its legal character and frame of mind would make it a rallying point in the constitutional debate that rumbled across England in the early seventeenth century, and that led up to the Civil War.

The power of the written word

The idea of a specific physical document that secured certain essential liberties of the subject seems to have emerged about 1225, with the charter of Henry III. John's Charter and those of 1216 and 1217, which we sometimes refer to as 'reissues', appear to have been viewed by contemporaries as three collections of liberties which were especially important. Royal charters were not new, but there were many things that distinguished that of 1215. It was not like a coronation charter, liable to be forgotten or even abrogated during the early 'honeymoon' year of a reign; it was not a commitment to right a certain wrong; it was not awarded to the baronial class against the rest of the realm. It was an award to the general community of the realm that ranged over many areas of government action and social life, wrung from a king in the fullness of his powers and of uncontested legitimacy, with provisos designed to ensure its terms were kept. The fact that the king died before he was able to finish it once and for all and that he was followed on the throne by a child at a time of civil war meant that authority had to adopt a conciliatory term if it was to remain in power. The royalists' adoption of the document kept the momentum going.

And documents were important – especially when they conveyed such complex concessions as this Charter. Kings did not like making concessions and if possible expected to recover any documentary concession. In January 1215 the barons had demanded John should confirm the coronation charter of Henry I. And they wanted a charter in the king's name that should be 'legally admissible evidence of an alienation of royal powers'. After June there was no chance that John would ever recover all the documents recording those momentous concessions. Even so, at the Treaty of Kingston in September 1217 it seems that Henry III's advisers expected the return of copies of John's Charter along with other records in French possession. At the end of the century King Edward I during his campaigns in Scotland made a point of recovering the documents relating to the agreement between the rebel barons of 1215 and the Scottish king, Alexander II.

The first known use of the phrase '*magna carta*' comes in a document where the clerk wanted to differentiate between the Charter of Liberties and the smaller Charter of the Forest. A few years later, a document describing the arrangements for the distribution of the two charters round the country in 1225 explained that the forest counties received two, i.e. one of each type: 'one concerning the liberties of the community' (*libertatibus communibus*) and the other 'concerning the liberties of the forests' (*libertatibus forestae*). The first, occupying a larger sheet of parchment, the clerk called the *maior carta*. The final stage in what one might call the grammatical evolution of the Charter came with the common form '*magna carta communium libertatum Angliae*', by which was merely meant 'the large charter containing the liberties of the community of England' but which bears a striking resemblance to 'the Great Charter of English liberties'. The fact that it acquired a distinctive identity, and above all a distinctive title from the start, gave it a powerful public image. With the words 'Magna Carta' the document became a slogan before it became a statute.

In the lead up to Runnymede, the Laws of Saint Edward the Confessor had been a rallying call, and although they are not referred to by name in the 1215 Charter, people generally assumed that this embodied customs which had ruled England in Edward's day. From that time on any questions as to what was meant by 'the liberties of England' could, in theory, be resolved by reference to the local archive. From 1225 nostalgic debate about the good old days and the customs that ruled then gave place in various well defined areas to quite concrete demands based on written agreement to be found in the king's charter, which his son Edward I was obliged to enrol with the statutes of the realm.

To what extent this text recorded the actual state of the law before the reign of King John was, however, quite another question. It was a time before statutes and even 'established' customs could be quite recent and in any case varied from one part of the country to another. In fact, the barons' claims that John had infringed established laws and customs accepted by his predecessors were political rather than historical statements. Precedents could be found for many of the clauses, but others were innovations, instances where the Charter states as law what its supporters wished to pretend was law. The most obvious example concerned 'scutage'; it had always been levied at the king's will, but the barons had claimed that it could be raised only with their consent.

Within three months of Runnymede, annulled by Pope Innocent, the Charter was a legal dead letter. John's death would place it squarely back in the political arena, but no one could have foreseen such a turn of events and in the autumn of 1215 it seemed the great baronial initiative had failed. Intended to bring peace, the Charter had provoked war; proclaimed as a statement of accepted laws and customs, it promoted fierce controversy. Even so, by establishing the idea of a written document as the final arbiter, the events at Runnymede changed the ground rules of debate. By the standards of the day, the Charter, with its royal seal, was a long and explicit document and it had been authenticated by the most solemn procedures and under the most dramatic circumstances.

The idea of a written constitution was a long time in the future and, ironically, it is generally agreed that England alone among the nations of Europe has never had one. Back in the 1290s there were those who would have disagreed. The anonymous legal treatise known as the Mirror of Justices put the matter in a nutshell: 'It is an abuse when the laws are not put in writing so that they may be published and known to all, whereas the law of this realm is founded upon the Articles of the Great Charter of Liberties.'

Liberties, money and politics

Henry III's charter of February 1225 tells us that 'in return for the concession and gift of these liberties the archbishops, bishops, abbots, priors, earls, barons, knights, free tenants and all the people of the realm have given a fifteenth of their movables'. In short, the bastion of England's liberties was bought.

Henry had been growing up among councillors keen to exploit the powers of monarchy and to remind him of his rights. He was a willing pupil. Late in January 1223 writs went out in the king's name ordering sheriffs to enquire into the rights that had been enjoyed by his royal father before the civil war. Alarm bells began to ring among England's great men when, in April, it was learnt that the Pope had ruled that in certain matters the sixteen-year-old king could be considered of age. The circle of favourites and royal advisers aimed to pre-empt complaints from suspicious barons by disclaiming any attempts to raise up evil customs. People were not reassured. In January 1224, as the winter court was coming to a close, Archbishop Langton asked that Henry confirm those liberties which had been won from his father and which he, when a boy, had confirmed by oath.

According to Roger of Wendover, William Briwerre, one of the royal councillors, answered on the king's behalf: 'The liberties you are talking about are not to be observed as of right, because they were extorted by force.' Of course, everybody present was quite aware of the facts – only ten years back many of them had prepared to go to war to enforce those liberties. But Briwerre miscalculated when he broke with the polite fiction that they had been freely granted. Langton cut straight to the heart of the case. 'If you loved the king William, you would not disturb the peace of the kingdom in this way.' The young king, watching the exchange, saw that the archbishop was about to flare up, and intervened. 'We have indeed sworn to observe these liberties, and what we have sworn to we are bound to abide by.' Tempers were calmed and the situation for the time being was stabilized. Later that year, with a campaign in Gascony draining the exchequer, money was needed and the royal advisers considered it wise to offer a confirmation of the two charters.

The 'fifteenth' was not the first instance of a tax on personal property – churchmen had long been familiar with such levies and churchmen, Langton at their head, were prominent in the regency council. It would not become a regular source of revenue from the laity for another fifty years. Being an innovation it could be levied only by consent and even then only in an emergency such as the war in Gascony presented. What one might call the cash-for-charters deal of 1225 established a precedent: a council of the chief tenants of the Crown could give consent on behalf of the whole realm. The arrangement foreshadowed the much later principle of taxation only by representation.

The idea that liberty belonged to the subject as of right was a long way in the future. We are not here dealing with human

rights in the modern sense of the term. It is a question of a
'concession and gift' negotiated with the influential minority
that made the payment of the agreed tax binding on the whole
community of the realm. As with modern parliamentary
taxation it depended upon a fiction – just as modern governments, regularly returned at election time on votes of a
minority of the electorate, are deemed to represent a 'democratic' majority of the voting population, so a small body of
the rich and powerful were held to embody the communal will.
At least the thirteenth-century community got something for
its money – a formal acknowledgement by government, unparalleled anywhere else in Europe, that it had to observe
certain norms and practices if it was receive the consent of the
governed.

Evidently the authorities were prepared for resistance. Local
justices were sent a special instruction that anybody who
withheld payment, even on the plea that they had taken the
pilgrim vows of a crusader, would have 'no share in the liberty
granted to our worthy men by our charters'. Chartered concessions forced from King John were now being used by the
councillors of his son as bargaining counters to extract new
taxes. The king learned the lesson well.

In 1237 Henry asked for a levy of a thirtieth, i.e. half that
demanded twelve years before. There was immediate opposition. His barons repudiated responsibility for the king's
financial difficulties and even charged him with having sought
a secret papal dispensation to absolve him from observing the
terms of the charters. Even the confirmation of 1225 had been
made while he was still a minor and people supposed that he
did not feel bound by commitments made on his behalf by
councillors, many of whom were now dead. In a dramatic
gesture to rebut such accusations, Henry met with his barons
under the auspices of the Archbishop of Canterbury and with

them pledged to observe the spirit of the Charter under pain of automatic excommunication in the event of any infringement. On 28 January he confirmed the Charter in person – there could no longer be any question but that it was binding on him. In return he got his thirtieth.

Sixteen years later, with the blessing of the Pope, Henry again applied to the great men for money, this time to help finance a crusade. The lay magnates grudgingly agreed an aid while the clergy made a grant of a tenth on their movables. The money was specified as being for 'the succour of the Holy Land against its enemies' and with the additional condition that it was to be spent only during the course of the actual campaign and under the supervision of baronial appointees. The idea of the Committee of Twenty-five dropped by the reissue of 1216 was still active. The grants were confirmed in solemn fashion in Westminster Abbey on 13 May 1253. They were linked to a confirmation of the charters and accompanied by the pronouncement of a solemn sentence of excommunication pronounced against all who should transgress them. The charters were formally confirmed on behalf of the king, while Bishop Grosseteste returned home and ordered the sentence read from every parish pulpit throughout his vast diocese of Lincoln. Once again the charters were linked to payment of tax and their constitutional importance made public by the most effective medium of communication then known.

Another fifteen years passed and Henry troubled his lay magnates once again for money. Again a crusade was the pretext, this time one that was to be undertaken by his sons, Edward and Edmund, and this time, according to the London chronicler, the grant was made by 'all the free men of the realm of England in townships as also in cities, boroughs and elsewhere'. Bishops, magnates and free tenants were summoned to

Westminster, while in London the reconfirmation of the charters was solemnly proclaimed at St Paul's Cross.

The link between the charters and taxation was becoming something of a tradition, but now the body summoned to grant the moneys and to witness the royal grant of liberties was something more than a council of magnates. Something very like Parliament was beginning to emerge. The link with finance was being expressed as a link with the wishes of the people. New constitutional equations were in the making and a power struggle between king and barons was once more a factor. The career of Simon de Montfort, Earl of Leicester and leader of the baronial opposition in mid-century was, for the Victorians, one of the great episodes in the struggle for constitutional liberty in England. His death at the Battle of Evesham in 1265 at the hands of Prince Edward, Henry's eldest son and his heir, was certainly a notable triumph for the royal party. But it was not a total victory, thanks to Magna Carta and its companion the Charter of the Forest.

The realm was however sufficiently pacified for Edward to fulfil his commitment to crusade and go to the Holy Land in support of the initiative of Louis IX, soon to be St Louis, King of France. After the death of his father in 1272, Edward was able to delay his return to his kingdom secure in the knowledge that his councillors could continue the royal government without danger of serious opposition. In fifteen years his wars in Wales broke the back of the opposition of the princes. But if the Welsh people were obliged to relinquish, if only for a time, their struggle for their freedom the opposition to Edward in his English kingdoms had not abandoned the struggle to maintain the ancient 'liberties of England' as embodied in the charters. In the mid-1290s civil war forced the king at the Michaelmas Parliament of 1297, however grudgingly, to promise a 'Confirmation of the Charters' and to agree that henceforth he would take no aids or taxes 'except by the common consent of the whole kingdom'.

Documents cannot bind governments against their will. But in England parchment did keep alive the idea that law should be paramount. Historians once characterized the politics of thirteenth-century England as 'the struggle for the charters', as baronial oppositions fought the Crown to enforce its observance of acceptable governmental practices, with the Charters of Liberties and of the Forest as the manifestos of their requirements. It looks very much like a constitutional struggle to enforce a written constitution, a struggle in which sectional interests were to the fore but the general benefit of the community was ultimately paramount.

With the 1297 'Confirmation', Magna Carta was enrolled on the statute rolls by Edward I in its 1225 form. In 1300 the king promised yet again to observe the charters, only to be absolved from his oath by the Pope five years later. The baronial opposition to his son Edward II tried new tools. In 1310 the group known as the Lords Ordainers concentrated on asserting the powers of the baronage within the royal great council and in the burgeoning institution called Parliament. There were references to the Charter but they seem incidental at first sight. This was because they were now part of the law and might be thought beyond controversy; this was deceptive. The fact that the charters were firmly embedded in English constitutional thinking is fully confirmed since the Lords Ordainers reserved to themselves the right to interpret them and to settle obscure points. Still more telling is the fact that although, so far as is known, no formulation of the coronation oath ever referred to Magna Carta, by the 1340s legal opinion held that for a king to infringe the Charter was to infringe the oath. The youthful Richard II, who acceded in 1377, was admonished by his first Parliament '. . . to keep the said charter as at his coronation he had been charged to do'. In the charter of this King's deposition twenty-two years later one of the charges laid against him was that he had breached the Great Charter of Liberties.

PART IV

LAW, LEGEND AND TALISMAN

From very early times the Great Charter was subject to confusion. The fact that there were two 'definitive' texts separated by a decade, that of 1215 and that of 1225, meant that even the most famous of all the clauses – that no freeman should be proceeded against except by 'the lawful judgment of his peers or by the law of the land' – has two numberings, appearing as Clause 39 in 1215 and as Clause 29 in 1225.

But then the very words 'Magna Carta' are, notoriously, often intoned merely as a slogan. In the spring of 2007 Gordon Brown, then the UK's chancellor of the exchequer, and Jack Frost, his campaign manager for election to leadership of the Labour Party, were listing it among the factors to be associated with the idea of Britishness; and it has been enlisted in many such a cause as a rhetorical flourish. But it has, too, often served as an inspiration for reform, change, even revolution.

15

THE EUROPEAN DIMENSION

Magna Carta was part of an English bureaucratic tradition of charter-making and heir to a series of coronation oaths and charters that stretched back over the generations. But England was by no means the only country in Europe where rulers granted liberties and concessions to their subjects, guaranteed by charter. To some it was merely a matter of common sense. In the preamble to a charter she granted to the commune of Ghent in the year 1192, Countess Matilda gave her view that it was not only in accordance with the law of God, but also with 'human reason that lords who wish to be honoured and well served by their subject will maintain their rights and customs for them'.

On the Continent, cities enjoyed something of a favoured status when it came to security of traditions and liberties. The great cities of northern Italy, Flanders and the German cities of the empire were all centres of immense power and wealth whose friendship was courted by kings, dukes and emperors. In the 1180s, indeed, Emperor Frederick I, 'Barbarossa', bought peace in a long drawn out struggle with the cities of Lombardy with a generous charter.

Best known of Magna Carta's continental contemporaries was the Golden Bull granted by Andrew II of Hungary in 1222. It had some striking points of resemblance. Where Magna Carta looked back to St Edward the Confessor, the Golden Bull purported to restore the customs of Hungary's first Christian king, St Stephen (d.1038), and like the Charter of John it guaranteed freedom from harassment without due judicial process. The appeal to tradition is found elsewhere. In 1266 Charles I of Sicily was required to restore the customs of William the Good (d.1180 and, incidentally, an uncle to John of England) while in 1314 Philip IV, granted a raft of concessions 'as they had been enjoyed at the time of St Louis IX' (d.1270).

But in the words of the modern German historian Ferdinand Seibt, 'English institutions were much more advanced' (*viel weiter gediehen*) at this period. The circumstances of Andrew's Golden Bull tell the story. It was forced on him by members of the lower nobility angered by royal connivance at the oppressions of the great magnates. In full, the crucial clause reads 'no noble shall be arrested or destroyed to please any powerful lord unless he has been first summonsed and convicted by judicial process'. As early as the 1030s Emperor Conrad II guaranteed to his military tenants that they could be deprived of their fiefs only 'according to the laws of our forebears and by the judgment of their peers'. Such a proviso was found in other European societies but these charters related to feudal tenants.

As the thirteenth century advanced, while the English continued their stubborn struggle for charters that could benefit

all classes of society thanks to the ever more generous interpretation of the magic term 'freeman', and in due course did,
other European countries found these grants of liberties increasingly limited to restricted and privileged groups of the
community. A Sicilian charter ensured that 'no services shall be
demanded from counts, barons and other nobles and knightly
men such as may not become their station'. Thirty years later
when King Philip IV of France, urged by his barons and
nobles, granted concessions and liberties, it was 'to the barons
and nobles of the realm of France' and amounted to the revival
of feudal jurisdictions, the right to private war and the exemptions of the nobility from royal jurisdiction. It was, in
essence, the foundation document of the French *noblesse*,
which met its Waterloo, with the proclamation of the French
Republic, in 1792.

16

MYTHS OF LIBERTY

The persistence of the Magna Carta legend is so much a part of the history of the English-speaking world that it may at first be difficult to realize how extraordinary it is. Other European countries had documents of a similar kind in their medieval past. Why should these be of merely antiquarian interest while the Charter persisted in the popular as well as in the legal memory of the English?

An important part of the explanation seems to involve a paradox. From the start the Charters (of Liberties and of the Forest) were the province of working lawyers; equally, from the start there was confusion as to the actual texts. Henry III's charter of 1225, with its many modifications of the Runnymede document, was the text that actually became statute law. And yet a highly intelligent man such as the historian Matthew Paris described it as 'the Charter of King John which Henry III swore to observe'. The barons of 1215 had claimed that they had merely formulated good and formal custom of venerable tradition that John had violated.

There were those who contested the claim at the time. In fact it was the reformulation of the second issue in 1217, the fruit of reworkings by expert lawyers, that provided the basis for 1225 and hence for the statute. But as the thirteenth century advanced, so all sections of the community of England accepted that it was the 1215 document that was being reaffirmed and confirmed, and as it was the barons who had forced that from the king so they could be seen as champions of the community. And of course, though much of both documents deal with baronial concerns, so both documents were granted to the freeman. In 1234 Henry III issued letters that made the point explicit: the charters are issued to all, both great and small, and what he has granted to his men should be granted by them to their men. The cynic's claim that the charters were to guarantee privileges for the social elite won by the social elite was gainsaid by the documents: and the theory was from an early date borne out in practice.

Despite the fact that the 1225 version omitted various clauses from 1215 and altered others, people came to look back on Magna Carta as unchangeable law. The idea soon came to transcend the fact. Interpretation of the famous clause proclaiming the right of a 'freeman' to be tried only by the 'lawful judgment of his peers or by the laws of the land' was of course crucial, and central to it were those words 'freeman' and 'peers'. Was this in fact a privilege reserved to freemen of noble birth? Did it, in fact, in the words of Sellars and Yeatman in *1066 and All That*, mean that a baron would be tried by a group of other barons 'who would understand', and did it, as they mocked, apply to everybody 'except the common people'?

The application of the terms depended on the courts. A ruling by a royal justice in 1302 that allowed 'trial by his peers' to a simple knight favoured a liberal interpretation and in 1354 a historic statute took the definition a wide stage further. It provided that no man 'of what state or condition so ever shall be put out of his land or tenement or put to death without being brought to answer by *due process of law* [emphasis added]'. This historic phraseology, in fact a paraphrase of the words of the Great Charter, would be enshrined in the American Bill of Rights as the Fifth Amendment to the Federal Constitution ratified by Congress in 1791. Many historians reckon that the 1354 statute means that the concept of 'freeman' now applied to all the king's male subjects – men of 'the common people' in fact! It seems that people at the time also held the view that the Great Charter offered protection to all. In the 1360s the peasants of a manor on the estates of Christ Church, Canterbury made a petition to the prior of the monastery in which they cited the Charter. Over a period of 150 years, the sonorous pledge of liberties granted at Runnymede 'to all the freemen of our kingdom' had seeped down to the grass roots.

This highlights one of the most significant features of the Charter of John and the 1225 issue by his son; a feature that marks them off from other, similar, royal charters whether in England or abroad. For they were granted 'to all the freemen of the realm . . . to them and their heirs from us and our heirs in perpetuity'. Usually a charter granted by a king was for his lifetime and expired when he died. Not so with Magna Carta. Most later kings honoured most of its provisos only when they were pressurized to do so. But the document was always there: a physical presence in every county, in the cathedral or other great church or other 'hoard' (the Old English word for 'archive' used in English-language proclamations of it), available on request for consultation and publicly read from time to time. It was a constant reminder that a king had given his word, that his successors were held to be bound by it and that, in consequence, there were principles of conduct and government thought to be above even the king himself. Richard II had been charged with breach of the Charter as one of the reasons for his deposition.

But times were changing and such appeals to the document became less frequent. The technicalities of the legal clauses were less relevant to later feudal society and the last confirmation was made by King Henry V. As the fifteenth century drew to its close, a century in which the realm had been troubled by civil wars, few people thought of restraining the royal power with charters; though the monarchy was about to advance claims for itself more extreme than ever before. At the end of that period Magna Carta, the English myth, would prove a potent weapon against the myth of the Divine Right of Kings advanced by the Scottish dynasty of the Stuarts.

The royal myth had deep roots. For centuries, England's kings had preened themselves as the successors of Arthur. The fact that most of his legend had been made up virtually out of whole cloth by the twelfth-century Welsh writer Geoffrey of Monmouth mattered little. It received a new lease of life with the victory of Henry VII on the field of Bosworth in 1485. Having only the flimsiest of hereditary rights to the crown and dubious antecedents even as an English nobleman (his mother was an English descendant of John of Gaunt's mistress whom he later married, and Henry's father a half-French Welsh gentleman), Henry Tudor, Earl of Richmond and protégé of the Duke of Brittany, made what he could of the fact that he had been born in a Welsh castle. By dint of patronizing Welsh harpers and calling his first son Arthur, he hoped to acquire vicarious virtue and perhaps, even, legitimacy by association.

Tudor propaganda is often praised for the success with which
it blackened the name of Richard III, whom Henry displaced,
but the fact that Henry and his dynasty are still considered
Welsh, when few rulers before and none since were as truly
English as they is a still greater tribute to its effectiveness.

But then the sixteenth-century court inhabited a world
of myth. The legend of England's conversion by Joseph of
Arimathea encouraged thoughts of an ancient British church
independent of Rome, which would match well with the claims
of Henry VIII to be independent of the papacy. Joseph, Brutus
and Arthur and the whole 'matter of Britain' fed the swelling
pretensions of the monarchy. As the English Reformation
advanced, its propagandists opened a new chapter in histor-
iographical revisionism with the case of Archbishop Thomas
Becket of Canterbury: heroic in his resistance to King Henry II,
martyred at the altar of his own cathedral, he had been until
then England's most loved and revered saint, but he was now
billed as the villain of the piece, a traitor who had sided with
the Pope against his sovereign. Enemy of the second Henry, he
received posthumous humiliation at the hands of the eighth
when, during the Dissolution of the Monasteries, his shrine at
Canterbury, one of the richest in all Europe, was despoiled of
its treasure. In a way, the Henrician reformation was the
culmination of a centuries-long struggle between the English
Crown and the Church. For its advocates King John himself
emerged as a champion of the monarchical cause.

Indeed, he acquired semi-heroic status as a victim of papal
intervention: the faithful Moses withstanding the oppressions
of the papal pharaoh yet forced by the power of the Church,
aided by the 'base rebellion' of the baronage to surrender his
kingdom. The assessment comes from John Bale's book *Kynge
Johan* written in the 1530s, when Henry VIII's struggle with
Rome was reaching its climax. The book provided the basis for

a play from 1590, *The Troublesome Reign of King John*, clearly known to Shakespeare. In Bale's opinion the king was a modern Joshua (the successor of Moses who had led the people of Israel into the promised land of Canaan) who was destined to lead his people the English into the promised land of freedom from papal tyranny.

It was John not the baronial opposition who was the hero of the Magna Carta moment according to Tudor apologists. For them it was always wrong to take up arms against an anointed king – memories of the conflicts of the previous century were as powerful arguments as any ideological consideration. This loyalist interpretation lingered. As late as 1611 John Speed in his *History of Great Britain* wrote that the barons rebelled to 'attain the shadow of seeming liberties', while his comment on the Committee of Twenty-five was scathing: 'Thus one of the greatest sovereigns of Christendom was now become the twenty-sixth petty king within his own dominions.'

In fact, Speed was unusual among his contemporaries in realizing that King John actually had issued a charter. In a lecture about Magna Carta, given at the University of Reading in 1968, Sir Herbert Butterfield commented, 'it seems clear that even the most scholarly people . . . had come to be unaware of the fact that Magna Carta was connected with King John'. To theatre-goers it can come as a surprise that Shakespeare's play on the life and death of King John contains not one reference to the Great Charter. Since he knew the chronicles of Ralph Holinshed (1st and 2nd editions [expurgated] 1577, 1587), and seems to have used them as one of the sources of the play, Shakespeare probably knew about the 1225 Charter but did not necessarily connect it with the reign of John, in conformity with the received educated opinion of his time.

The establishment view is best explained by the conventions of the law books. The volumes of the statutes of England which began to appear in printed form in the sixteenth century opened with Magna Carta, but the text they used was given as that of the ninth year of Henry III, i.e. the issue made in that king's name in 1225. Presumably the lawyers believed this to be the original grant. Commenting on the statute in his *Interpreter* law dictionary published in 1607, John Cowell wrote: 'I reade in Holinshed that King John, to appease his barons, yielded to lawes or articles of government much like this Great Charter, but we nowe have no ancienter written lawe than this.'

Whatever the prevailing orthodoxies of legal opinion, historians such as John Speed clearly understood the link with the reign of John. In the early 1600s the Charter was moving firmly into the arena of public debate and was beginning to acquire iconic status. Sir Henry Spelman, historian and antiquary (d.1641), considered the statute the 'most majestic document and a sacrosanct anchor to English liberties' while MP William Hakewill (d.1655) exulted in this 'the most ancient statute law . . . sealed and won with the blood of our ancestors'. Where Speed had derided the Charter in 1611, ten years later the Great Protestation of 1621 claimed that '. . . the Liberties of Parliament are the ancient birthright of the subjects of England'. Speaking on the motion, Sir Edward Coke MP, a former chief justice, appealed directly to 'Magna Carta . . . called . . . the Charter of Liberty, because it maketh freemen'. It was a remarkable and contentious interpretation when it equated the concept of legal liberties – i.e. exercise of legal entitlements – with the freedom of the individual: an interpretation that would earn critical censure from any modern historian today. At the time it earned Coke seven months in the Tower of London from James I on a charge of treason. The battle with Parliament would be inherited by James's son Charles I, the second Scottish king to interfere in English affairs, to deadly effect. Looking always for ways to raise money, Charles tried to raise a forced loan and met with opposition from five gentlemen, the 'Five Knights', who refused to pay despite the 'special mandate of the king'. He ordered their imprisonment. Parliament raged that this contravened Clause 39/29 of Magna Carta. Charles's attorney general, a post that even then combined judicial functions with those of government, retorted that there was nothing explicit on the matter 'in all the statutes and records'.

The question of arbitrary arrest had been raised under King Edward III in the fourteenth century, while in the reign of his father the Ordainers, by reserving to themselves the exclusive right to interpret all doubtful passages in Magna Carta, had hoped to pre-empt any awkward claims as to its meaning by opposition groups. Of course in their case the opposition meant the king himself, Edward II, and his supporters. The Ordainers' attempt to return to the principles of Runnymede so long as they held the military advantage in the civil strife they themselves had provoked ultimately failed. When the king's party overthrew them, all talk of the Charter ceased.

In the seventeenth century debate over the Great Charter would lead to an issue of life and death as King Charles I learnt to his discomfiture on 30 January 1649 on the scaffold in Whitehall. For the time being Parliament aimed to wrest the initiative just as the Ordainers had done. A bill for the 'renewing of Magna Carta' was proposed in 1621. The objective was, in fact, to guarantee the subject against arbitrary loss of liberty by establishing Clause 39/29 as unquestionably part of the law of the land in its own right. The case of the Five Knights added the question of non-parliamentary taxation to the issue of wrongful imprisonment. It failed to reach the statute book. Then in 1628 Sir Edward Coke, having survived his humiliations at the king's hands and once again in Parliament (member for a Cornish constituency) introduced a bill of liberties with which he proposed 'to explain Magna Carta and put it into execution'. The debates that followed between the two houses of Parliament and between Parliament and the king were prolonged. Charles proposed to make formal confirmation of the Charter as his predecessors had done but adamantly refused to entertain any Act of Parliament to curtail his prerogatives as king. Coke countered with what amounted to a compromise. The procedure he proposed did not follow the formalities of a parliamentary act but it would curtail the king's prerogative by a declaration of the law in such terms as would be binding on judges irrespective of the king's wishes in the case. The result was the famous Petition of Right of 1628.

With a glance in the direction of the Five Knights case there were clauses that ensured against taxation in any form except such as was imposed by Parliament. Central was the clause against imprisonment without due cause shown which quoted the terms of the Charter. It also quoted the 1354 statute embodying the phrase 'due process of law'. The Petition also made provisions against martial law. It was read three times in each house of Parliament and the king signified his acceptance but not in the time-honoured phrase used to authenticate an Act of Parliament, '*le roi le veult*', 'the king wishes it'. Had this form of words been used the Petition would, in effect, have been an Act of Parliament, the very thing the king had refused to concede. A new formula was devised, '*soit droit fait comme est désiré*', 'let right be done as is desired'. It could be argued that a distinction seems to be suggested between the doing of 'right' and the 'wish of the king'; over the centuries there have been those who have found that an aura of principle surrounds the 'Petition': a factor rarely associated with an Act of Parliament.

When the Petition of Right received the royal assent in its uniquely solemn words, Magna Carta should have been relegated to the historical record once and for all. After all, the Petition embodied those essential English freedoms held to have been confirmed at Runnymede, stripped of the anachronistic provisos and guarantees relevant to an outdated feudal society. Furthermore, King Charles had been forced to make his assent not to a select body of barons and wealthy churchmen whom later ages might *deem* to have been representative of the whole community of the realm, but in Parliament which *was*, so far as anything could be in the 1620s, the representative of the community of the realm. This meant that from that point on Parliament had become the trustee for the liberties of the subject. The struggle for those liberties was to be tied in with the struggle for the survival of Parliament itself.

Why did the English go historical at this time and dig up the Charter? An answer may emerge if we look back to the original struggle against King John. Some of the barons in the opposition had been prepared to go to war on the king and hang the consequences. But challenge to the royal power was a hazardous business, and it remained so down to the seventeenth century. We have seen that in the lead up to Runnymede the opposition, rebutting the charge of rebellion, looked for a respectable front by appealing to past precedents – the charter of John's revered ancestor Henry I or the putative Laws of Edward the Confessor. Similarly, the fledgling opposition to the Stuarts, parliamentary and legal, used supposed precedents in developing a systematic attack on royal claims, claims that had entirely legitimate bases. When he proposed the idea of a petition to the king to resolve the question of the 'Five Knights', Coke asserted that such had been 'the ancient way, until the unhappy division between the houses of Lancaster and Yorkshire [sic!]'. It had not been. Equally unhistorical was the claim that taxation without parliamentary consent was contrary to Magna Carta. In both cases recourse to a fictional past was called in to redress the balance of the present and false precedents were cited to cover the assertion of new rights.

The tactic was repeated time and again. The origins of the House of Commons were fancifully found among the ancient Britons so as undermine any claim to seniority by the institution of monarchy; the fourteenth-century tract on 'How a parliament should be held', *Modus tenendi parlamentum*, was attributed to the time of Edward the Confessor – a claim that the barons at Runnymede could not have made, devoted though they were to the memory of the English saint-king, since the tract had not been yet written! Trial by jury, indeed most of the liberties and institutions of England, were traced to an ever receding antiquity. All were enjoyed as of right; none was owed to concessions by the Crown. In this world view Magna Carta was not something new but simply a restatement of literally age-old privilege.

The programme of opposition by creative antiquarian research brought history to bear on the actual practice of the royal courts. But such appeals to the Great Charter could work in the reverse direction. An attack mounted by radicals in Parliament in the 1640s against the institution of the episcopacy was countered by champions of the old order with an appeal to the first clause of the Charter with its guarantee of the rights of the Church. By now the war of words was about to break out into fighting in earnest. The eventual military triumph of Parliament would relegate the speculations of the antiquarians to scholarly debate and analysis. The Restoration of the monarchy in 1660 changed the landscape of debate once more. In the introduction to his *Old English Liberties*, published in 1684 only months before the death of Charles II,

Robert Brady described Magna Carta as merely a feudal document which was intended to serve the interests of the leading landholders. 'Sir Edward Coke', opined Brady, 'hath a fine fetch to play off the Great Charter and interpret it by his modern Lawe.' In place of heroic English noblemen struggling for their birthright and that of the whole nation, Brady proposed a selfish squabble within the Norman ruling class to claw back their privileges.

Four years later the scene had shifted yet again. The autocratic and uncompromising rule of Charles's brother, King James II, seemed to endanger the English protestant aristocratic establishment. The protestant Dutch prince, William of Orange, and his English wife Princess Mary, King James's daughter, invaded the country by invitation. James ignominiously fled London without a shot fired and Parliament's battle for supremacy over the Crown seemed assured when William and Mary accepted 'The Declaration of Rights' as the condition of their being offered the throne. This deemed James to have abdicated and the throne, as a result, to be vacant. On becoming sovereigns in 1689, William and Mary formally assented to an Act Declaring the Rights and Liberties of the Subject and Settling the Succession to the Crown. Thus was the crown of England assigned to its new incumbent and the succession to that crown defined by Act of Parliament. It was a revolution but a revolution without bloodshed. To contemporaries it seemed a glorious triumph for Parliament and the ancient liberties of the subject. It made no claim to prescribe the rights and liberties of other peoples – only the right to be governed according to the ancient rights and liberties of Englishmen (even if under a Dutch king!). This seemed good enough to those who devised it. No wonder people spoke of the Glorious Revolution.

In England Magna Carta, the Great Charter of English Liberties, was now a museum piece, though for many it continued to be recalled with veneration. The fact that it continued in the front ranks of freedom's banners was largely due to the thousands of Englishmen and women who flooded across the Atlantic to colonize a New World where, 102 years later, another Bill of Rights would be promulgated by the citizens of the Republic.

17

AN OLD CHARTER IN
NEW WORLDS AND NEW TIMES

English trading ventures to the New World date from the mid-sixteenth century, but the first successful settlement was established at Jamestown, Virginia, in 1607. The pioneers set sail on the last day of December 1606 under the auspices of the Virginia Company of London and a royal charter granted by King James I. Drafted under the direction of Sir Edward Coke, it declared that 'the persons which shall dwell within the colonies shall have all Liberties as if they had been abiding and born within this our realm of England or any other of our said dominions'. The guarantee, in one form or another, appears in the founding charters of Massachusetts (1629), Maryland (1632), Maine (1639), Connecticut (1662), Rhode Island (1663) and others, such as Georgia in 1732. The 'Liberties' thus conferred might sometimes be open to debate, but few doubted the Great Charter of Liberties, that is Magna Carta, to be their foundation. And exposure to the air of America was to breathe new life into the old document. In the spring of 2007 the Lincoln Cathedral Great Charter was on display at the Contemporary Art Center of Virginia, at Virginia Beach, to commemorate the Jamestown fourth centenary.

We can say that for American history, the influence of Magna Carta lay not in the encounter of King John and the barons at Runnymede in 1215 but in Coke's colourful if essentially inaccurate version of it and his exalted conception of the common law. In 1647 the governor and assistants of the young Commonwealth of Massachusetts ordered two copies of Coke on Magna Carta, along with various other books on English law, 'to the end we may have better light for making and proceeding about laws'.

It has been estimated that by 1640 some 20,000 British emigrants had settled along the eastern seaboard of the United States. Their leaders were early aware of the need to establish the rule of law on firm foundations, lest the magistrates should, in John Winthrop's pleasant euphemism, 'proceed according to their discretion'. Accordingly, it was agreed 'that some men should be appointed to frame a body of grounds of law, in resemblance to a Magna Carta, which . . . should be received for fundamental laws'. The 1641 Massachusetts Body of Liberties guaranteed that:

No man's life shall be taken away, no man's honour or good name shall be stayned, no man's person shall be arrested, restrayned, banished nor anywayes punished, no man shall be deprived of his wife or children, no man's goods or estaite shall be taken away from him . . . unless by virtue of some express lawe of the country warranting the same.

The first Massachusetts Body of Liberties attempted to combine the principles of a theocratic state with those of the Common Law, but in the revised version which shortly followed religious content gave place in many sections to practical legal concerns. Other law codes followed the example, that of Rhode Island eschewing all use of Holy Writ in favour of Magna Carta.

By this time the very words 'Magna Carta' and 'Great Charter' had acquired an almost mystic incantatory quality. Instructions issued in 1618 by the Virginia Company to Sir George Yeardley, the colony's governor, came to be known as the 'Great Charter' by Virginian historians and writers. They required him to organize the election of a representative assembly, abolished martial law and made important changes in the terms and conditions of land tenure. Half a century later the proprietors of the colony of North Carolina authorized the governor to grant land on the same terms and conditions as the 'Great Deed of Grant' of Virginia, which they considered 'a species of Magna Carta'. The words became a common term for various documents of special constitutional significance. From the outset, American legislators were governed by the precept that fundamental legal principles should be embodied in written form. In a sense, indeed, the early colonial charters were forerunners of the Constitution of the United States. The colonists liked to regard their charters as solemn contracts between themselves and the king. For its part, the Crown was always jealous of the royal prerogative. As British colonial and commercial policy developed, so the Americans came under increasingly tight imperial control through Crown and parliamentary agencies.

In 1638 the Assembly of Maryland agreed an Act whereby 'the inhabitants shall have all their rights and liberties according to the Great Charter of England'. The Act was disallowed by King Charles I's attorney general because, among other things, he considered it inconsistent with royal prerogative.

In Massachusetts, protest by leading citizens that, through high-handed actions of the governors, men could no longer feel secure in the enjoyment of their lives, liberties and estates as free-born Englishmen led to an order of the General Court that the Body of Liberties be thoroughly compared with Magna Carta and the principles of common law. The General Court sent an address to Parliament in London to prove that the government of the colony was framed in accordance with 'the fundamental and common laws of England and that rule by which all kingdoms and jurisdictions must render account of every act and administration in the last day'. This they did by presenting selections from the colony's law, English law and the text of Magna Carta itself in parallel columns. Parliament was no doubt impressed by the antiquarian learning of the colonists, and their respect for their English legacy.

In most colonies, the charters which conferred powers of local legislation were followed by moves in the written laws of these new dominions to establish their claims to rights under the common law independently. The Rhode Island charter defined Magna Carta's famous words '*lex terrae*', 'the law of the land', to mean the law of the General Assembly of Rhode Island and not the law of England unless this had been adopted by the assembly as part of the laws of the colony. It was a forward-looking proviso.

In 1692 William Penn, who while still in England had argued the rights of the colonials as Englishmen to the protection of Magna Carta as construed by Coke, published an edition of the Charter together with the confirmations of Edward I. Penn's collection was prefaced with a heartfelt address to his readers not to give away anything of Liberty and Property that at present they do enjoy, but take up the good example of our ancestors and understand that it is easy to part with or give away great privileges, which be hard to be gained if once lost.

As American lawyers began to develop their own, independent traditions, the appeal to Magna Carta and the rights of 'every free-born English subject', perennially popular with defendants, occasionally provoked some asperity from the bench. Subjected to yet another harangue on ancient liberties one Massachusetts judge was moved to remark, 'we must not think that the laws of England follow us to the ends of the earth'. But in conflicts with the home government the Charter was sovereign. Almost exactly a century before the Declaration of Independence it featured in what has been called the 'first colonial rebellion again English taxation'.

In 1680, the New York state government confronted an angry opposition movement. The state's governor, Sir Edmund Andros, was well liked by James, Duke of York, for his profitable administration of the colony; New Yorkers protested against the regime as oppressive and high-handed, and charged mismanagement, extravagance and 'discrepancies in the financial reports'. Summoned to London, Andros embarked for England in October leaving instructions that the administration of the colony 'remain as then settled' until his return.

The administration's revenue derived from a long-contested customs duty levied under an order which expired in November and which Governor Andros neglected to renew. This aristocratic disregard for detail spelt trouble for his deputy William Dyer. When the order expired, New York's merchants, pleading the letter of the law, withheld payment of customs. Dyer impounded a ship and its cargo and the storm broke. The owners brought suit against him in the colonial court of assize for unlawful seizure of property and further accursed him of 'the subversion . . . of the ancient fundamental laws of the Realm of England contrary to the Great Charter of Liberties and the Petition of Right . . .'.

The court ruled that Dyer was to answer to the Privy Council in England. Both he and Andros were of course acquitted, though neither was returned to duty in New York. The colonists now petitioned for an assembly elected by the freeholders, as was customary in the government of other colonies. In October 1683 Thomas Dongan, an Irish gentleman, arrived as governor briefed to establish an elected assembly and frame a charter. Dongan's statute for New York's 'charter of liberties' embodied many of the principles of Magna Carta and was welcomed by the state legislature. It never received approval from London, where it was regarded as 'savouring too strongly of popular freedom and as counter to the prerogatives of the legal supremacy of parliament'. New York was still without an assembly. But the charter of liberties was not forgotten.

All legislation in the American colonies required the assent of the Crown. Whereas the royal veto had long been discredited in British affairs, the imperial veto exercised by the Crown in Parliament and applied by the colonial governors was used by the government at Westminster to safeguard the authority of Parliament. That was the intention, but America's eighteenth-century colonial legislatures frequently by-passed the veto, re-enacting the rewording measures as they saw fit, to preserve what they conceived as their liberties, among which provisions based on Magna Carta were prominent.

As the century progressed the Charter was called on in the most unexpected causes. In Virginia in the 1750s the legal profession had sunk so low in popular estimation that moves were made to expel all lawyers from the state, or at least to prohibit any person pleading in any judicial proceedings for reward. Bowing to public opinion, governor and council approved the measure but only on condition that the proposed legislation did not infringe the terms of Magna Carta.

Even the great pre-Revolutionary battle cry, 'No taxation without representation', would be justified by appeal to the Great Charter. That it was bad history is neither here nor there. Almost every appeal to Magna Carta over the past two centuries had been in the same category. English liberties had been won by parliamentary opposition to arbitrary taxation, and seventeenth-century English parliamentarians had traced the tradition behind their victories back to Magna Carta. As a matter of sober historical fact, the very word 'parliament' was unknown to King John and his barons, but 'history', in the sense of what actually happened in the past, had little to do with the power of Magna Carta to shape the British constitution. 'Magna Carta-ism', as we might call it, continued as creatively in the New World as it had been in the old. Myth-making lay at the heart of the process, and the American revolutionaries proved worthy heirs to the tradition.

In one sense, it could be said that the American War of Independence was fought to vindicate rights won in England and embodied in the doctrines of common law, the principles of the Bill of Rights and the idea of Magna Carta. Fuelled by the tradition of English constitutionalism, the war was sparked by that fiery pamphleteer Tom Paine, whose writings, above all the *Rights of Man*, provided the touch-paper. But it was wedded also to the idea of an Englishman's birthright, and Magna Carta came into play here as the inspiration of revolutionary attitudes to government and the concept of liberty. From an early date the fact that the Charter had been forced from the king was seen as more important than almost any of the actual clauses of the document. A dissident group of barons and churchmen were mythologized into champions of the people. This, combined with a flattering history of the power of Parliament, made Magna Carta a symbol of the concept of the sovereign power of the people to impose their will on the government. In the American context this gave rise to the idea that the expression of the people's will concerning the fundamental rights retained by them was to be recorded in a written document.

From this it was perceived that a document of fundamental liberties, because it embodied the will of the people and the concepts of fundamental law, must be superior not only to the executive but even to the legislature. As the Supreme Court case of Hurtado v. California in 1884 made clear, 'In this country written constitutions were deemed essential to protect the rights and liberties of the people against the encroachments of power delegated to their governments, and the provisions of Magna Carta were incorporated into the Bill of Rights.' The concept of a written constitution, introduced by America, was to be adopted by almost every nation in the world except Britain.

The final transformation of the Charter into a truly mystic principle of government was the proposition, embodied in the Ninth Amendment of the American Constitution, that that written document, though it specified the limits of government power, was merely recording rights that had existed prior to the promulgation of the charter, and where rights were not stated they were to be retained by the people.

Within a few years of the signing of the Constitution itself a series of amendments to it were passed. But whereas the advisers of King Henry III aimed to safeguard the authority of the legislature and executive by their work, the Fathers of the Republic sought to strengthen popular liberties. And whereas the ultimate interpreters of the medieval statute came to be the legislature/executive itself, in America the final arbiter was the Supreme Court, held to be above both legislature and executive.

Of the role of Magna Carta in the United States, it has been said that it:

> provided the starting-point for framing standards appropriate to safeguarding the liberties of a people living under a regime socially, economically and politically about as far from 1215 as it is possible to conceive. Having served its function of having put law on the right track, it receded into the background.

Yet the ancient document continued to exert its spell over the Supreme Court judges, tempting them, from time to time, into flights of rhetoric as soul-stirring and unhistorical as anything conceived by Lord Coke. Delivering judgment in the case of Murray's Lessee v. Hoboken Land and Improvement Company in 1856, Mr Justice Curtis lyrically described Magna Carta as

> the affirmance of the ancient standing laws of the land as they existed among the Saxons ere the power of Norman chivalry, combined with the subtlety of Norman lawyers, had deprived the Saxons – who then formed and whose descendants still form the mass of the English nation – of their ancient political institutions.

In 1941, summing up the case of Bridges v. California, Mr Justice Frankfurter opined that 'the administration of justice by an impartial judiciary has been basic to our conception of freedom ever since Magna Carta'. By a trick of history, in that very year of 1941, the Lincoln Cathedral Magna Carta was actually in the United States. Two years earlier it had been sent for exhibition at the New York's World's Fair, but before it could be sent back to England, the United Kingdom had declared war on Germany. The precious document, described by one newspaper as 'the ever-living fountain from which flow those liberties which the English world enjoys today' was placed for safe keeping along with the United States Constitution in Fort Knox. It remained there throughout the Second World War and was returned only in 1947.

The following year, when the Universal Declaration of Human Rights was presented for adoption by the General Assembly of the United Nations, Eleanor Roosevelt, chairwoman of the committee charged with the task of drafting the text, described it as 'a Magna Carta for the future'. In 1957 the American Bar Association erected a commemorative pillar at Runnymede, near the Commonwealth War Memorial there, carved with the words, 'To commemorate Magna Carta, symbol of Freedom Under Law'. In 1963 Mr Justice Goldberg, in the case of Kennedy v. Mendoza Martinez, commenting on the Fourteenth Amendment, observed: 'Dating back to Magna Carta, it has been an abiding principle governing the lives of civilized men that no freeman shall be taken or imprisoned or disseised or outlawed or exiled . . . without the judgment of his peers or by the laws of the land.'

The Lincoln document itself crossed the Atlantic twice more, in 1976 for the bicentennial celebrations of the Declaration of Independence, when Queen Elizabeth II, King John's successor, was welcomed as a guest, and again in 1987 for the bicentenary of the writing of the United States Constitution.

In the former colonies of the American States, respect for the Great Charter vaunted by their English ancestors survived even a bloody war for independence. In Australia, where independence was peacefully won, the tradition of respect also continued. A child in a secondary school in Sydney in the 1940s might know little or nothing about the history of Asia, continental Europe, or even the Australian continent; but a good deal about King John and Runnymede.

In 1952, Australia's Parliamentary Librarian paid some £12,500 sterling, after private negotiations in England, for an undistinguished piece of parchment of no literary value, dating from the late thirteenth century and measuring some 20 by 16.5 inches (510 by 420 millimetres). The price paid was not considered exorbitant, and this extremely unexciting document was put on public display in the Public Area of Parliament House, Canberra. This was a copy of the Confirmation of Magna Carta bearing the seal of King Edward I and the date of 12 October 1297. It had been put up for sale by the King's School, Bruton, Somerset, England, where it had shortly before been discovered among the school's muniments by the son of the headmaster. This was, at the time, one of the two versions of Magna Carta still in private hands. The other, belonging to the Brudenell family, was to be later acquired, as we saw, by billionaire businessman Mr Ross Perot and exhibited near the Declaration of Independence, the Bill of Rights and the United States Constitution, at the National Archives Rotunda in Washington. Both parchments are part of the diffusion of the centuries-old fall-out from 1215.

In fact, we find mention of the Charter in connection with Australia from the very earliest, inglorious days of the penal settlement era of the island continent. In his *Plea for the Constitution* of 1803 Jeremy Bentham, Utilitarian philosopher, international lawyer and lifelong campaigner for civil liberties, aimed to expose: 'The enormities committed to the oppression of British subjects, innocent as well as guilty, in the breach of Magna Carta ... by the design, foundation and government of the penal colony of New South Wales'. That Bentham, as famous for his general contempt for all things 'medieval' as for his passion for human dignity, should appeal to the Charter speaks volumes for the power of its slogan.

The English – and here Bentham shared the common view – held that the liberties of England had existed from time out of mind. It was supposed that they could be rediscovered, by historical research if need be, and re-established where they had been abrogated. In this thought-world, even Magna Carta was but the restatement of the liberties vouchsafed to Englishmen from the first. The idea was so deeply imprinted that it survived transplantation to the American colonies. (The fact was, the colonists looked upon themselves as Englishmen entitled to the rights of Englishmen of which they regarded Magna Carta to be the chief embodiment.) During the Bill of Rights parliamentary debates of 1689 Sir Robert Howard MP (proudly quoted by his New Zealand descendant, John Howard, on a Magna Carta website) asserted that: 'The several charters of the people's rights, most particularly Magna Carta, were not grants from the king, but recognitions by the king of rights that have been reserved and that appertained unto us by common law.'

In 1988 New Zealand's Parliament adopted the vital clause of the 1297 Statute through the Imperial Laws Application Act (1988) First Schedule, while in Australia, Brisbane's Expo 88 gave the Lincoln Charter privileged display. It was flown out on a plane of the Queen's Flight. On the Expo site it had its own pavilion. Only two other displays were accorded this distinction – one for Captain Cook, the other for the Vatican.

In the 1790s, in his *Reflections on the Revolution in France*, Edmund Burke wrote:

> From Magna Carta . . . it has been the uniform policy of our constitution to claim and assert our liberties, as an entailed inheritance derived to us from our forefathers and to be transmitted to our posterity . . . without any reference whatever to any other more general or prior right.

The idea that the Charter was for those who live in England or who considered themselves Englishmen or heirs to the English tradition – a manifesto not of revolution but for the restoration of liberties that Englishmen had enjoyed time out of mind – made such an impression outside England that the pioneer German sociologist Max Weber (d.1920) inclined to the view that the very idea of natural law derived in part

> from the idea particularly indigenous to England that every member of the community has certain natural rights. This idea of birthright arose essentially under the influence of the popular conception that certain rights confirmed in Magna Carta . . . were the habitual Liberties of all Englishmen as such.

In fact, in eighteenth-century England the Charter fell out of view, as an 'obsolete, an old-fashioned law', to quote the radical MP Sir Francis Burdett, Bart., 'not suited to the refinements of modern times'. Parliament by contrast was in the full pomp of its self-importance. In 1810 a radical member was imprisoned by order of the House of Commons 'for publicly questioning their proceedings in a disrespectful tone'. Burdett, the Member for Westminster, declared the action to have violated common law, Magna Carta and trial by jury. He in his turn was arrested on a breach of privilege charge and imprisoned for a time in the Tower of London. Burdett was no slouch at PR: when the officers came to effect his arrest he and his family were listening to his fourteen-year-old son read an English translation of the original Latin Magna Carta.

At about this time, the radical press revived the Charter's cause. The satirical weekly *The Black Dwarf* opposed Parliament's seven-year suspension of Habeas Corpus (1794–1801), a measure that 'descended in part from that traitor of olden times, Magna Carta, though fortunately incapable of intervening in the affairs of government . . . being now very old and infirm he seldom stirs abroad.'

In fact he did stir abroad some thirty years later thanks to the London Working Man's Association. In 1838 it launched the six-point People's Charter for parliamentary reform. It seems reasonable to suppose that it was as an implied rebuke to the very old and infirm gentleman's charter that this brash newcomer called itself the 'People's' Charter. Whatever the intention, the Chartists could not avoid the association. At a mass meeting held on Hartshead Moor in Yorkshire (one of the Reverend Patrick Brontë's curacies) the lead speaker, the Reverend Joseph Raynor Stephens, proclaimed: 'We stand upon our rights, we seek no change, we say give us the good old Laws of England. And what are these Laws?' 'Magna Carta,' roared back the crowd, we are told. 'Aye!' continued the orator, comfortingly oblivious to what might be the historical reality. 'Aye! Magna Carta. The good old laws of English Freedom. Free meetings, freedom of speech, freedom of worship, freedom of homesteads, the free and happy fireside, and no workhouses.'

The mother of all wish lists for the working class of England's industrial revolution, it shows that Raynor and his audience accepted the barons' Great Charter as the automatic rallying cry for Englishmen's freedoms however defined. Another Englishman, the artist J. M. W. Turner, noted for his passion for England if not for his poetry, jotted in his

Devonshire coast notebook for 1811, 'Thus native bravery Liberty decreed/Received the stimulus act at Runnymede.'

For nineteenth-century Americans the Charter was the root of the United States Constitution. A ruling by the Supreme Court in the case Hurtado v. California in 1884 set out the position (see Introduction, page xix). The Charter has been invoked in American law courts until quite recent times and was clearly seen as native to the American tradition; we have noted Mr Justice Frankfurter's opinion of 1941 and twenty-odd years later Mr Justice Goldberg's observation of the abiding principle of Magna Carta. That one of the world's great judicial systems should cite as normal precedents and statute law from that of another is surely a remarkable fact, worth reflecting on.

Today, thanks in part to the bloody-mindedness and PR know-how of England's Anglo-Norman baronage, thanks to the death of a king before he could bring them to heel, and thanks to ex-colonials in two continents surprisingly keen to champion fundamental constitutional provisions of their former imperial masters, the world at large knows what is meant by the rule of law.

It is often said that Britain has no written constitution. In fact in the two principles that override all others – the account-ability of government to the governed and liberty from arbitrary arrest and imprisonment – it has the world's oldest.

Writing in the *Independent* of London of 26 August 2003, Simon Carr observed that Magna Carta's purpose was to limit the power of the state. No doubt the European Union of today, in which binding treaties and 'constitutions' to create state power are negotiated in secret without appeal to public opinion, would have approved the action of Innocent III when he cancelled an attempt to *limit* state authority. Thanks to the papal annulment, Magna Carta became a rallying cry before it became a statute. Perhaps Europe's governors should arrange for the incineration of the surviving copies, for such is the durability of the medieval record that one cannot rely on obsolescent technology or disc corruption to do the job. Indeed one hopes that for years to come authority will continue to be irritated by this mischievous sheet of parchment.

CHRONOLOGY

FROM THE 'CONFIRMATION OF THE CHARTERS' TO THE PRESENT

1321 *July*. Parliament banishes Edward II's ministers for advising the king to act against Magna Carta.

1333 The last payment of the tribute to Rome incurred by John's surrender of the kingdom to the Holy See in 1213.

1340 *29 December*. Archbishop Stratford preaches a sermon followed by a speech in English, dealing with alleged infringements of Magna Carta.

1366 Repudiation of English homage to Rome.

1376 The Good Parliament.

1377 Richard II's coronation pledge.

1399 Richard II abdicates.

1413 Henry V reissues the Charter, the last king to do
–22 so.

1442 A petition in Parliament appeals to Magna Carta that

in certain cases noble women should be guaranteed trail by their peerage in their own right.

1472 Edward IV's Long Parliament re-enacts the sections of
–75   the Charter relating to hindrance of river traffic by the levees at weirs and mills, which were to have been pulled down.

1536 In the Pilgrimage of Grace uprising, rebels against Henry VIII charge that the king did not give due respect to Magna Carta.

1607 The charter granted by King James I to the pioneers at Jamestown, sponsored by London's Virginia Company, drafted under the direction of Sir Edward Coke, declares that 'the persons . . . within the colonies shall have all Liberties as if they had been abiding . . . within this our realm of England . . .', liberties with their origins in the Great Charter.

1628 Charles I agrees the Petition of Right, which enshrines the principle of no imprisonment without due process of law.

1638 The Assembly of Maryland agree an Act whereby 'the inhabitants shall have all their rights and liberties according to the Great Charter of England'.

1641 The Massachusetts Body of Liberties is framed 'in resemblance to a Magna Carta, which . . . should be received for fundamental laws'.

1663 The Rhode Island charter defines Magna Carta's famous words '*lex terrae*' ('the law of the land') to mean the law of the General Assembly of Rhode Island and not the law of England.

1680 New York state resists proposed taxation as 'contrary to the Great Charter of Liberties'.

1689 In the Bill of Rights parliamentary debates Sir Robert Howard MP, asserts: 'The several charters of the people's rights, most particularly Magna Carta, were not grants from the king, but recognitions by the king of rights that have been reserved and that appertained unto us by common law.'

1679 Habeas Corpus Act is passed.

1759 Sir William Blackstone issues his Commentary on Magna Carta. Blackstone's classic work, *Commentaries on the Laws of England* (1765–69), was profoundly influential not only in English but American law studies.

1776 The Virginia Declaration of Rights includes a guarantee against loss of a man's liberty or property 'except by the law of the land or the judgment of his peers'; all other states framed bills of rights containing in some form or another the guarantee against arrest or imprisonment or loss of rights 'without due process of law'.

1790 In his *Reflections on the Revolution in France*, Edmund Burke writes: 'From Magna Carta . . . it has been the uniform policy of our constitution to claim and assert our liberties . . . without any reference whatever to any other more general or prior right.'

1791 *15 December*. The principle of 'due process of law' is enshrined in the first ten Amendments to the United States Constitution, adopted on this day and known collectively as the Bill of Rights.

1803 Jeremy Bentham, the Utilitarian philosopher and campaigner for civil liberties, publishes *Plea for the Constitution*. He aimed to expose 'The enormities committed to the oppression of British subjects . . . in the breach of Magna Carta . . . by the design, foundation and government of the penal colony of New South Wales'.

1810 Sir Francis Burdett, MP for Westminster, sent to the

Tower of London for declaring Parliament to have violated Common Law, Magna Carta and trial by jury.

1838   At a mass meeting held on Hartshead Moor the Reverend Joseph Raynor Stephens, Chartist orator, proclaims Magna Carta to be 'the good old Laws of England'.

1839   *7 June*. King Kamehaha III promulgates the Declaration of Rights, called Hawaii's Magna Carta.

1856   Mr Justice Curtis cites Magna Carta in the case of Murray's Lessee v. Hoboken Land and Improvement Company.

1884   A ruling by the United States Supreme Court in the case Hurtado v. California affirms the provisions of Magna Carta as essential to protect the rights and liberties of the people against the encroachments of their governments.

1888   James Bryce, the British jurist, historian and statesman (and later England's ambassador to the United States) publishes *The American Commonwealth*, which becomes highly popular. He dubs the Bill of Rights 'the legitimate child of Magna Carta'.

1904   Edward Jenks's article 'The Myth of Magna Carta' denounces the Charter for preserving class distinctions and embodying vested interests.

1905   W. S. McKechnie publishes *Magna Carta: A Commentary on the Great Charter of King John*, the most comprehensive legal commentary since Runnymede.
        In the case of Ghia Gee v. Martin, counsel appeals against a Commonwealth of Australia Act on the grounds of inconsistency with Magna Carta.

1935   Prime Minister Baldwin in a speech defying European 'tyrants' vaunts Magna Carta as the talisman of British liberties.

1939   The Lincoln Cathedral Magna Carta (1215) is sent

for exhibition at the New York World's Fair. In September Britain declares war on Germany. As a result, Magna Carta remains in America, in Fort Knox, to avoid the hazards of U-boat attacks on the Atlantic crossing.

1941   Mr Justice Frankfurter, summing up in the case of Bridges v. California, observes: 'The administration of justice by an impartial judiciary has been basic to our conception of freedom ever since Magna Carta.'

1941   *December*. The United States enters the war with Germany. The 1215 parchment is placed for safekeeping along with the United States Constitution in Fort Knox. It remains there throughout the Second World War and is returned to Lincoln only in 1946.

1948   Universal Declaration of Human Rights is presented for adoption by the General Assembly of the United Nations. Eleanor Roosevelt, chairwoman of the committee which had been charged with the task of drafting the text, describes it as 'a Magna Carta for the future'.

1952   The Australian Federal Government acquires the 'Bruton' Magna Carta, a confirmation of the 1225 charter made by Edward I in 1297; it is displayed in Parliament House, Canberra.

1957   At Runnymede the American Bar Association erects a commemorative pillar, carved with the words 'To commemorate Magna Carta, symbol of Freedom Under Law'.

1963   Mr Justice Goldberg cites Magna Carta in the case of Kennedy v. Mendoza Martinez.

1976   The Lincoln Cathedral Charter is sent to the United States for the bicentennial celebrations of the Declaration of Independence.

1978   The Lincoln Charter is displayed in Auckland, New
        Zealand.

1983   The Ross Perot Foundation acquires the 'Brudenell'
        1297 Inspeximus Magna Carta, issued in the name of
        Edward I.

1986   The Lincoln Charter tours the United States, commem-
–87   orating the bicentenary of the writing of the Constitu-
        tion in the summer of 1787.

1988   The Lincoln Charter is displayed at Brisbane's Expo 88.
        New Zealand's Parliament adopts the vital clause of
        the 1297 Statute through the Imperial Laws Applica-
        tion Act (1988).

1990   *January*. The Lincoln Charter visits Canada, being
        displayed at Calgary and Saskatoon.

1997   *12 October*. On the 700th anniversary of the affixing of
        the royal seal of Edward I to the 'Inspeximus' Magna
        Carta on display in the Parliament building, the Hon-
        ourable Sir Gerard Brennan AC, KBE, Chief Justice of
        the High Court of Australia, dedicates 'Magna Carta
        Place' in the Parliamentary Triangle, Canberra.

2001   *26 September*. 'Magna Carta Place' is formally opened
        in the presence of the Prime Minister of Australia, the
        Honourable John Howard MP, 2001 being the cen-
        tenary year of the Australian Federation's indepen-
        dence.

2003   *October*. Appearing before Mr Justice Ouseley in the case
        of the Chagos Islanders v. Attorney General and Others,
        counsel attempts to persuade the court to recognize a new
        tort of 'unlawful exile', claiming it to be a continuing tort
        based on rights deriving from Magna Carta.

2006   *30 May*. The date on Magna Carta, 15 June 1215, tops
        an opinion poll as the best day for the proposed annual
        commemoration of 'Britishness'.

2007   *April–July.* The Lincoln Cathedral Magna Carta is displayed at the Contemporary Art Center of Virginia, Virginia Beach, as part of the celebrations of the fourth centenary of the foundation of Jamestown. In July the Charter travels to Philadelphia to be displayed under the aegis of the National Education Association at the National Constitution Center, where actor James Earl Jones assists at the unveiling ceremony.

18 December. The 1297 'Inspeximus' Magna Carta of Edward I, auctioned at Sotheby's New York, is acquired by American businessman Mr David Rubinstein.

APPENDIX

THE CHARTER OF LIBERTIES
GRANTED BY KING JOHN IN 1215

The 'freeman'

The Charter uses the term 'free man' in a characteristic manner, its meaning varying slightly from clause to clause. Sometimes it can mean an under-tenant – see Chapters 15 and 30; sometimes a baron of status – see Chapter 34 where it refers to a man with the right to hold a court of more than petty manorial jurisdiction. Such courts enabled a lord to enforce law and order in the manor and take profits from his tenants, but also settled disputes between villagers as to grazing rights, for example, and issued rulings on the use of common land. In Chapter 39 the application is to any man in all or any of these categories.

The Charter assumes legal parity of all freemen. The Charter was concerned with granting liberties to the kingdom; it

assumed that the liberties in question were held by a community not by individuals. The Committee of Twenty-five was to
act in concert with 'the commune of the whole land'; the
monastic chronicler from Dunstable writes of the Charter as
concerning 'the liberties of the realm of England'. It is not the
province of any one class of society. Elsewhere in Christendom, as in the kingdom of Sicily for example, the rights of
freemen stopped short at the holders of fiefs and did not apply
to people of lower rank.

The text

In medieval Latin and dealing with many concerns which have
long since lost their relevance, in some cases even their meaning, the text of the Great Charter can nevertheless have
resonances even today. What follows is a summary of the
contents of the entire document, parts being given in free
translation, others being merely summarized (these are shown
in italics). The actual text runs unbroken but by long established modern convention it is divided into sixty-three clauses
(some historians make only sixty-one divisions, running what
are here given as the final three clauses as one).

For treatment of topics in the main body of the text see index
headings. There are some more detailed comments in this
summary, given in square brackets and in italics.

An asterisk indicates clauses not in the Charter issued in
1225.

The Charter

John by the grace of God, King of England, Lord of Ireland,
Duke of Normandy and Aquitaine, and count of Anjou [*it was
eleven years since King Philip Augustus of France had driven*

*John from Normandy and the Angevin family's ancestral lands
of Anjou, but titles die hard – to this day, Queen Elizabeth II is
titled 'Duke of Normandy' in the Channel Islands*], to the
archbishops, bishops, abbots, earls, barons, justiciars, foresters, sheriffs, stewards, servants, and to all his bailiffs and liege
subjects, greetings [*the document is addressed not only to
those who are to benefit from it but also to those of the King's
officers who are to implement its provisions*]. Know that, with
respect for God and for the salvation of our souls and of all our
ancestors' and heirs', and to the honour of God and the
advancement of Holy Church, and for the emendation of
our realm, by advice of Stephen Archbishop of Canterbury,
Henry Archbishop of Dublin, bishops William of London,
Peter of Winchester, Jocelyn of Bath and Glastonbury, Hugh
of Lincoln, Walter of Worcester, William of Coventry, and
Benedict of Rochester, of master Pandulf [*the papal legate*], of
brother Aymeric [*master of the kinghts Templar in England*],
and of the noble men William Marshal, earl of Pembroke [*the
most honoured knight in Europe*], William, earl of Salisbury
[*the King's half-brother*] . . . [*Fourteen other 'noble men' – at
this time the words mean 'men of note or distinction' rather
than aristocrats of technical rank – are named, among them
Hubert de Burgh whose defence of Dover would be vital to the
royal cause in the looming civil war and who was destined for
a prominent role in the next reign.*]

We have granted
[1] that the English church shall be free . . . and shall have her
liberties inviolate *notably* . . . the freedom of elections, which
is reckoned most important . . . and which we of our pure
and unconstrained will [*This is no cliché. The rights granted to
the Church are described as given voluntarily, those granted
to the lay freemen are not, leaving the king free to claim, as he
did, that the Great Charter had been extorted under duress.*]

did grant . . . by charter before the discord arose between us
and our barons . . . And we have also granted to all freemen of
our realm, for us and our heirs forever, all the underwritten
liberties to be had and held by them and their heirs, of us and
our heirs.

[2] *'Relief' payments (the feudal equivalent of death duties)
shall be* according to the ancient custom of fiefs.

[3] *An heir who is under age at the death of his father shall
have his inheritance without the payment of a relief or a fine.*

[4] *The guardian administering the lands of an under-age heir
is to take only reasonable customary dues, revenue and reasonable services and is not to 'waste' (i.e., destroy or overexploit)
men or goods on the estate. If the unscrupulous administrator
is a royal appointee, for example a sheriff, or someone who has
bought the right to administer the lands from the king, the king
will extract compensation from him on behalf of the heir and
appoint two scrutineer administrators.*

[5] *Moreover the guardian is enjoined to return the property,*
its houses, parks, fishponds, stanks ['*stagna*'], mills and other
things pertaining to the land *in good repair and fully stocked
with* ploughs and wainage [see page 100] according as the
season of husbandry shall require and the revenues of the land
can reasonably be expected to yield.

[*The meaning of the word 'stank' is debated by scholars – it
may signify merely a specific type of fishpond, fish-farming
being widespread in the Middle Ages, or the standing pond of a
watermill. It would be interesting to know whether the clerks
who framed the Charter meant 'mills' to include the comparatively modern windmills as well as watermills.*]

[6] *Heirs shall be married without disparagement with due
notice given to the next of kin.*

[7] *A widow is henceforward to be assured of the rights in her
'dower' (dos) – the portion of her husband's lands specifically set*

*aside for her widowhood; her 'marriage portion' (maritagium) –
that portion of his lands which her father had made over to her at
the time of her marriage; and her inheritance (hereditas) – any
lands bequeathed to her personally, by relations or friends
perhaps, after her marriage. She was also guaranteed forty days'
(in legal jargon the widow's quarantine, from the Latin word for
'forty') residence in the house of her husband after his death,
during which time the dower had to be made over to her. The
1217 issue of the Charter also provided for a widow to receive
estovers from the estate, i.e. supplies for her daily maintenance
during the quarantine period.*

[8] No *widow shall be compelled to marry, though if she does
marry she must have the consent of the lord from whom she
holds her lands, whether the king or some other.*

[9] Neither we nor our bailiffs are to seize any land or rent in
payment for any debt if the chattels of the debtor are sufficient
to repay the debt . . . nor shall those who stood surety to the
debtor be distrained for so long as the debtor has the where-
withal to pay the debt . . .

*[10] If one who has borrowed from the Jews . . . die before
that loan be repaid, the debt shall not bear interest while the
heir is under age . . . [*During the heir's minority he who held
the wardship of the estate drew its revenues. Since the heir had
nothing with which to pay the interest this clause was certainly
fair to his interests – equally it was unfair to the moneylender.*]

*[11] And if anyone die indebted to the Jews, his wife shall
have her dower and repay no part of the debt; any children of
the deceased who are under age shall receive maintenance in
keeping with the holding of he deceased; the debt shall be paid
out of the residue of the estate . . . and the same shall apply to
debts owed to others than Jews.

*[12] Neither aid nor scutage shall be imposed on our king-
dom without the common counsel of the kingdom *except for*

ransom of the king, knighting his eldest son, or for one marriage of his eldest son, or for one marriage of his eldest daughter . . . Let aids from the city of London be decided in the same way.

[13] And the city of London shall have all its ancient liberties and customs by land and water; *the same to apply to all other cities and towns and ports.*

*[14] And to obtain the common counsel of the kingdom on the assessment of an aid or a scutage, we will have the archbishops, bishops, abbots, earls and great barons individually summoned by our letters; *others holding in chief, i.e, directly from the king, would receive a general summons through a royal officer such as the sheriff. The summons was to give at least forty days' notice, but the meeting would go ahead on the given day even if not all those summoned appeared.*

*[15] Conditions governing aids levied by the king are to apply also to those levied by lords on their tenants.

[16] *Demands for military service shall not exceed what is legally due by terms of the tenure.*

[17] *The court of common pleas shall have a permanent venue and no longer follow the royal court on its travels across the country.*

[18] *Certain assizes concerning local landowning titles are to be decided by the king's travelling justices in the county court, assisted by four knights of the county, four times a year.*

*[19] *The clause provides for assizes covered by Clause 18 which for any reason cannot be settled on the day of the county court.*

[20] *A freeman shall be amerced only reasonably for a small offence and even in the case of a grave offence shall not be penalized so heavily that he cannot maintain himself in a*

fitting way of life; a merchant must be left with sufficient stock to continue in business and even a villein shall not lose his 'wainage'. No amercement can be imposed except by the oath of honest men of the neighbourhood.

[21] *Earls and barons are to be amerced through their peers.*

[22] *The Clause deals with the amercement of clerics.*

[23] No village or individual shall be compelled to make bridges at river banks, except those who of old were legally bound to do so.

[24] Pleas of the crown shall not be held by our sheriffs, constables, coroners or other bailiffs.

*[25] *The clause forbids sheriffs to raise rents and levies arbitrarily.*

[26] *The clause concerns debts owing to the king by the estate of a deceased landowner. The king's officer may catalogue the chattels of the deceased before witnesses on the property, up to the value of the debt, so that nothing be removed before the death is discharged.*

*[27] If a freeman die intestate, his chattels shall be distributed by . . . his nearest kinsfolk and friends, under supervision of the church . . .

[28] No bailiff of ours shall take . . . provisions from anyone without immediately tendering money therefor . . .

[29] *Knights owing castle-guard cannot be compelled to give money in lieu if they wish to serve in their own persons or to provide a competent substitute.*

[30] *No sheriff or bailiff of ours, or other person, shall requisition the horses or carts of any freeman.*

[31] *. . . nor wood . . . for castle building or any other work without the agreement of the owner.*

[32] *The lands of convicted felons, which by tradition fell to the Crown for a period, are henceforth to be returned to the lord of the fief in which they lie after a year and a day.*

[33] All kydells [*i.e, fish weirs*] shall be removed from the rivers Thames and Medway, as throughout all England, except from the seashore.

[34] *The government writ praecipe, which concerned property disputes and effectively removed such cases from the jurisdiction of the territorial lord to the king's court,* shall not in future be issued to anyone concerning any tenement so that a freeman may lose his court.

[35] Let there be one measure of wine throughout our whole realm; and one measure of ale; and one measure of corn, namely 'the London quarter'; and one width of cloth – whether dyed or russet, or halberget [*possibly a heavy material used for the haybergeon body vest worn by knights under a coat of mail*], namely, two ells [about 7 feet 6 inches (2.3 meters)] within the selvedges; let it be the same for weights as for measures.

[36] In future no payment shall be offered or accepted for a writ of inquisition of life or limb, but it shall be freely available . . .

[37] *In this clause the king agrees that where a man may hold small parcels of land from him, or owe service by minor feudal obligations known as 'small or petty serjeanties', but holds the bulk of his land from another lord by major obligations, the royal government will not exploit these petty dues to claim the right to administer the land during the minority of an heir.*

[38] *The clause forbids royal officials to put a man on trial* (ponat ad legem, *to his 'law',*) *on their own unsupported complaint but requires them to back it up with credible witnesses.* [*The term was causing trouble for commentators as early as 1300.*]

[39] No freeman shall be taken or ['vel', *the Latin word used here, can also mean 'and', a fact which has caused endless debate among historians and lawyers*] imprisoned or [*here the*

unambiguous 'aut' *is used*] disseised or exiled or in any way destroyed nor will we go upon him or send upon him, except by the lawful judgement of his peers or [*vel*] by the law of the land. [40] To no one will we sell, to no one will we refuse or delay, right or justice.

[41] *The clause guarantees freedom of movement to foreign merchants in time of peace and provides that in time of war they shall be held safe but secure until the government can discover how English merchants are being treated by the belligerent power.*

*[42] It shall be lawful in future for anyone . . . to leave our kingdom and to return, safe and secure by land and water . . . reserving always to the allegiance due to us.

[*The clause excepts convicts and restricts its terms in time of war, but the modern tourist licensed to travel with a passport which remains the property of his government should perhaps look back on the good old days of King John with nostalgia.*]
[43] *A technical clause concerning land held of an escheated estate.*

[44] Men who live outside the forest need no longer attend before our Justiciars of the Forest on a general summons . . . [exceptions include anyone who has offered himself as surety for someone charged with a forest offence].

*[45] Only men who know the law of the realm and mean to observe it well shall henceforward be appointed as justices, constables, sheriffs or bailiffs.

[46] All barons who have founded abbeys, for which they hold charters . . . or of which they have long-continued possession, shall have the wardship of them, when vacant . . . [*The clause is to protect a baronial right against the king, not to protect the abbeys in question.*]

*[47] *All land afforested in our time shall be immediately disafforested,* all river banks put 'in defence' are likewise to be

returned to their former state. [*To 'defend' a river meant to fence off bridal paths and make other provisions to give the royal hunt free course in following hawks and falcons.*]

*[48] All evil customs connected with forests and warrens, foresters and warreners, sheriffs and their officers, river-banks and their wardens, shall immediately be inquired into in each county by twelve sworn knights . . . and shall, within forty days of the said inquest, be utterly abolished . . . provided we have intimation thereof. [*It seems the commissions of knights carried out their work and, although nothing survives, their reports may have formed the basis for the 1217 'Charter of the Forest'.*]

*[49] We will immediately restore all hostages and charters delivered to us by Englishmen, as sureties of the peace or of faithful service. [*A glimpse of the unacceptable face of royal 'protection'.*]

*[50] We will entirely remove from their bailiwicks, the relations of Gerard of Athée . . . Engelard de Cigogné . . . Philip Mark . . . and others [*The men named in the clause were professionals, foreigners, low-born and well hated by the Anglo-Norman baronage.*]

*[51] As soon as peace is restored we will banish from the kingdom all foreign-born knights . . . and mercenary soldiers [*probably John's most loyal as well as most effective servants, like the mercenary captain Faulkes de Bréauté*].

*[52] If anyone has been dispossessed or removed by us, without the legal judgment of his peers, from his lands, castles . . . or from his rights, we will immediately restore them to him; and if any dispute arise let it be decided by Twenty-five barons to be mentioned below . . . Moreover, for all those possessions from which anyone has . . . been removed by our father, King Henry or our brother, King Richard, and which we retain in our own hand . . . we shall have respite

until the usual term of crusaders (*crucesignatorum*) . . . but immediately on our return from the pilgrimage we shall grant full justice.

*[53] *The respite of the crusader is extended to afforestations, wardships, and abbeys on lands other than those of the king.*

[54] No one shall be arrested or imprisoned upon the appeal of a woman, for the death of any other than her husband. [*Women could appoint a champion in the trial by battle, men had to fight for themselves.*]

*[55] *All fines and penalties [i.e. amercements] made and imposed unjustly and against the law of the land are to be remitted or otherwise dealt with as shall be decided by the Committee of Twenty-five barons set up by Clause 61 of the Charter to see that its terms are carried out.*

*[56] If we have dispossessed any Welshmen of lands or liberties or other things without the legal judgment of their peers in England or in Wales, they shall be immediately restored to them . . . *disputes to be settled by judgement of peers according to English law, Welsh law or the law of the Marches according to the location of the tenement.*

*[57] *This, the second of three clauses concerning the opposition barons; Welsh allies headed by Llywelyn, provides that they shall be restored to any lands or liberties unjustly taken from them by John's brother [Richard I] or his father [Henry II], with the proviso that the king shall enjoy the respite allowed a crusader in all cases concerning which proceedings were instituted before he took the cross.*

*[58] We will immediately free the son of Llywelyn and all the hostages of Wales, and charters made over to us as securities for the peace.

*[59] *Alexander II King of Scots is to be treated on the same terms as the barons of England in the matter of his sisters and the hostages he gave as security and concerning his franchises,*

unless it ought to be otherwise according to charters which John had received from Alexander's father William the Lion [d.1214], the questions to be settled by the judgment of the king's peers in John's court.

[Although the seventeen-year-old Alexander II of Scotland was not a party to the Charter, the barons wanted all the allies they could get and included this as a bait to the northern monarch. The question naturally arose, how could the king of Scots have peers – i.e. equals in rank? The issue revolved around the question of the homage which the kings of England reckoned was owing to them from the Scottish ruler – just as the kings of France reckoned the English ruler owed them homage. William had in fact done reluctant homage to John with the saving clause 'reserving always his own right'. Then on 1 August 1209 Alexander did homage on behalf of his father in regard to other castles and lands, while his sisters Margaret and Isabel were handed over as wards of John, being held in close but honourable confinement in Corfe Castle, Dorset. Needing John's military help against a pretender to the Scottish throne, in 1212 William even made the fourteen-year-old Alexander a ward of England to be married at John's discretion over the next six years. Finally, in October 1213, Pope Innocent ordered both William and Alexander to do homage to King John.

[60] . . . the customs and liberties aforesaid, the observance of which we have granted . . . as pertains to us towards our men, shall be observed by all of our kingdom, clergy as well as lay, as pertains between them and their men.

*[61] . . . moreover . . . we give and grant to our barons the under-written security, namely, that the barons shall choose Twenty-five barons of the kingdom they wish, who must with all their might observe, hold and cause to be observed, the peace and liberties which we have granted and confirmed to

them by this present charter of ours, so that if we, or our justiciar, or our bailiffs or any one of our officers offend in any way against anyone or transgress any of the articles of the peace or the security and the offence be notified to four of the aforesaid Twenty-five barons, the four shall report to us or our justiciar and petition to have that transgression rectified without delay. And if we shall not have corrected the transgression within forty days . . . the four barons shall report to the rest of the Twenty-five and [*they*] together with the commune of the whole land (*communa tocius terre*), shall distrain and distress us in all possible ways, as by seizing our castle, lands, possessions, and in any other way open to them, *though without violence to the king, queen or their children* until they deem that redress has been done . . . *This astonishing clause goes on to enjoin everyone in the realm to swear loyalty to the Twenty-five in helping them* to 'molest' *the king* 'to the utmost of their power' *and any who do not take the oath will be compelled to do so by the king himself. Finally, the clause provides for majority decision to govern the actions of the Twenty-five.*

*[62] We completely remit and pardon to everyone any ill will hatred and bitterness that has arisen between us and our men during the time of discord between us . . . And on this head, we have caused to be made for them letters testimonial patent of the lord Stephen Archbishop of Canterbury, or the lord Henry Archbishop of Dublin, of the bishops above mentioned and of Master Pandulf [*the papal legate*] concerning this security and the concessions aforesaid [*i.e., in fact, the Charter*].

[Letters containing the text of the Charter were issued.]

*[63] Wherefore it is our will, and we firmly enjoin, that the English church be free, and that the men in our kingdom have and hold all the aforesaid liberties, rights and concessions . . . for themselves and their heirs, of us and our heirs . . . for

ever . . . An oath, moreover, has been taken as well on our part as on the part of the barons, that all these conditions . . . shall be kept in good faith and without evil intent. Given under our hand . . . in the meadow which is called Runnymede, between Windsor and Staines, on the fifteenth day of June, in the seventeenth year of our reign.

SELECT BIBLIOGRAPHY

Appleby, John T., *John King of England* (New York, 1959)
————*England without Richard 1189–1199* (London, 1965)
Baggley, J.J., *Historical Interpretation 1066–1540* (Harmondsworth, 1965)
Bale, John, *Kynge Johan* (London, 1539)
Barker, J.R.V., *The Tournament in England 1100–1400* (Woodbridge, 1986)
Barlow, Frank, *The Feudal Kingdom of England* (London, 1955)
Bazeley, M., 'The Extent of the English Forest in the Thirteenth Century', *Transactions of the Royal Historical Society,* 4th series, iv (Cambridge, 1921)
Bechmann, Roland, *Des arbres et des hommes: La forêt au moyen-âge* (Paris, 1984)
Bentham, Jeremy, *Plea for the Constitution* (London, 1803)
Beresford, M.W., *New Towns of the Middle Ages* (New York, 1967)
Blackstone, Sir William, *The Great Charter and Charter of the Forest, to which is prefixed the History of the Charters* (London, 1759)
————*Commentaries on the Laws of England* (London, 1765–9)
Brady, Robert, *An Introduction to the Old English History* (London, 1684)
Breay, Claire, *Magna Carta, Manuscripts and Myths* (London, 2002)
Bryce, James, *The American Commonwealth* (London and New York, 1888)
Butt, Ronald, *A History of Parliament: The Middle Ages* (London, 1989)
Butterfield, Sir Herbert, *Magna Carta in the Historiography of the Sixteenth and Seventeenth Centuries* (Reading, 1969)
Cam, Helen M., *Magna Carta – Event or Document?* (Selden Society Lecture, London, 1965)

Cheney, C.R., *From Becket to Langton* (Manchester, 1956)
——— 'The Eve of Magna Carta', *Bulletin of the John Rylands' Library,* xxxviii (Manchester, 1955)
——— 'The Twenty Five Barons of Magna Carta', *Bulletin of the John Rylands' Library,* i (Manchester, 1968)
Church, S.D. (ed.), *King John: New Interpretations* (Woodbridge, 1999)
Churchill, Winston S., *A History of the English Speaking Peoples* (New York, 1956)
Clanchy, M.T., *England and its Rulers 1066–1272* (London, 1983)
Collins, A.J., 'The Documents of the Great Charter of 1215', *Proceedings of the British Academy,* xxxiv (London, 1948)
Cowell, John, *The Interpreter* (London, 1607)
Cronne, H.A., *The Reign of Stephen* (London, 1970)
Danziger, Danny and Gillingham, John, *1215: The Year of Magna Carta* (London, 2003)
Davies, R.R. *The Age of Conquest*, vol. 4 in *The Oxford History of Wales* (New York, 2000)
Davis, G.R.C., *Magna Carta* (London, 1963)
Davis, R.H.C., *King Stephen* (London, 1967)
Duby, Georges, *The Legend of Bouvines* (Berkeley and Los Angeles, 1990)
Eadmur, *Eadmeri Historia Novorum in Anglia et opuscula duo Vita Sancti Anselmi et quibusdam miraculis ejus* (London, 1884)
Frame, R., *Colonial Ireland 1169–1369* (Dublin, 1981)
Geoffrey of Monmouth (trans. Lewis Thorpe), *History of the Kings of Britain* (Harmondsworth, 1966)
Gerald of Wales (ed. J.S. Brewer, J.F. Dinnock and G.F. Warner), *Giraldus Cambrensis, Opera,* 8 vols, Rolls Series (London, 1861–91)
Gillingham, J., *The Angevin Empire* (London, 1984)
Hastings, Adrian, *Elias of Dereham, Architect of Salisbury Cathedral* (Much Wenlock, 1997)
Hindley, Geoffrey, 'Old Charter in New Worlds: Magna Carta in Pacific Settings, from California to Canberra and Beyond', *Le Commonwealth: modifications de l'apport culturel britannique* (Université Le Havre, 1999)
Holt, J.C., *Magna Carta,* 2nd edition (Cambridge, 1992)
———*Magna Carta and Medieval Government* (London, 1985)
Hoveden (ed. W. Stubbs), *Chronica Rogeri de,* 4 vols, Rolls Series (London, 1868–71)
Howard, A.E. Dick, *The Road from Runnymede* (Charlottesville, 1968)
Jeffreys, Stephen, *Tourney and Joust* (London, 1973)
Jenks, Edward, 'The Myth of Magna Carta', *Independent Review,* iv, pp. 260–73, (London, 1904)
Jennings, I., *Magna Carta: Its Influence on the World Today* (London, 1965)
Jones, J.A.P., *King John and Magna Carta* (1971)
Kearney, Hugh, *The British Isles: A History of Four Nations,* 2nd edition, (Cambridge, 2000)
Keen, M.H., *Chivalry* (New Haven and London, 1984)
Keeney, B.C., *Judgement by Peers* (Cambridge, Mass., 1949)
Labarge, M.W., *Gascony, England's First Colony* (London, 1980)
McFarlane, K.B., *The Nobility of Later Medieval England* (Oxford, 1973)
McKechnie, W.S., *Magna Carta: A Commentary on the Great Charter of King John,* 2nd edition (Glasgow, 1914)

McKisack, May, *The Fourteenth Century 1307–1399* (Oxford, 1959)

Maddicott, 'Magna Carta and the Local Community', *Past and Present, 102* (Oxford, 1984)

'Melrose Chronicle', *see* Stephenson, Joseph

Myers, Henry A. and Herwig, Wolfram, *Medieval Kingship* (Chicago, 1982)

Neale, J.E., *Elizabeth I and Her Parliaments* (London, 1953)

Painter, Sidney, *William Marshal* (Baltimore, 1949)

Pallister, Anne, *Magna Carta: Heritage of Liberty* (London, 1971)

Poole, A.L., *From Domesday Book to Magna Carta* (Oxford 1955)

Potter, K.R. (ed.), *Gesta Stephani: the Deeds of Stephen* (London, 1955)

Powell, W.R., 'The Administration of the Navy', *English Historical Review,* lxxi (Oxford, 1956)

Powicke, F.M., *King Henry III and the Lord Edward* (Oxford, 1947)

————*The Loss of Normandy* (Manchester, 1961)

Prestwich, Michael, *Edward I* (London, 1988)

Ralph of Coggeshall (ed. J. Stephenson), *Radulphi de Coggeshall Chronicon Anglicanum*, Rolls Series (London, 1875)

Rheinstein, Max, *Max Weber on Law in Economy and Society* (Cambridge, Mass. 1954)

Richard of Devizes (ed. J.T. Appleby), *Chronicon Richardi Divensis de tempore Regis Richardi Primi* (London, 1963)

Richardson, H.G. (ed.), *The English Jewry under the Angevin Kings* (London, 1960)

Roger of Howden, *see* Hoveden

Roth, C., *The History of the Jews in England* (Oxford, 1964)

Round, J.H., 'An Unknown Charter of Liberties', *English Historical Review*, viii (Oxford, 1893)

Russell, C., *The Crisis of Parliaments English History 1509–1660* (Oxford, 1971)

Rutland, Robert A., *The Birth of the Bill of Rights* (Chapel Hill, 1983)

Seibt, Ferdinand, *Glanz und Elend des Mittelalters* (Berlin, 1987)

Smith, Elsie, *The Sarum Magna Carta* (Salisbury, 1967)

Sotheby's, *The Magna Carta* (New York, 2007)

Speed, John, *History of Great Britaine* (London, 1611)

Stenton, D.M., *English Justice between the Norman Conquest and the Great Charter* (London, 1965)

Stephenson, Joseph, *Medieval Chronicles of Scotland* (Lampeter, 1988)

Stoel, Caroline P. and Clarke, Ann B., *Magna Carta to the Constitution* (Portland, 1986)

Stubbs, William, *Constitutional History of England*, 3 vols (Oxford, 1897)

Thompson, Faith T., *The First Copy of Magna Carta. Why It Persisted as a Document* (Minnesota, 1925)

————*Magna Carta: Its Role in the Making of the English Constitution 1300–1629* (Minneapolis, 1948)

Thorne, Samuel E., *et al. The Great Charter. Four Essays on Magna Carta and the History of Our Liberty* (New York, 1965)

Turner, Ralph V., *King John: England's Evil King?* (Stroud, 2003)

Warren, W.L., *King John* (Harmondsworth, 1966)

————*Henry II* (London, 1973)

————*The Governance of Norman and Angevin England 1086–1272* (London, 1987)

Whittingham, Selby, *A Thirteenth-century Portrait Gallery at Salisbury Cathedral* (Salisbury, 1979)

Wickson, R., *The Community of the Realm in Thirteenth-century England* (London, 1970)

Williams, G.A., *Medieval London from Commune to Capital* (London, 1963)

Young, Arthur, *Travels in France* (London, 1792)

Young, C.R., *The Royal Forests of Medieval England* (Leicester, 1979)

INDEX